Hurricane Mitigation for the Built Environment

Hurricane Mitigation for the Built Environment

Ricardo A. Alvarez

CRC Press is an imprint of the
Taylor & Francis Group, an **informa** business

Cover image provided by Ana-Maria Alvarez.

CRC Press
Taylor & Francis Group
6000 Broken Sound Parkway NW, Suite 300
Boca Raton, FL 33487-2742

First issued in paperback 2021
First issued in hardback 2019

© 2016 by Taylor & Francis Group, LLC
CRC Press is an imprint of Taylor & Francis Group, an Informa business

No claim to original U.S. Government works

ISBN 13: 978-1-03-224265-1 (pbk)
ISBN 13: 978-1-4987-1498-3 (hbk)

DOI: 10.1201/b19474

This book contains information obtained from authentic and highly regarded sources. Reasonable efforts have been made to publish reliable data and information, but the author and publisher cannot assume responsibility for the validity of all materials or the consequences of their use. The authors and publishers have attempted to trace the copyright holders of all material reproduced in this publication and apologize to copyright holders if permission to publish in this form has not been obtained. If any copyright material has not been acknowledged please write and let us know so we may rectify in any future reprint.

Except as permitted under U.S. Copyright Law, no part of this book may be reprinted, reproduced, transmitted, or utilized in any form by any electronic, mechanical, or other means, now known or hereafter invented, including photocopying, microfilming, and recording, or in any information storage or retrieval system, without written permission from the publishers.

For permission to photocopy or use material electronically from this work, please access www.copyright.com (http://www.copyright.com/) or contact the Copyright Clearance Center, Inc. (CCC), 222 Rosewood Drive, Danvers, MA 01923, 978-750-8400. CCC is a not-for-profit organization that provides licenses and registration for a variety of users. For organizations that have been granted a photocopy license by the CCC, a separate system of payment has been arranged.

Trademark Notice: Product or corporate names may be trademarks or registered trademarks, and are used only for identification and explanation without intent to infringe.

Publisher's Note
The publisher has gone to great lengths to ensure the quality of this reprint but points out that some imperfections in the original copies may be apparent.

Library of Congress Cataloging-in-Publication Data

Álvarez Salaverry, Ricardo A., author.
  Hurricane mitigation for the built environment / Ricardo A. Alvarez.
      pages cm
  Includes bibliographical references and index.
  ISBN 978-1-4987-1498-3 (alk. paper)
    1. Hurricane protection. 2. Coastal zone management. 3. City planning--Environmental aspects. I. Title.

HV635.5.A48 2016
624.1'76--dc23   2015027181

Visit the Taylor & Francis Web site at
http://www.taylorandfrancis.com

and the CRC Press Web site at
http://www.crcpress.com

Contents

Foreword xi
Preface.. xiii
Author's Notes xv
Acknowledgments.. xix
Author xxi

Chapter 1   The Art and Science of Hazard Mitigation 1

Chapter 2   Two Hurricanes in Three Weeks....................................... 11

Chapter 3   Hurricanes, Vulnerability, and Causes of Damage 27

Hurricane.. 27
We Need to Be Educated... 28
Vulnerability.. 30
Damages 31
    Damaging Components 31
        Wind Pressure... 32
        Windborne Debris 32
        Torrential Rain.. 32
        Flooding.. 33
        Hydrodynamic Pressure from Storm Surge............... 33
        Wave Impact 34
        Hydrostatic Pressure due to Flooding....................... 34
        Floating Debris 35

Chapter 4   Wind and Water.. 37

Air We Breathe.. 37
Wind 40
    Wind Behavior.. 40
        Wind Speed Increases As It Flows at Higher Elevations
        above Ground.. 40
        Static Wind Pressure Diminishes As Its Velocity
        Increases and When Wind Encounters an Object in Its
        Path, It Increases Its Velocity to Surmount It 41
        Characteristics of Wind Flow Will Change in Response
        to Changes in the Terrain over Which It Flows......... 42
    Turbulent Flow... 43

v

vi Contents

Wind Effects 44
   Positive Pressure 46
   Suction 47
   Drag 48
   Shaking 49
   Vibration 49
   Vorticity 50
   Stagnation 51
   Drift, Overturning, and Uplift 52
   Eddies 54
   Missiles 54
Water 56
  Water Behavior 57
   Water Is a Heavy and Incompressible Fluid 57
   Water Pressure Increases with Depth 57
   Characteristics of Water Flow Change in Response to
   the Characteristics of the Terrain over Which It Flows 57
   Sea Water Is Salty 58
   Water in the Oceans Reacts to the Gravitational
   Attraction of Sun and Moon 58
   Sea Surface Water Temperature Varies Considerably
   Depending on Latitude 59
  Water Effects 60
   Hydrostatic Pressure 60
   Hydrodynamic Pressure 62
   Tides 63
   Waves 63
   Storm Surge 65
   Flooding 66
   Erosion 68
   Leveling-Off 68
   Debris 70
   Whirlpool 72

Chapter 5 Hurricanes and the Built Environment 75

Foundation 76
Structure 77
  Connections 77
  Redundancy 77
  Overcapacity 78
Building Envelope 78
Exterior Infrastructure 82
Sails, Wind-Catchers, and Wind Tunnels 84

Contents   vii

Symmetry, Continuity, Centricity, Aerodynamics, and
Hydrodynamics 86
    Symmetry 90
    Centricity 91
    Continuity 93
    Aerodynamics.. 95
    Hydrodynamics.. 96
Structural Integrity... 97
One Hurricane Is All It Takes 98

Chapter 6   Cancun: A Mexican Gate to the Caribbean 101

My First Visit to Cancun 101
1979 Atlantic Hurricane Season... 102
1988 Atlantic Hurricane Season... 103
2005 Atlantic Hurricane Season 103
Paradise 104

Chapter 7   Cyclones of Quintana Roo 107

Chapter 8   Hurricane Gilbert—1988... 113

Balance of Hurricane Gilbert... 115
From the Lesson Book of Hurricane Gilbert 116
Typifying Damage Caused by Hurricane Gilbert 117
    Damage to the Beach.. 118
    Damage to Outdoor Infrastructure... 118
    Damage to Foundations... 120
    Damage to Building Envelope.. 120
    Damage to Building Interior 122

Chapter 9   Ten Years Later—Higher Vulnerability.. 123

Preliminary Assessment.. 124
Potential for Damage.. 125

Chapter 10 Hurricane Wilma—2005... 129

Balance of Hurricane Wilma 132
    Wilma Lesson Book 134
Typifying Damages Caused by Hurricane Wilma.............................. 137
    Destruction of the Beach 138

viii   Contents

Damage to External Infrastructure 140
Damage to Building Foundations 140
Damage to the Building Envelope 142
Damage to the Interior of Buildings 145
Other Damages 147

Chapter 11 Classification and Mitigation of Damages 149

Beach Damage 149
    Mitigation 151
Building Damage 152
    Foundations 152
        Mitigation 153
    Structure 154
        Mitigation 155
Roofs 155
    Main Tile Roofs 156
    Secondary Tile Roofs 157
        Mitigation 158
    Flat Roofs 159
        Mitigation 160
    Skylights 161
        Mitigation 162
    Metal Roofs 163
        Mitigation 163
    Decorative Artisan Roofs 164
        Mitigation 164
Building Envelope 165
    Reinforced Concrete or Masonry Walls 166
        Mitigation 166
    Glass and Architectural Metals 167
        Mitigation 168
    Other Exterior Walls 170
        Mitigation 172
External Infrastructure 172
    Retaining Walls 173
    Terraces and Swimming Pools 174
    Balconies and Railings 174
    Exterior Ceilings 174
    Roof-Mounted Equipment 175
    Other Exterior-Mounted Equipment 177
    Parking Lots 177
    Exterior Lighting, Masts, and Traffic Lights 178
    Piers, Tiki Huts, and Others 180

Contents ix

Landscaping and Gardens 181
Signs and Billboards... 181
Mitigation.. 182
Building Interior.. 188
Contents 192
Mitigation.. 194

Chapter 12 Future Impacts... 197

Natural Factors 197
Climate Change 198
Global Warming 198
Sea Level Rise 200
Multidecadal Cycles of Tropical Cyclone Activity 201
Anthropogenic Factors 202

Chapter 13 Hurricane-Resistant Buildings 205

Macro Approach...208
Project-Specific Approach..209
Shape Factor 211
Foundation.. 212
Structure 217
Building Envelope 218
Exterior Walls..220
Roofs.. 221
Exterior Openings..227
Skylights 229
Ventilation Components 230
Other Building Envelope Components 233
Building Shape and Proportions...234
Slenderness 235
Continuity of the Building Envelope 235
Sails and Wind-Catchers 236
Wind Tunnels...237
Internal Infrastructure 239
Electrical..239
Mechanical 241
Plumbing..243
Communication Systems 245
Waste Management...247
Building Interior and Décor 247
Finishes, Decorative Elements, and Built-In Furniture 249
External Infrastructure 249
Vicinity 250

Chapter 14 Climate Change: An Exacerbating Factor 255

Specific Problems 261
Links between Hurricanes and Climate Change 262
Expected Consequences of Business-as-Usual Approach 262
A Paradigm Shift Is Needed 263
Recommendations and Timelines 264

Index 269

Foreword

This book draws on the intimate experience of Ricardo Alvarez with damage from hurricanes gleaned from post event assessments and studies conducted over a span of more than 25 years. It is clear that the author shares the joy of those who choose to build, live, work, and play in coastal areas where sun, sand, and a warm climate make life so enjoyable. In the midst of this celebration of life, he calls the reader to both recognize the risks that accompany living in these areas, which all too often are subject to the dangers of hurricanes, and to take the actions necessary to help minimize hurricane risks in a cost-effective manner.

What I like most about the book is that it is written from a personal perspective using examples from observation and research. The book is approachable and easy to read as it does not rely on equations and scientific jargon to describe and try to quantify hurricane effects. It does not get bogged down in spelling out the steps and calculation that one would follow to design or retrofit a building to reduce its vulnerability to hurricane wind- and water-related damage. Instead, it uses a liberal sprinkling of analogies to help the reader develop a better intuitive feel for the effects of wind, rain, and surge associated with the impact of a hurricane on buildings, developments, and communities.

This book presents examples of vulnerabilities that are exposed and damage that frequently occurs and provides specific practical recommendations for the types of mitigation actions that represent best practices. This book will serve as a good practical guide to the kinds of issues that need to be considered and addressed during the design of new buildings and developments or the retrofit of existing buildings.

One of the author's messages to design professionals is that they need to look beyond historical data and events and define design criteria based on expected future events that include potential increases in surge-related risks due to sea level rise.

Ricardo's role in managing Federal Emergency Management Agency (FEMA) mitigation efforts in South Florida following Hurricane Andrew includes founding the Laboratory for Structural Mitigation at Florida International University (FIU) where his work with airboats planted the seeds for FIU's Wall-of-Wind test facility. At FIU, he taught courses on hazard mitigation and vulnerability assessment for 16 years and served as deputy director of the International Hurricane Research Center. Descriptions of damage and its consequences are infused with, and informed by, this experience and by very personal encounters with buildings impacted by hurricanes and the people who experienced these events. He is not afraid to state his opinions and clearly identifies when the observations and suggestions are his opinions.

Alvarez drives home the point that for buildings and communities located in hurricane-prone regions, it is not a question of whether the area will be impacted, but when it will be impacted. The book makes a strong case for taking responsibility to understand the vulnerabilities of buildings and structures to hurricane impacts. As such, he rightly urges developers, designers, and owners to incorporate that knowledge into the design of new buildings or the retrofit of existing buildings to reduce hurricane damage and the potential for extended loss of use that frequently follows these events.

Timothy Reinhold, PhD
Tampa, Florida

Preface

It is our responsibility to know and take ownership of our own vulnerability; it is only thus that we shall be able to implement effective mitigation measures to protect ourselves and our buildings from the expected impacts of hurricanes.

Ricardo A. Alvarez
2007

I learned that I wanted to be an architect when I was about 7 years old not because I knew then what that profession was, but because my father asked me what I would like to be when I grew up after he had seen me spend most of my summer vacation excavating around our backyard, building towers, bridges, and other structures. I answered I wanted to build houses and buildings and he said, "so you want to be an architect." Having set my professional objectives at such an early age, I never deviated as I went through primary and secondary school, often imagining how a building pictured in my mind would actually look like in reality. It helped me a lot that I enjoyed drawing and could quickly sketch what I saw or any idea in my mind as long as I had pencil and paper at hand. What I most remember from those long-ago days are two things: First, how much I enjoyed watching a building job site as workers excavated, erected scaffolding, and the building emerged from the ground up until one day there it was! Scaffolding came down and as if by magic a brand new building stood there, shining in the sunlight. Second, I was always asking or imagining how a building would react when hit by one of those earthquakes that every so often shook my hometown. My main concern was: What may cause a building to be damaged or perhaps fall down under the impact of a hazard?

I carried all those questions with me as I started my architectural studies in California where, in addition to learning about space and light and the famous dictum of *form follows function*, I began to develop a strong interest on how buildings perform while interacting with natural hazards such as earthquakes, floods, or hurricanes, and what could be done through design to minimize damage.

This strong focus with encouragement from my professors shaped my design philosophy in such a way that I soon realized it was not enough for me as an architect to design a building. I also needed to know how it would stand up and why it might fall down under external forces, as well as how the structure and all components of a building work together. I needed to know how to build the building.

Guided by these ideas, I saw the need to go beyond the typical two-dimensional boards showing site plans, floor plans, elevations, sections, details, and a nicely rendered perspective when presenting a project in my design lab. I started building scaled models of the whole building or of some section of it to test them under various loading conditions, learning a lot from this research.

In my fourth year of architectural studies, I worked on the design of an Olympic stadium with a roof consisting of a membrane supported by a network of cables tensed between structural members. In order to understand how such a cable structure and roof would behave under windy conditions, I built a model of a section of the building and tested it using a regular electric fan as the wind source. During these tests, I discovered that the edge of the roof fluttered under the wind, and soon realized that this condition could become a major problem and potential cause of damage in a full-scale building.

In looking for solutions to this fluttering problem, my first reaction was to strengthen the cable structure by increasing the tension of the main cables, which did little to stop the fluttering. Back to the drawing board and research, I explored how aeronautical engineers had tackled and solved similar issues with the wings of airplanes as they interact with strong winds aloft. Based on what I learned, I redesigned the leading edge of the roof, introducing components that modified the wind flow counteracting and totally dampening the fluttering effect. Problem solved!

I did not know it at the time, but I had in fact just had my first taste of the practice of hazard mitigation by implementing a specific measure, on the roof of my building, to reduce the potential for damage from the impact of wind, which is exactly what hazard mitigation is. I learned invaluable lessons from that experience, one of them being that the best time to mitigate expected impacts is during the design phase of a new building. I also learned the value of empirical knowledge and of research and testing in designing and implementing mitigation solutions.

These remembrances show, and in such light I share them here, the foundation upon which I have specialized in the practice of hazard mitigation and related fields of vulnerability assessment, risk management, emergency management, and climate change. Each architect has traveled his or her own road to become a design professional and each individual's story is unique, but the story shared before and this entire book are offered to highlight the unique contribution architects and other building design professionals can and should make to the field of hurricane mitigation, which can benefit so many in vulnerable communities throughout the world.

Author's Notes

This is a book about hurricane mitigation based on a methodology for analysis and application developed over the course of many years of practice in this field, and on findings from that field work and research spanning from 1988 to the present in the aftermath of dozens of major hurricanes that have made landfall across the southern and gulf coasts of the United States, Mexico, and the Caribbean. The similarities in development, design, type of construction, amenities, and other characteristics between the hotel strips and beach-front tourist resorts in these regions are such that, save rare exceptions, all of the lessons learned in one place regarding causes of damage and effective mitigation are perfectly usable or adaptable across borders.

The years of work and applied research on how buildings and infrastructure perform and sustain damage under the impact of natural hazards have provided many of the examples, photos, illustrations, and case studies cited used here. Of those, many are derived from my field work and a technical report I coauthored with Dr. Timothy "Tim" Reinhold, PhD and Dr. Hugh Gladwin, PhD, at the request of the state government of Quintana Roo, Mexico, in the immediate aftermath of Hurricane Wilma in Cancun, Cozumel, Playa del Carmen, and surrounding areas in late October 2005, describing the vulnerability of the region and recommendations for mitigation.

The seed for this volume was planted long ago in California where, as a student of environmental design, architecture, and urbanism, I began building models of structures and buildings to help me visualize how these would interact with and perform under the effect of natural forces, such as seismic waves, wind, rushing waters, etc. In 1988, in the aftermath of category 5 Hurricane Gilbert, I had my first chance, as a professional, to assess at close range damage caused to buildings and the natural environment by a major hurricane in Cancun, Mexico. In the aftermath of Hurricane Andrew (1992), I had the opportunity to conduct a large damage assessment effort involving more than 5000 damaged buildings and facilities in Miami-Dade County before being tasked by the Federal Emergency Management Agency (FEMA) with managing the hazard mitigation effort for Hurricane Andrew and three other declared major disasters in Florida. The knowledge I gained from direct observation of damage in the field, during that post-Gilbert visit to Cancun in 1988 and during my post-Andrew collaboration with FEMA, was so amazingly vast and comprehensive, as building after building "told" me their stories of interacting with a major hurricane in highly graphic and palpable ways, that it would have been impossible to acquire by way of theoretical, analytical, or experimental studies regardless of how many years I would have invested in such an effort. This is a book that also reflects 20 years of study dedicated to the topic of climate change, more specifically the adaptation of the coastal built environment to sea level rise as an exacerbating component of storm surge and wave action during hurricanes.

I offer these lines as testament to the invaluable benefits derived from an experiential approach to learning about these incredibly interesting and complex issues. A great value of the empirical approach is that nature itself is your laboratory, offering a wealth of detailed findings that would be impossible to approximate in a controlled experimental laboratory environment despite advances in instrumentation and modeling capabilities. On the other hand, we must recognize the advantages derived from the ability of using instrumentation to acquire data and visualizing performance in real time, something that is extremely difficult and vastly more dangerous to do during a real-life hazard event. The truth is that we need to take advantage of both approaches to learn about the performance of buildings under hurricane impacts, the damage caused by such impacts, and the kinds of mitigation measures that will be effective in reducing the potential for damage from recurring future impacts. Toward that end, I believe this book takes an important initial step by documenting hurricane damage graphically and textually by type and cause and by offering recommendations for mitigation by building system or component.

On the topic of using both the empirical and experimental approaches, I submit there are current efforts underway that are advancing in that direction. Certainly, the work done in Florida for the past 15 years under the *Coastal Monitoring Program* (Reinhold, Gurley, Masters, Pinelli et al.), which includes outfitting houses with sensors and other instrumentation and data acquisition and transmission equipment, allows measurements to be taken in real time and safe observations to be made during an uncontrolled natural real-life event under conditions that only nature can provide. This program also includes the deployment of hurricane-resistant towers outfitted with meteorological instrumentation and data acquisition and transmission equipment in order to capture the characteristics of actual hurricane wind fields in real time. This applied research program combines both approaches quite effectively.

My work is founded on the belief that nature recognizes no political or geographical boundaries and that natural processes and the hazards generated will affect an entire region regardless of how many different countries or communities are in it. In this regard, countries have a lot to learn from one another in terms of consequences of impacts and mitigation successes. Adhering to the no-boundary concept, I will be using observations and applying lessons learned in the Cancun region in Mexico to arrive at conclusions about the causality of damage and make recommendations about effective mitigation alternatives that may be implemented in the United States and in many other hurricane-vulnerable coastal regions in other countries. In this regard, I would say there is no shame in copying the good and in learning from the successes and experiences of others.

All of this is about the intersection of sea level rise and hurricanes as much as it is about the unavoidable and much desired linkage and collaboration between the emergency management and climate management sectors. And it is also about the need for many other sectors, such as building design professionals and policy makers, to jump into the fray and join others in the design and implementation of actual solutions to protect against expected adverse consequences from climate-exacerbated hurricanes.

This shares a foundation with my previous work *Paraiso protegido: hacia una cultura de mitigacion (Paradise Protected: Toward a Culture of Mitigation)* published in Spanish (ISBN 978-607-401-556-0; Editorial M.A. Porrua, Mexico, D.F., Mexico, 2012), which was mostly based on the field study and report for the State Government in Quintana Roo following Hurricane Wilma (2005). But it has a much broader focus that includes climate change and the linkage with hurricanes through the exacerbating elements of sea level rise and storm surge.

Author's Notes

I started this as a narrative about technical, engineering, and scientific issues regarding the impact of hurricanes, the design of buildings and infrastructure in hurricane-vulnerable regions, and the exacerbating aspects of sea level rise and global warming, but along the way, thanks to a fresh perspective and valuable input from my friend and colleague, the architect Carlos Constandse of Cancun, Mexico, it evolved into a book about technical issues written in nontechnical language. This approach will benefit those in the trenches of developing a new project in a vulnerable coastal location, those investing their hard-earned monies to generate new development and sources of work, as well as those responsible for the protection of life and property and the integrity of the built environment.

I write about a quest to develop a body of knowledge, a theory of hazard mitigation, using an approach based on observations of actual damage caused by hurricane impacts complemented by applied research and testing that have generated the knowledge and findings about vulnerability, damage, causality of damage, risk, the performance of buildings interacting with damaging components of hurricanes, and the effectiveness of mitigation measures in reducing the potential for damage to the built environment from recurring hurricane impacts.

In conclusion, I want to share the following: Hurricanes must not be an obstacle for us to live, play, invest, build, and, in one way or another, enjoy and benefit from all that is offered by so many beautiful places as there are in the coastal regions of Florida, the Gulf of Mexico, and the U.S. Atlantic seaboard, as well as in Quintana Roo, the Caribbean, and elsewhere. We possess the knowledge and the methods needed to design and construct hurricane-resistant buildings in a cost-effective manner. We have within ourselves the capability of avoiding a repeat of the damage the next time. We must become educated to acquire a culture of hurricane mitigation to protect our buildings and the human life and human activity they shelter.

Let this book be a contribution to the protection of the built environment that is already in place and the practice of mitigation through the use of design criteria by building design professionals, as well a guide for those business entrepreneurs and visitors who are planning to invest and develop new infrastructure in hurricane-vulnerable regions everywhere. I encourage everyone to integrate the concepts of mitigation in the practice of their jobs or professions.

> The greatest satisfaction that can be derived by those who practice hurricane mitigation goes well beyond the reduction of potential damage and ensuring the functional continuity of their projects, to also include the enormous satisfaction of having contributed to saving the lives of many without those so protected even knowing about it.

Ricardo A. Alvarez
North Miami Beach, Florida

Acknowledgments

In thinking about those whom I have to thank for supporting me and helping make this book possible, I am reminded of Sir Isaac Newton saying, "If I see far it is because I stand on the shoulders of giants." I am not comparing myself to Newton or claiming that I have seen far, but just saying that this book is a reality because I walk in the company of loved family, friends, colleagues, and mentors who have inspired, and urged me on, as I have put pen to paper (in reality, mostly fingers to keyboard) to share my thoughts, opinions, ideas, and recommendations about topics that I believe are of the utmost importance for the future of humankind and the coastal built environment in hurricane-vulnerable regions.

First, I thank my wife Marcia for her unwavering support and for allowing me to rely on her clear intellect and constructive criticism to rescue me those times when I got mired in muddled sentences of my own creation. I thank my son and namesake Ricardo Ramon "Ric," whom I have often used as a sounding board to discuss scientific and technical aspects and the most effective ways to communicate those in "day-to-day" language. I am also grateful to my daughter Ana-Maria who contributed her talents in art, computer animation, and research to design the cover of my previous book and some of the graphics that illustrate this work and help clarify important content herein. I also owe my heartfelt thanks to a family member who may not have, at least for now, any idea of how much he has contributed to my work. My grandson Gabriel, who reached the ripe old age of seven in October 2014, loves to read scientific books, engages in mental math games with me, and beats me at tic-tac-toe almost every time we play, and who has the ability to express thoughts and ideas about difficult concepts in such a clear and concise manner that it has inspired me greatly.

I want to thank my good friend Frank Reddish (1939–2009), a mathematician and engineer, whom I met in 1993 when he worked for the State of Florida during the post-Hurricane Andrew recovery phase. Frank moved on to become Director of Hazard Mitigation for Miami-Dade County's Office of Emergency Management and founder of the Local Mitigation Strategy. Frank and I collaborated on several hazard mitigation projects in what was truly a pioneering effort of translating regulatory language into actual applications in the field. Frank invited me to meetings of the Miami-Dade County Local Mitigation Strategy (LMS) to share my findings from research work or my views on sea level rise as an exacerbating factor of storm surge and wave impacts during hurricanes. Frank and I shared the view that closer collaboration between emergency and climate managers is essential for the protection of our vulnerable communities. In a sense, many of the presentations that Frank invited me to make in front of the LMS group were trial runs for many of the concepts and topics discussed here, and for this I am grateful.

A heartfelt word of thanks goes to my colleague and good friend Jose Mitrani, a structural engineer and former chair of the Department of Construction Management at FIU, who has contributed much to the strengthening of building codes and hurricane mitigation initiatives in Florida. Jose is the person who challenged me to share my practical experience and knowledge of hurricane vulnerability and hazard mitigation by teaching on these topics at Florida International University (FIU). Jose was also instrumental in connecting me with the International Hurricane Research Center.

I could not have tackled many of the topics covered here without the enriching experience of having conducted applied hurricane research with Timothy Reinhold, an internationally known and pioneering wind engineer and current senior vice-president for research at the Institute of Business and Home Safety (IBHS), when he was a professor at Clemson University. What I have learned from Tim regarding wind pressure and building performance is not only truly invaluable, but it also emboldened me to have the temerity to use plain language in discussing sometimes complex technical issues. And for this, I will remain indebted to Tim. I would also like to thank Dr. Hugh "Huq" Gladwin, PhD, a respected anthropologist dedicated to the human impact of disasters, with whom I have also collaborated on hurricane mitigation research and educational initiatives going back to 1998. The foundation of this book is much stronger as a result of his and Dr. Reinhold's invaluable support and shared knowledge.

Author

Ricardo A. Alvarez is an internationally known consultant, subject-matter expert, applied research scientist, former college professor, author, and speaker, focusing on the performance of the built environment in the context of vulnerability to natural hazards, risk management, hazard mitigation, emergency management, and adaptation to climate change.

He began focusing on how buildings perform under the impact of natural hazards as an architecture student in California, complementing his design work by conducting research using small-scale models to visualize the behavior of structures under various loading conditions, and how damage takes place under such impacts. Early in his career, he had a chance to convert the knowledge he had acquired through analytical and experimental research into actual practice when he experienced a major earthquake in his native Nicaragua and had the opportunity of assessing damage on numerous buildings, and of formulating plans for repairs and reconstruction with the objective of making buildings stronger against future expected impacts.

That early experience taught him invaluable lessons that contributed to a philosophy of design and professions, which he had begun formulating as a student, learning about building performance under external impacts. Among these lessons, the value of empirical knowledge acquired through field work and observation of damaged buildings in the aftermath of a disaster have become central to Ricardo's approach to reducing the potential for damage to the built environment from expected impacts of natural hazards.

Another valuable lesson Ricardo has incorporated into his philosophy of work is that a practical methodology toward hazard mitigation based on empirical knowledge, complemented as needed by experimental and analytical work, will be effective independently of the type of natural hazard prevailing in any given region. Ricardo's lifetime work is proof of this. He has over the years successfully converted this method into a multihazard approach to mitigation that has worked effectively in cases of hurricanes, floods, and other hazards, and as a foundation for his work on adaptation of the built environment to climate change.

Ricardo has engaged in vulnerability, risk, and damage assessment field work in the United States and other countries posthurricanes Gilbert, Andrew, Mitch, Opal, Ivan, Katrina, Wilma, and many more, developing an empirical approach for characterizing impacts, assessing the causality of damage, and identifying effective hazard mitigation and adaptation measures to reduce the potential for damage to the built environment.

He was the principal investigator (2000–2004) conducting research funded by the State of Florida Residential Construction Mitigation Program and has directed more than 1400 hazard mitigation projects since 1993, many of which have involved work at major hospitals and other critical facilities. Ricardo taught "Vulnerability Assessment and Hazard Mitigation" graduate-level courses at Florida International University (1995–2010) and "Risk Management and Hazard Mitigation in the Private Sector" (2003–2006) for the CMBA at Florida Atlantic University. He developed a certificate in "Emergency Management and Hazard Mitigation" (1996–2000) for EM professionals and a "Developing a Culture of Mitigation through Education" (2001–2005) K-12 program designated as a best practice by FEMA in 2004.

Ricardo has been engaged in work related to global climate change since 1997. In 1998, he was the managing director for the "Climate Change and Extreme Events Workshop" for the First National Assessment of Global Climate Change Consequences in the United States, leading to a report to the Congress in 2000. Ricardo authored a white paper, "The Need for Action to Confront Potential Consequences of Global Climate Change on a Regional Basis" (U.S. South Atlantic Coastal Areas of Florida, Georgia, North Carolina, South Carolina plus Puerto Rico, and the U.S. Virgin Islands), which set the agenda for discussion at that workshop. Since 2004, Ricardo's main focus has been on the combined impacts of storm surge and sea level rise, the potential for damage to buildings, infrastructure, and the urban environment in the coastal region, and the need for implementing adaptation measures on an individual building basis as well as at regional scales.

He is known for pushing the envelope and engaging in pioneering work on various fronts. Examples of this pioneering spirit include the development in 1996 of the concept of *sheltering in place* as a major practical and effective alternative to the evacuation of major hospitals in coastal regions vulnerable to hurricanes; the development of an *encapsulation* solution developed in 1999 to provide a hurricane-resistant envelope for the Miami Children's Hospital; 2 years of research leading to a new method of anchoring roof sheathing in houses, which resulted in a 130% increase in wind-uplift resistance without increasing the cost of construction; and his position, submitted at a time when the focus was on mitigation by reducing emissions, that society needed to at the very least dedicate equal emphasis to climate change adaptation as it did to mitigation of climate change. A current and more recent example of this forward vision and pioneering spirit is Ricardo's challenge to the research and engineering communities of Southeast Florida to engage in applied research to demonstrate whether the permeability (porosity) of the limestone ocean substrate can be overcome, which he has issued in the context of the feasibility of implementing regional protective works to protect human activity and the way of life of our coastal regions to the expected impacts of storm surge and waves being exacerbated by sea level rise.

Ricardo is a former deputy director of the International Hurricane Center (1997–2004). He has served in the Miami-Dade County Local Mitigation Strategy Steering Committee (LMS), the Florida State Hazard Mitigation Plan Advisory Team (SHMPAT), and the CLEO Institute Advisory Board. He is a published author with two books, a book chapter, and numerous published articles. His first book was published in Spanish, *Paraiso Protegido: Hacia una cultura de mitigacion*

(2012) (ISBN 978-607-401-556-0) by Editorial M.A. Porrua, Mexico D.F., Mexico. *Hurricane Mitigation for the Built Environment* is his second book, and he is working on a third book, *Vulnerability Assessment: An Empirical Approach*. Ricardo is a research affiliate at the Florida Center for Environmental Studies at Florida Atlantic University and is a principal at Mitigat.com, Inc., a Florida-based consulting firm focusing on vulnerability assessment and mitigation.

Born in Bluefields, on the Caribbean coast of Nicaragua, at 3 years of age, Ricardo and his family moved to the capital city of Managua, where he grew up and graduated from the prestigious La Salle (Instituto Pedagogico de Varones) school. Ricardo was 8 years old when he discovered that he wanted to be an architect. It was then his father, a medical doctor and surgeon, having watched him excavating and building in the yard for days on end during the summer, asked what he wanted to be when he grew up. Ricardo responded, "I want to build houses," to which his father declared, "So you want to be an architect," and so it was decided.

Ricardo attended the University of California at Berkeley, the California State Polytechnic University (Cal Poly) at San Luis Obispo, California, the Instituto Centroamericano de Administracion de Empresas (INCAE), and MBA school in Managua, Nicaragua. At the INM Systems Science Institute in Beverly Hills, California, he completed a broad field of studies in environmental design, architecture, city planning, business administration, and systems and project management.

Ricardo and his wife Marcia, an educational psychologist and kindergarten ESOL (English as a second language) teacher, have two children. They have resided in Southeast Florida since 1979. Ricardo has traveled to 28 different countries and is fluent in English and Spanish, in addition to having communicative competency in four other languages.

Ricardo's dedication to his hazard mitigation and climate change adaptation work is best expressed in the words of a speaker at a major event, hosted in 1998 by the University of Quintana Roo, in Chetumal, Mexico, who thanked Ricardo for his contributions by saying "We thank you for all you have done and continue to do to protect property and the life of so many from the impacts of natural hazards, without those who are so protected even knowing about it."

1 The Art and Science of Hazard Mitigation

Mitigation is about lowering the risk and reducing the effects of disasters ... To successfully mitigate against disaster will require the combined talents and concerted efforts of all levels of government, academia, professionals and voluntary organizations, the corporate sector, and all Americans.

William J. Clinton
President of the United States, December 6, 1995

We cannot stop the forces of nature, but we can and must prevent them from causing major social and economic disasters.

Kofi Annan
Secretary-General of the United Nations, 1999

Hazard mitigation, specifically hurricane mitigation, offers the most practical and effective way to reduce the potential for damage to the built environment, to protect life and property, and to achieve resilient communities in vulnerable coastal regions around the world. Hazard mitigation is a tried-and-tested approach that can benefit many, but only to the degree that it is adopted as an essential component of daily practice by architects and other design professionals with support from planners and policy makers, and that of an informed general public. Despite considerable progress in the practice of hurricane mitigation highlighted by a range of success stories, the reality is that the vulnerability of the coastal built environment and potential for damage to the full spectrum of human activity continues to increase as the hazards are exacerbated by the inexorable push of global warming and sea level rise, and as urban development and population continue to grow in the coastal region. It is clear we must look at hurricane mitigation with a sense of urgency while actively pursuing it as common practice. I offer here a roadmap for understanding hurricane mitigation, both from a historical perspective and from the critical role it can play in protecting hurricane-vulnerable communities well into the foreseeable future.

Practitioners in the field of emergency management here in the United States have in one form or another addressed the topic of hazard mitigation, hurricane mitigation, for more than 25 years now. For some in hurricane-vulnerable coastal communities, the term *hazard mitigation* has become synonymous with federal funding programs that have contributed significant amounts of monies to a wide range of measures expected to be effective in reducing potential damages to buildings and infrastructure from the recurring impacts of future hurricanes. The enactment of new laws or revision of existing laws have enhanced the practice of hazard mitigation and contributed to the formation of a cadre of hazard mitigation practitioners participating in formally organized working groups and professional associations.

Formal education and outreach efforts supported by the Higher Education Project launched by Federal Emergency Management Agency (FEMA) in the mid-1990s, have added an academic perspective through the offering of courses and degree programs that is enriching this field.

But it was not always like this and much essential and important work remains to be done. What many take for granted today relative to hazard mitigation did not exist back in 1992 after Hurricane Andrew had devastated a vast region of South Florida. Except for those who had been directly engaged by public agencies to assess the feasibility of enhancing hurricane-damaged buildings during the repair–reconstruction process, design professionals such as architects and engineers rarely participated in the practice of hazard mitigation. Recent hurricane impacts on coastal communities in the United States (i.e., Sandy in 2012) have highlighted important challenges ahead.

Departing from those early days without a generally accepted theory of how hazard mitigation should be practiced, and without literature or reference materials other than those in the code of federal regulations or agency memoranda and manuals addressing regulatory and programmatic issues, these pages describe how the practice of hurricane mitigation emerged in the field through a true learn-by-doing process to reach the stage where it is today.

On the topic of mitigation, a prior definition of terms is critical in promoting meaningful discussion in an environment of clarity and mutual understanding between all parties involved. To that end, the root of the terms *hazard* and *mitigation*, their etymology, usually offers the simplest, clearest, and briefest definition possible:

> *Hazard*: From the Arabic noun *az-zahr* = dice, chance, uncertainty, danger, risk, source of danger, obstacle
> *Mitigation*: From the Latin verb *mitigare* = to soften, to alleviate, to make less harsh, to diminish

It is quite clear what these two words mean. When we combine both to create the term *hazard mitigation*, it is clear we are speaking of diminishing the danger posed by a hazard.

When I first got involved in this field by providing professional services to FEMA in the aftermath of the Hurricane Andrew (August 1992) disaster in southeast Florida, there was a legal definition of hazard mitigation found in Title 44 of the Code of Federal Regulations, 44 CFR for short, which read as follows:

> *Hazard mitigation* means any cost-effective measure that will reduce the potential for damage to a facility from a disaster event (44 CFR, 206.201(f)).

The above definitions, both the etymological and the regulatory, are normative in that they tell us the *what* but not the *how*.

The regulatory definition in 44 CFR is specific in establishing the following criteria for hazard mitigation:

- Hazard mitigation measures must be *cost effective*, which means the benefits of implementing mitigation measures must exceed or at a minimum be equal to the cost. This addresses the legal requirement for all projects to be funded in whole or in part by federal funds.

- The purpose of hazard mitigation is the reduction of potential damage, which means future damage that may be caused by hazard events. This makes it clear that hazard mitigation is preventive in nature not remedial.
- For regulatory purposes, hazard mitigation is linked to a disaster event, which in the context of 44 CFR means a *declared major disaster* referring to the legal requirements for a major disaster declaration by the President of the United States.

This definition sets the rules for the practice of hazard mitigation funded by federal programs but it also establishes, in my opinion, a sound practical foundation for privately funded mitigation projects.

This definition however is not *prescriptive* in that it does not say how to go from its regulatory language to implementation of cost-effective measures to reduce the potential for damage to a facility from some future hazard event. Other than specifying that mitigation measures must be cost effective, it says nothing about what kinds of measures or how to implement them. It specifically states that damage reduction is the objective, but says nothing about what kinds of damage or from what causes? It requires cost effectiveness to satisfy legal financial requirements, but it leaves implicitly, a need to show effectiveness in damage reduction and offers no guidance on how to do this. In summary, this 44 CFR definition provides the basic legal requirements for federally funded hazard mitigation project, but it is not a user's or design manual for mitigation practitioners.

This specific definition in 44 CFR is what I found when in the late spring of 1993, FEMA requested that I take charge of managing the hazard mitigation program in the aftermath of Hurricane Andrew and for three other declared disasters in Florida. This was my starting point, a regulation that had been published in 44 CFR back in 1988 with the passage of the *Robert T. Stafford Disaster Relief and Emergency Assistance Act (Public Law 93–288 as amended)* to modify the *Disaster Relief Act of 1974*, and a lot of confusion in the field where federal, state, and local representatives could not even agree on what constituted an eligible mitigation project.

Before I share with you how a viable and effective, often pioneering, hazard mitigation practice emerged and evolved out of this muddled base after Hurricane Andrew let me share with you another definition for hazard mitigation in 44 CFR—a much newer one that was incorporated in 2002 when *mitigation planning* became a requirement under amendments to the Stafford Act, one that in my opinion adds a new perspective to the topic and reads as follows:

> *Hazard mitigation* means any sustained action taken to reduce or eliminate the long-term risk to human life and property from hazards (44 CFR 201.2).

I believe it will be of interest and beneficial to many, new and veteran, practitioners of hazard mitigation to learn how the true practice of hazard mitigation was developed and became a reality in the field, the product of a concerted, pragmatic, and decisive learn-by-doing effort, in those hectic days following the impact of what was at the time considered to be the costliest natural disaster to ever hit the United States.

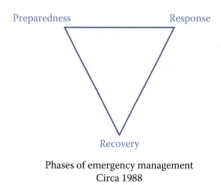

Phases of emergency management
Circa 1988

FIGURE 1.1 Schematic of the phases of emergency management before the practice of mitigation was fully developed and embraced as the foundation of emergency management.

To put that effort in context, let me start by presenting a graphic that describes the model of emergency management practice that was current back in 1992–1993. This is represented in Figure 1.1.

I still remember the training material from FEMA referring to emergency management (EM) as a three-legged stool, where the seat was the practice of EM and *preparedness*, *response*, and *recovery*, the so-called three phases of EM, were the legs supporting the stool, a rather simple, but effective description and illustration of what EM was. Please note that there is no mention of mitigation here.

So this is how the effort started from the meager foundation of a regulatory definition and a partial diagram describing what emergency management involves, by setting three clear objectives for the teams charged with managing the recovery effort in the region devastated by Hurricane Andrew, as follows:

- Establish and use a common language with definition of terms understood and accepted by all involved.
- Define hazard mitigation in terms of actual field applications.
- Design a method to convert legal regulatory language into actual brick-and-mortar or nuts-and-bolts applications in the field.

Establishing a common language was simple enough because most of the terms needed were already defined in 44 CFR, and we were able to segregate terms into two groups, one for terms with a regulatory meaning, and the other for practical terms involving the application of mitigation measures. This and a series of training workshops soon got almost everybody communicating in the same language and understanding each other.

In the process of tackling actual projects in the field and discussing options to protect buildings from future impacts, while gaining experience through practice, it was realized the reduction of potential damage is the common denominator of all mitigation projects. Mitigation is about *damage reduction!* This startlingly simple yet monumental conclusion led me to test proposed mitigation alternatives by asking the following question: Will this reduce potential damage? This simple, straightforward

The Art and Science of Hazard Mitigation

test worked very well at the time and has continued to work equally well over the many years I have engaged in the practice of hazard mitigation.

Important as this progress was, the biggest challenge still remained the need to develop methodology to move from the regulatory language in 44 CFR to actual implementation of solutions in the field. This was much more challenging than anything done before in this discipline, becoming a work in progress with all involved parties learning by doing in a process requiring periodic recalibration, corrections, and constant debate, which continues today.

In reality, this methodology required the development of a *theory of mitigation* to guide the practice by way of an empirical approach. In doing this, there was a great benefit in being able to inspect a the damaged building and establish the causality of the damage, by identifying actual causes of direct damage and linking these to the actual effects from the impacts. Repeating this process in project and after project, a method was developed, tested, calibrated, and refined, which worked well in assessing the potential for damage, in identifying mitigation alternatives, in analyzing these for effectiveness in terms of damage reduction and other criteria, in estimating costs, and in evaluating implementation variables.

This methodology was based on the following parameters:

- Approach each and all projects without preconceptions.
- Apply the method and let it work.
- Use regulatory language in 44 CFR to establish eligibility of each project and compliance with all applicable regulations as a first step.
- If the building has been damaged, research the hazard conditions that prevailed and caused the observed damage on a site-specific basis. Set this as a benchmark to characterize actual impacts and extrapolate to other hazard conditions.
- Identify a range of alternatives for mitigation measures; initially concentrate on damage-reduction capabilities only, not on cost.
- Assess the effectiveness of each identified alternative in terms of structural capability, technical aspects, and logistics. For example, does the specific mitigation measure require deployment each time there is a hurricane warning? Is equipment required for deployment? What about periodic maintenance?
- Initially, look at the big picture in terms of damage reduction, effectiveness, and practical application, but leave construction details and costs for later. Let your imagination be the initial guide.
- Establish a design concept and estimate the initial cost and any recurring maintenance cost if applicable. Estimate the expected service life of each proposed mitigation alternative.
- Complete a benefit–cost analysis of each proposed alternative using methodology approved by the government funding agency.
- Compare alternatives and recommend a preferred alternative.
- Implement.

This was the methodology developed during the Hurricane Andrew recovery phase, which set a foundation that still works today 23 years later, and which has worked effectively in thousands of mitigation projects worth billions of dollars across the United States. I believe we will all agree this is a rather direct approach based on sound scientific, engineering, and economic analysis principles.

Looking back, I cannot help but think that what most emergency managers take for granted today in terms of methodology for hazard mitigation analysis, took a lot of effort, collaboration, and leadership under the rather difficult circumstances of postdisaster recovery in a multiyear process involving many players. This took place in the trenches from the ground up, something really developed and tested in the field and later adopted as policy by the agency. I am quite proud of my contribution to that effort and also should be the many others who collaborated in this enterprise.

While going through the process I have just described, it became clear that all three of the elements of emergency management (see Figure 1.1) share the common goal of damage reduction. Why do we prepare? To be ready for eventual hazard events, some would say. But if you really think about this, it becomes clear that we prepare in order to minimize adverse consequences from the impact of a hazard; in other words, to reduce damage. What are the main objectives of response operations following the impact of a hazard? Most would correctly mention search and rescue, saving lives, restoring communications, removing debris to open roadways and provide access to affected communities, etc. Here again, careful analysis of each of those outcomes will show that the ultimate and common objective is the reduction of damage; from saving lives to reducing human suffering, it is all the same: damage reduction. A similar exercise regarding recovery activities will make us reach the same conclusion: it is all about reducing damage. What this meant for us at the time was that damage reduction, mitigation, is central to the practice of emergency management. This was reflected in a new graphic (Figure 1.2) that modified the one shown in Figure 1.1.

Over the years as I have continued being involved in multiple facets of hazard mitigation, from directing actual projects to conducting applied research or teaching graduate-level courses about this subject matter, I have discovered ways to enhance the methodology and guide the process toward new solutions for damage reduction.

Phases of emergency management
1994

FIGURE 1.2 Schematic of the phases of emergency management showing mitigation as the core and common denominator for the practice of this discipline.

The Art and Science of Hazard Mitigation

It would take too long to mention or describe all of these, but I would like to itemize just a few that I have found particularly effective, and which I have incorporated into my own practice of this discipline:

- Before you mitigate, assess vulnerability! Assessing vulnerability on a site-specific basis allows a project team to
  - Characterize expected impacts in terms of external forces acting on a building.
  - Project expected impacts over the service life of a new or existing building.
- Always use a multihazard approach.
- Always incorporate mitigation elements in design criteria for a new building.
- Consider incorporating mitigation criteria via retrofitting of existing buildings.
- Always consider the feasibility of incorporating mitigation measures during the repair or reconstruction of a damaged building.
- Always take advantage of a hazard event to assess causes of damage and causality by inspecting damaged buildings in the affected area as soon as it is safely possible after the actual impact.
- In assessing vulnerability on a site-specific basis, always consider the character of the vicinity and surroundings to identify sources of potential damage.
- In assessing vulnerability, always look for and assess local or vicinity natural or anthropogenic features that may act as impact modifiers during a hazard event.
- Always consider the benefit of incremental mitigation, meaning what you implement today by way of mitigation measures should not be the end of the road. Future mitigation measures may address changing conditions, introduce desirable redundancy and enhanced protection, and improve the effectiveness of previous mitigation efforts.

All of the above summarizes fairly well the road that took us to where we are today in terms of the theory and practice of hazard mitigation. What I have not mentioned up to now are some of the obstacles and remaining gaps we must address to enhance and strengthen mitigation practice going forward.

Take for example the role of building codes and consider whether they can be considered as mitigation. I will agree that having a building code is much better than having no code, but in the end, it will all depend on what type of code is adopted, whether it is a prescriptive or a normative code, and on what hazard impacts it addresses. In my experience, most building codes establish minimum standards for building design and construction on the basis of specific hazards by location, while also striving for balance between life safety and affordability of construction. Based on this, building codes may certainly be considered mitigation contributors, but only to a point because they typically do not address the worst case in terms of expected hazard impacts, which means there will be future impacts that may generate external loading conditions exceeding by far the design criteria of the affected building, causing extensive catastrophic damage.

The benefits of building to an enhanced code versus a weaker prior code or no code at all have been made clearly evident during the impact of hurricanes. I still remember buildings on the Gulf Coast of central Florida after the passage of Hurricane Charlie in 2004, where it was rather clear how houses built to the new Florida Building Code had performed much more effectively than neighboring units built to a previous code.

What I find concerning in this respect is the prevailing view among most building design professionals that all they are obligated to do is meet the pertinent building code. While this is true from a legal point of view, I submit it is not the best from a professional perspective. After all, if you know that expected impacts may exceed the requirements of the building code, why would you not as a design professional address such expected impacts via design criteria?

Another example is the confusion that arises from the ever-changing lingo used in various sectors that work on the impacts of hazards. Some 20 years ago, the "term du jour" was *sustainable development*, and I still remember how the term was used by many in the emergency management and social research sectors, and how the topic was frequently discussed and presented at conferences and workshops everywhere. I also remember vigorous debates about what this term really meant until it faded away into obscurity and *sustainability* arrived. Does sustainability mean the same as sustainable development? Can these terms be used interchangeably? What do we mean exactly when we say sustainability? Is sustainability related to or based on *preparedness*? What about the term *mitigation* that has been used by emergency managers for over 30 years with one meaning, and just 10 years ago, the climate change sector started using mitigation in an entire new way leading to confusion when representatives from both sectors communicated with each other. What about the term *adaptation* used by climate managers to mean pretty much the same that emergency managers mean when they say mitigation. More confusion occurs. What about the current "term-du-jour" *resilience*, which I have seen defined as "The ability to prepare for and adapt to changing conditions and withstand and recover rapidly from disruption. Resilience includes the ability to withstand and recover from deliberate attacks, accidents, or naturally occurring threats and incidents." I see all of the elements of emergency management in this definition, as well as some of the lingo prevailing among climate managers. So, is resilience the new sustainability or could it just be the new preparedness?

This confusing state of affairs in terms of the language we use to define or discuss a broad range of activities addressing hazard impacts reminds me of what was happening more than 20 years ago, in the aftermath of Hurricane Andrew, as we began to tackle the hazard mitigation issue.

Perhaps, it is time we had another "agreement on a common language" exercise. I submit this is not only necessary but also highly desirable especially now when we are promoting intersectorial collaboration between climate managers and emergency managers, between *mitigators* and *adaptators*. Until this takes place, the current linguistic confusion is hurting efforts toward reducing the potential for damage from the impact of hazards to our coastal communities.

From all of these "happenings," we can only conclude that hazard mitigation is a work in progress, and I trust it will remain so. It benefits from the foundation laid long ago, but it suffers from the growing pains of many sectors dedicated to similar pursuits and common objectives that speak in "different languages."

Hazard mitigation will benefit from enhanced education across all sectors of society, from design professionals to planners, developers, scientists, policymakers, and the general public, all will benefit from learning more about these topics and also from learning a "new" common language to facilitate communication. I am talking about an education enterprise spanning from K to 20, where universities will equip professionals in many disciplines, but especially building design professionals, with the knowledge and tools needed to confront expected hazard impacts through comprehensive and enhanced hazard mitigation practices.

This educational effort needs to be complemented by a paradigm shift in professional licensing practices to one in which all professionals involved in the planning, design, and protection of the built environment will be required to demonstrate knowledge and competency in addressing the impacts of hazards to which a community is vulnerable, through effective hazard mitigation practices, in order to obtain or renew a professional licence to practice.

Hazard mitigation will benefit from current and future research efforts that may lead to new methods of construction, or new building materials or systems, or even new technologies for embedding sensors and instrumentation in buildings, so that they may report on their own performance while interacting with external forces generated by natural hazards, perhaps even pinpoint the exact component that may be compromised, or damaged, or near failure, so that appropriate action may be taken to prevent or reduce the potential for damage. Toward this goal research conducted by IBHS at its full-scale testing facility in North Carolina, or sponsored by the National Institute of Building Sciences (NIBS), or by Factory Mutual Insurance to enhance the performance of buildings, or the "code plus" voluntary standards advocated by the IBHS FORTIFIED Program or the Federal Alliance for Safe Housing (FLASH) Blueprint for Safety are already making an important contribution.

And the journey continues. Mitigation, just like vulnerability, must be a dynamic and interactive process: dynamic because it must continuously adjust to evolving and changing hazard conditions, and interactive because as buildings and structures already incorporating mitigation elements interact with hazards, we can learn a lot from their performance, which can contribute to enhancement of existing mitigation concepts or the development of new ones.

This is hazard mitigation—a blend of science, engineering, technology, and art where the use of imagination is not optional, but absolutely required. It is all about damage reduction. Hurricane mitigation and climate change adaptation of the built environment must be a constant and ever-evolving pursuit in our coastal regions in Florida, the same as those in Cancun and other parts.

2 Two Hurricanes in Three Weeks

Tropical cyclones have destructive capacity, through the combined effects of wind and water, for causing significant, even catastrophic, damage to buildings and infrastructure. No hurricane is too small or too insignificant to be dismissed as *just another minor storm*, in the now infamous words of a local weather forecaster spoken as Hurricane Wilma approached South Florida from the west before causing more than 30 deaths and $20+ billion in damage to an entire region. Perhaps surprisingly to many, no direct hit or landfall is needed for significant damage to occur in the built environment, a fact sadly made evident in 2012 to residents of coastal communities in southeast Florida that sustained $100+ million in damage when tropical cyclone Sandy tracked more than 200 miles off shore on its way to a devastating encounter with New Jersey, New York, and other northeastern communities.

Yes, there is a significant potential for damage from the impact of hurricanes along the coastline from Texas to Maine, the same as in Mexico, Central America, the Caribbean nations, the Philippines, Southeast Asia, Japan, Australia, and so many other areas worldwide. This potential for damage is increasing with the exponential growth of population and urban development in the coastal regions and the exacerbating effects of global warming and sea level rise. It is this potential for damage that the practice of hurricane mitigation can counteract and reduce.

In considering such potential for damage and the benefits of hurricane mitigation, it is critically important to understand the human dimension in all of this. While the structural devastation and physical damage to buildings is the most visible after a hurricane impact, the most severe and long-lasting damage is the loss of life; the injuries, both physical and psychological; the human suffering; and the long-lasting trauma and mental health impacts that affect so many of the victims and survivors of these natural events. In the end, the central and most important objective of practicing hurricane mitigation is to reduce the human impact in terms of death, injury, and economic losses that so affect individuals, families, and the functioning of entire communities. The main reason we want to incorporate hurricane mitigation through design criteria is to strengthen the building so that it will better protect human life and activity sheltered within it.

To help us keep our focus on the human aspects of hurricane impacts and mitigation, this chapter offers an anecdotal review of a true human story within the context of hurricane vulnerability.

Starting with my first visit to Cancun in 1979, and throughout the many other times I have been in Quintana Roo, I have always noted how similar that region of Mexico and Florida are, especially when it comes to their shared vulnerability to hurricanes. Their geography and geology, as well as their flora and fauna, are quite similar. Even more surprising is how both places share a similar evolution in their respective historical development. Both Quintana Roo and Florida were populated by important native cultures that eventually suffered the adverse consequences of European colonization. Each of these places became, at some point in their histories, the newest and last frontier to be respectively developed and conquered in Mexico and the United States. Both Florida and Quintana Roo have at some point attracted visionaries who have taken advantage of their natural beauty, the sand, the sun, and the sea to create wonderful resorts and places to play such as Cancun and the Maya Riviera in Quintana Roo, and Miami Beach and the *Sun Coast* in Florida. Both places make tourism their main economic engine.

Similarities do not however end there. Quite interestingly, and much more related to the topic of this book, are the similarities relative to hurricanes. Quintana Roo and Florida share the dubious distinction of being the two most hurricane-vulnerable places in the Atlantic basin. Both states have been the target of major hurricanes and numerous threats of impacts over the more than 150 years that we have been keeping records of tropical cyclone activity in this region.

In Florida and also in Quintana Roo, there are countless newly arrived residents from other states and countries whose only knowledge of what a hurricane impact is comes from television or other news media. There are also many others who have resided in Quintana Roo or Florida for several years, but who have never directly suffered the brunt of the worst conditions during a hurricane and may, consequently, have totally erroneous ideas about the power and behavior of these natural hazards.

It is because of these similarities and concerns that I now share a real-life story— one that I believe is not only of interest, but also creates a proper context for sharing knowledge, information, and advice through these pages. Please be aware that in deference to the privacy of the real protagonists of the story, fictitious names are used.

Recently widowed Marlene had moved from her native Ohio to Miami Beach, in warm and sunny Florida, in 1977 to live in the house she and her husband had bought, a few years before, to escape from the cruel Cleveland winters and enjoy wonderful annual vacations in the heavenly climate of the Florida beaches.

Marlene still remembered how some friends in Cleveland had tried to dissuade her from her planned move by talking about the annual hurricane season and the high risk she would run by becoming a permanent resident of the Florida coastal region.

With such thoughts all but fading memories after 15 years of living in paradise, in early 1992, Marlene still did not know how it felt to experience the direct hit of a hurricane, for in all these years, she had only once felt hurricane strength winds, which, in her own words, were *not a big deal*. Not a single hurricane came even close to Florida's shores in 1977 and 1978, but in early September of 1979, Marlene thought her time had come when the National Hurricane Center (NHC) used television and radio to inform that they were monitoring what they called a *tropical wave*, which had generated near the Cape Verde islands off the coast of Africa. The report indicated the tropical wave looked quite organized in satellite imagery, generating copious amounts of rain and showing signs of potential further strengthening and, this was the worrisome part, that given certain possible conditions, it might eventually pose a threat to the east coast of the United States.

Two Hurricanes in Three Weeks

At first, Marlene paid little attention to the daily reports given on TV during the six-o'clock news. Given the warm and sunny weather prevalent over south Florida at the time, an Atlantic storm thousands of kilometers away appeared so distant that why worry about it.

On 27 August, as was her custom, Marlene called her daughter Miriam who lived with her husband and two young children in Homestead, a vibrant Florida agricultural community located some 60 km to the southeast of Miami Beach. Over the telephone, mother and daughter chatted about myriads of things, and then, almost in passing before hanging up, both mentioned that the storm had become a hurricane and been given the name of *David*. Later that day, at night before going to bed, Marlene called her other daughter Helena who was recently married and lived in the Hawaiian Islands. Phone calls to Helena during week days had to be made close to midnight Florida time, because of the 6-h difference in time zones with Hawaii.

29 August: The news told of Hurricane David hitting the island of Dominica with sustained winds of 230 kph, the strongest tropical cyclone to hit that island nation in the twentieth century. With more than 260 mm of intense rain dumped in just a few hours, the hit on Dominica was catastrophic. More than 50 were dead, over 200 were injured, and a total of 60,000 people or more than 70% of the total population were left homeless. Close to 75% of the banana and coconut crops were totally lost.

In light of the disaster caused by David in Dominica and the distinct possibility that several other nations in the Lesser Antilles would be similarly impacted, the tone of the newscasts on TV changed radically. Soon, there were also rather graphic images of structural damage and human suffering in Martinique, Guadalupe, and other places in the Caribbean as Hurricane David continued its advance toward the United States. Marlene and her daughter Miriam started to pay closer attention to the tropical weather reports broadcast by radio and television. In south Florida, county and municipal emergency management officials initiated preliminary preparations, including issuing periodic informative bulletins for the general public.

On 31 August, the eye of Hurricane David tracked within 128 km south of Puerto Rico where more than 500 mm of rain fall over mountainous regions. The U.S. and British Virgin Islands were also impacted by extreme rain.

Once over the central Caribbean that same day, Hurricane David reached category 5 strength, with maximum sustained winds of 276 kph and higher gusts, while its central barometric pressure fell to 924 millibars, all of which are characteristics of a damaging major hurricane. That afternoon, category 5 Hurricane David made landfall in the Dominican Republic, where the interaction of the cyclone with the mountain ranges of Santo Domingo and also in Haiti caused extreme rainfall and flash floods, while its winds were considerably weakened for the same reason.

That evening, Marlene and her neighbors Susan and Stuart talked about the news of the disaster David would most probably cause in the Dominican Republic and Haiti. Marlene was now worried about how strong and damaging the hurricane had become, but even more about the reports being issued by scientists at the NHC, which were already giving some probability to a possible landfall on the shores of Miami. Trying to calm her down, Stuart told her that he and Susan had lived there since 1962 and had seen Hurricane Cleo come over the area with 145 kph winds, and then a somewhat weaker Hurricane Donna in 1965. "Neither Cleo nor Donna were the big thing, although I have heard the Miami hurricane of 1926 was quite destructive. But I wouldn't worry too much about David being too dangerous because, as the meteorologists are saying, it will weaken considerably as it moves over the mountains of Hispaniola," Stuart said.

Stuart's words had a certain ring of truth and certainty, but even so Marlene could not help but feel a certain pang of uncertainty, and for the first time accepted that she really had no idea of what the impact of a major hurricane would be like. With these worries and a sense of confusion in her mind, Marlene initiated the daily ritual of her phone visit with her daughter Miriam in Homestead, who told her that she had heard on the radio that Miami Beach would have to be evacuated should Hurricane David track in that direction. That night, after talking with her daughter Helena over the telephone, Marlene slept restlessly.

Everything suddenly changed on 1 September when the 6:00 p.m. evening news on TV reported an estimated 1000 dead in the Dominican Republic as a result of flash floods caused by the clash between the cyclone and the mountains in the island. Beyond this sad and sobering piece of information, there was positive news regarding the hurricane, which had weakened considerably during its passage between Haiti and Cuba and was now just a tropical storm with maximum winds barely reaching 110 kph. At dusk that day, while taking a long leisurely walk along the beach with a view of a wonderful sunset, a temperature of 29°C, and a delicious breeze coming over the ocean, Marlene remembered her neighbor Stuart's words and decided that she truly had nothing to worry about. She felt even more optimistic after talking to Helena who told her that there had not been a single hurricane over the Pacific near Hawaii, where the climate was as warm and radiant as the one in Miami Beach. That night, Marlene dreamt she was in Kauai with Helena and the news reported a violent hurricane had devastated Miami.

"Nature tolerates no jest, for the errors and omissions are those of men." These words of the great philosopher and poet Goethe resonated loudly and clearly, before the changes that took place on 2 September.

As if to make fun of Marlene's new-found optimism and the calming words of Stuart, the next day, tropical storm David came over the warm waters of the eastern Bahamas and began to strengthen again. Near Andros Island, the winds of the storm had climbed to 130 kph, as torrential rains fell over a large region, with more than 200 mm over the Bahamas in just a few hours. Unexpectedly, the tropical cyclone started veering toward the northeast in the direction of the coastline of southeast Florida, the paradise where Marlene and her neighbors were planning to spend their remaining days enjoying the sun, the sea, and the climate.

The news flashes of the day finally destroyed what remained of Marlene's optimism. The hurricane continued to gain strength and was aiming directly for Miami Beach and Miami, its winds were getting stronger, and the central barometric pressure was now at 965 millibars. That morning, emergency management officials issued a hurricane watch for Dade County but around noon upgraded it to a full hurricane warning; hurricane shelters were staffed and opened at several school buildings, and a mandatory evacuation order was issued for most of the coastal communities, including Miami Beach. Although evacuation was obligatory, the authorities concentrated their efforts in evacuating the elderly and infirm who lived mainly in multistory buildings near the beach, but by and large left others basically free to decide whether to evacuate or not.

In the early afternoon, Miriam called and pleaded with her mother to go and stay with her far inland in Homestead, far away from the coast. Marlene considered the possibility of actually leaving and taking her daughter up on her offer, but she also thought of Susan and Stuart's comments about the solid reinforced masonry construction of their houses in Miami Beach, with strong tile roofs, and either aluminum awnings or thick wood shutters to protect their windows. Eventually, the opinion of her neighbors who had indeed had previous experience with hurricanes prevailed over that of her daughter, who had only been residing in Florida for a little over a year and had never been in a hurricane. Marlene decided to shutter-up her windows and ride out the storm in her own house.

By nightfall, the weather had changed; the sky that had been bright and sunny that morning was now overcast and dark while a strong breeze blew from the northeast. There was however a strange and silent calm in the environment. The eleven-o'clock news reported that the eye of Hurricane David was 300 km to the east, while the storm continued to move toward Miami Beach. Somewhat exhausted from all the agitation of the day, Marlene fell into a fidgety sleep until just past midnight when she was awakened by the whistling sound of the wind and the knocking of the wooden shutters against the house. It was raining heavily and even with the shuttered windows she could see the continuous flashing of lightning, although the little thunder she heard sounded somewhat muffled.

The power went off around 4:00 in the morning, sinking the house, and the whole neighborhood, into total darkness except for the eerie and continuous flashing of lightning.

The terrible sound of the wind, the thunder, and the knocking of the shutters continued for what seemed to Marlene like an eternity until, after dawn, little by little, the noise began to subside and by around 10:00 in the morning, it was not even a shadow of what it had been during the night. Using her battery-operated radio, Marlene heard the news that as Hurricane David emerged from over the Bahamas en-route toward Southeast Florida, it began to change course as it got nearer to the Gulf Stream—the strong ocean current that flows north by northeast paralleling most of the eastern coast of Florida—and had started to track more or less along the Gulf Stream. A few hours later, the news came over the radio that David had made landfall to the north of Palm Beach County, approximately 100 km to the north of Miami Beach, shortly before noon. As if by magic, power was restored and everything started to return to normalcy (Figure 2.1).

Marlene emerged from her house and started to open the shutters; a couple of downed trees laid on the street nearby, and there were tree leaves, small branches, and debris everywhere. The outside of her house was covered by hundreds of leaves stuck to the still wet walls. Although it was still cloudy, a moderate wind was blowing from the west, and it appeared as if the sun could penetrate the cloud cover at any moment. Shortly thereafter, her neighbors came over and Susan's first words were, "What did you think of it? I told you nothing would happen!" Then her phone rang and she rushed inside the house to pick it up; it was her daughter Helena calling

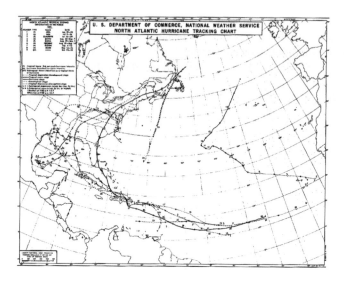

FIGURE 2.1 Track of Hurricane David, which came near Miami and Miami Beach on September 3, 1979 and made landfall to the north of the city of Palm Beach. David was the first hurricane to hit the densely urbanized region of southeast Florida since Hurricane Cleo (1964) and Hurricane Donna (1965) had made minor impacts. (Adapted from NWS—Department of Commerce.)

from Kauai where it was only 7:00 in the morning. As they embarked in animated conversation, Marlene thought to herself: "To tell the truth a hurricane is not that big of a deal."

As an offside to this story, I believe it is important to note that in 1979 there was not a single tropical cyclone in the northeastern Pacific basin, where hurricanes that may eventually impact Hawaii usually form.

After the Hurricane David scare, Mother Nature kept hurricanes mostly away from Florida for the next 13 years. There were some threats in 1981, when Hurricane Dennis came near and touched Florida's coast on the Gulf of Mexico, and then in 1985, when Hurricane Bob traversed the Florida peninsula some 180 km away from Marlene's home. In 1987, Hurricane Floyd brushed the Florida Keys and the southern tip of the peninsula to then continue tracking toward the northeast and away from the coast.

That was all that took place over the 15 years Marlene had been calling Miami Beach home. Neither Bob nor Dennis or Floyd compared in the least to Hurricane David, and if this had really been the most intense of them all, well perhaps her neighbors Susan and Stuart had been right all along: "Hurricanes are no big deal, nothing ever happens." After David and the other threats she had endured over the years, Marlene truly felt quite experienced in matters of hurricanes, to the point where it was now she who gave advice to those newly arrived to the paradise of Florida's beaches by telling them, "There is nothing to worry about, nothing ever happens! Hurricanes in Florida are not that big a deal."

Two Hurricanes in Three Weeks

The 1991 Atlantic hurricane season was a rather calm one, generating only four tropical storms and four weak hurricanes, only one of which came near the coast, but never made landfall.

Enter 1992. The "official" start of the Atlantic hurricane season on June 1, 1992 came and went as did the whole month of June, and when July 1 arrived, there was not a single cyclonic threat anywhere in the Atlantic basin. July's days followed one another in quiet succession until there we were, in August of 1992—that time of the year when all take advantage of the last few days of vacation before the start of a new school year.

For Marlene, Susan, Stuart, Miriam, and most of us who resided in this corner of Florida at the time, it was a summer like the many others we had grown used to over the years. This was just another warm and humid August with the typical pattern of almost daily afternoon showers and thunderstorms.

Satellite imagery on August 14, 1992 showed a region of disturbed weather to the south of the Cape Verde Islands that appeared to be one more *tropical wave* of the many that are generated over equatorial Africa, in assembly line fashion, to then emerge over the warm waters of the eastern Atlantic, and which are routinely assessed by scientists at the NHC to determine if they warrant additional scrutiny for signs of potential further development. In this specific case, the initial assessment showed a system with good organization moving in an environment that appeared conducive for further strengthening, which caused NHC meteorologists to carry out an analysis of intensity of the system using what is known as the *Dvorak technique* (Figure 2.2).

Around noon on 16 August, the tropical wave became a *tropical depression*; we were witnessing the infancy of a tropical cyclone. Eighteen hours later, already 78 days into the 1992 Atlantic hurricane season, the system had strengthened to *tropical storm* status with maximum sustained winds of 63 kph and was christened with the name of *Andrew*, the first-named storm of the season, as it moved generally westward toward the Lesser Antilles.

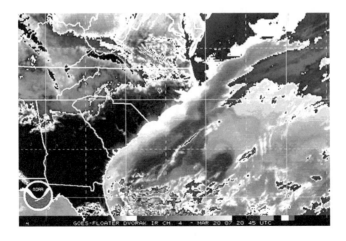

FIGURE 2.2 Satellite image showing data used by NOAA NHC to assess the intensity of a tropical cyclone using what is known as the Dvorak technique. (Adapted from NOAA.)

Between August 17 and 20, tropical storm Andrew encountered quite an adverse atmospheric environment, including wind shear, which weakened it so much that satellite imagery showed a storm system with a rather disorganized and shaggy appearance on the brink of being torn apart.

Many of us, including Marlene and her neighbors, paid little to no attention to the meteorological information embedded within the weather reports on TV, which highlighted the fact that Andrew was the first tropical cyclone of what had thus far been a rather dull 1992 Atlantic hurricane season and mentioned the possibility that it could go on to become the first hurricane of the season. The sad reality was that most of us were happily suffering from cases of *hurricane amnesia*. We had grown used to seeing tropical cyclones emerge over the distant horizon to then just move away from Florida's coasts, and in consequence, few, if any, of us really worried about what course Andrew might follow.

Tropical storm Andrew survived its passage through the adverse environment it had encountered over the open waters of the Atlantic to the north of the Virgin Islands and Puerto Rico and had in fact begun to grow stronger and better organized as it approached the Bahamas from the east. In the morning of 22 August, Andrew intensified and became the first hurricane of the 1992 Atlantic hurricane season, immediately entering a period of rapid intensification that saw its maximum sustained winds reach velocities in excess of 240 kph and its central pressure drop to 922 millibars by the next day. By then, the hurricane was over the Bahamas, moving west in the direction of Miami.

Suddenly, the realization was that Andrew posed a serious threat to Miami and neighboring communities in south Florida. The news media in collaboration with the Office of Emergency Management in Dade County launched an intense and immediate campaign to alert the public to the fact that there was a major and still intensifying hurricane at the doorsteps of south Florida. A hurricane watch was issued for the coast of southeastern Florida. Hurricane shelters were staffed and activated, while an evacuation plan for the coastal zone was also activated. Big and beautiful cruise ships that were docked at Miami left port to sail away from the possible impact zone. Tourists and many residents rushed to the airport to find seats on flights leaving Miami. A hurricane warning was issued later that morning of August 23, 1992.

As if awakening from a dream, Marlene thought this threat really was different. Television images were showing a map of the projected trajectory of Hurricane Andrew as a straight line right through Miami. Emergency management officials and weather reporters were emphasizing the fact that this was a rather strong category 4 hurricane; also that a ridge of high pressure to the north would keep Andrew on its then current westward track for a possible landfall in the region of Miami. When Marlene talked with Miriam around noon, she decided to shutter her house and go to Homestead to ride the storm out at her daughter's home.

By late afternoon on 23 August, tens of thousands of people were already in Red Cross-operated shelters and it was estimated that more than half a million others had already left town for points in north and central Florida. The few major roadways heading north in this long and narrow peninsula were already loaded with vehicles of all sorts when the first bands of rain and strong winds could be felt along the coastal region. International airports in Miami, Fort Lauderdale, and Palm Beach were under siege by thousands who frantically tried to get seats in the few flights left, before all operations were suspended for reasons of public safety.

Although Andrew weakened some during its crossing over the Bahamas, once over the Florida straits nourished by the warms waters of the Gulf Stream, it regained category 4 strength, and it continued getting stronger.

In Miriam's house, Marlene felt a lot safer than at her own house so close to the coastline. All windows were "protected" by wide strips of heavy duct tape that would prevent flying glass, in the event window panes were to be broken by flying debris. They had enough bottled water to last them for 3 or 4 days, plus the bathtub had also been filled with water after having been cleaned with bleach. In addition, canned food, a battery-operated radio, flashlights, and a portable stove for cooking were the emergency provisions planned by Miriam and her family.

Since 6:00 p.m., Channel 4 TV had concentrated on broadcasting continuous information about the approaching hurricane, also taking a growing stream of calls from viewers worried about how to better protect themselves from the approaching impact, and dispensing advice and answers to their questions. With frequent regularity, the station broadcasted the latest bulletins from the NHC and the Dade County Office of Emergency Management. Marlene and her daughter and son-in-law watched a news flash around 10:00 p.m., which indicated the hurricane appeared to be taking more of a northeastern track, so Andrew might eventually make landfall near the northern end of the county, some 70 km north of their house in Homestead. Even with the worry and uncertainty they all felt, the news gave them a measure of relief when they thought Hurricane Andrew might come over land far from where they were, so they decided the best thing was to try and get some sleep.

Both small children soon fell into a deep sleep, undoubtedly exhausted; on the other hand, the adults were only able to catch a few winks of restless sleep. For a hurricane supposed to be veering toward the north and away from them, the winds they felt in Homestead certainly appeared to be getting progressively more intense. A few minutes past midnight, the howling of the wind became louder; gusts of wind made the entire house and especially the windows utter all manner of noises, almost like painful grunts, which were rather worrisome to the occupants. George, Marlene's son-in-law, got up to turn on the TV; Channel 4 continued broadcasting reports about the hurricane's progress and intensity and also answering the many calls coming over the telephone. Outside their house, in addition to the progressively louder howl of the wind, they could hear the equally loud and worrisome sounds of unknown objects crashing against the exterior of the house. With each new gust, the windows vibrated furiously. Then, in an instant, the power went off; after a couple of failed attempts at being restored, everything was covered by the most frightful darkness.

By then, extremely worried by what clearly appeared to be a monstrous hurricane, they decided to take refuge in the main bedroom. The children were still asleep on heavy blankets on the floor, while the adults crowded together on the bed, paying attention to their battery-operated radio and any information or report that could provide some idea of what was happening or about to happen relative to the hurricane. Little by little, they all succumbed to sleep, but with each new and louder roar of the wind and each new gust that appeared to be trying to rip the house apart, they were brusquely startled out of their restless sleep.

When they thought what they felt and heard could not get any worse, suddenly they heard a terrible and even louder noise while their ears felt as if they were going to explode, all of a sudden the wind penetrated their house. Everything in the room was flying about crashing against the walls, the roof trusses moaned, and pieces of ceiling fell on them together with rain. The hurricane was inside the house with them! Very scared and confused, they took refuge, as best they could, inside the closet trying to shield themselves from the hurricane with pillows and blankets. The light closet door threatened to disintegrate at any moment, and even in that shelter of desperation they still felt debris and rain falling upon them.

After what had felt to them as an eternity, the terrorized occupants of the improvised shelter realized the horrible roar of the hurricane was not as loud as before. They could see a sliver of daylight under the door and heard static coming from the radio. The closet door only shook sporadically as wind gusts continued to blow from time to time.

Slowly and carefully George opened the closet door and stuck his head out. There was daylight and light rain coming into the room through broken windows, and large sections of the ceiling and roof that were missing, having been ripped apart, exposing the interior of the house to the elements. The bed and bedroom furniture as well as the carpet were covered by debris and soaking wet.

Miriam burst into tears sobbing rather loudly as her startled children asked: "What happened mommy, what happened?" Marlene, stiff and in pain from the hours of crouching uncomfortably on the closet floor, could not even utter a word. They could hear excited loud voices outside, and once in a while still another gust of wind lashing at the house like some kind of rear guard whip from a retreating Hurricane Andrew on its way to the Gulf of Mexico.

Without going into the details, I can say that Miriam and George's house was declared a total loss, uninhabitable. In contrast to this, Marlene's house in Miami Beach suffered exterior damage, but not a single drop of rain penetrated its interior. Hurricane Andrew did not change course as it had been indicated it might have, but simply kept on marching to the west, making landfall in the southern region of Dade County, and destroying most of the city of Homestead and nearby communities (Figure 2.3).

Hurricane Andrew was a category 5 storm as it made landfall in Florida. Everything considered, the good news is that it was a rather small and compact tropical cyclone that generated little rain, and which moved at 30 kph as it crossed the Florida peninsula. An analysis of the scientific data and meteorological observations revealed the hurricane had a maximum sustained wind speed of 276 kph.

Hurricane Andrew caused 65 deaths and physical damage totaling $41.0 billion (1992).

Three days later, Miriam, George, and their two young boys were living in a tent together with five thousand other survivors of the disaster in another 1200 tents, in an instant city erected by the National Guard. Marlene had managed to make it back to her house in Miami Beach, where power was still out and the clearing of debris from the streets had yet to begin, while the authorities were still not allowing the

Two Hurricanes in Three Weeks   21

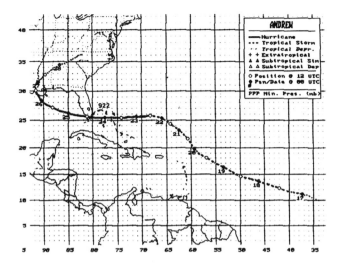

FIGURE 2.3 Map showing the track of Hurricane Andrew from the time it became a tropical storm on August 17, 1992 until it made landfall in Southeast Florida 12 km ENE of Homestead as a category 5 hurricane in the early morning of August 24, 1992. Hurricane Andrew continued traversing the Florida peninsula to emerge over the Gulf of Mexico toward a new landfall in Louisiana near Morgan City 2 days later as a category 3 hurricane. This graphic is based on a *Preliminary Report on Hurricane Andrew* (A16—28 August 1992) prepared by NOAA, and subsequent revisions of December 10, 1993 and February 7, 2005.

return of residents to the southern third of the island. Thanks to a field communications center installed by the telephone company, Marlene had been able to talk with Helena who had begged her to go and spend at least a month with her family in Kauai or at least until some semblance of normalcy had returned to Florida. On the first of September, Marlene boarded a flight in Miami on her way to Hawaii; she had accepted the invitation of Helena and her husband.

After a rather slow and difficult process of checking in for her flight, in an airport still in the midst of clean-up operations and repairs, the flight from Miami to Los Angeles had been quiet and uneventful, allowing Marlene to get some much-needed sleep.

This was Marlene's first ever visit to Hawaii, and she was instantly captivated by the climate and the colors of the tropics, as well as by the kindness and friendliness of the people and their exotic faces, a reflection of their Polynesian, Asian, and European ancestry. Gathering her luggage to then check-in for her flight to Kauai was quite an efficient process, but also one that transpired in a somewhat slower, more peaceful, friendly, and amiable manner than what one would normally experience at large international airports.

The 40-passenger twin engine jet-prop lifted off punctually from Honolulu and offered a continuous stream of spectacular views of the archipelago along its route. Not too long afterwards, the captain announced the plane was descending and on its final approach for landing in Kauai. Marlene happily embraced and kissed her daughter, whom she had not seen for 3 years, and her son-in-law.

On the trip from the airport to Helena's house, Marlene could not cease admiring the incredible vegetation and the wonderful landscapes that appeared everywhere as glimpses of paradise. Giovanni and Helena's house had walls of concrete blocks and a rather steep corrugated metal roof with wide eaves. All windows had wooden jalousie shutters similar to those at her house in Miami Beach. The numerous trees around the house and throughout the surrounding neighborhood had thick trunks, dense canopies, and lot of flowers the color of fire. The front yards, sidewalks, and streets were covered by a reddish and yellow carpet of fallen flowers. There was no doubt in Marlene's mind, Kauai was another paradise! For the first time in too many days, Marlene felt relaxed, at peace, rested, and happy taking in the beauty of the place and seeing her daughter. Although in the back of her mind she still saw, like in flashes, the images of Miriam and George and their two beautiful children sheltered in a field tent back in Florida.

A few days before Marlene flew to Hawaii, in fact even before the terrible impact of Hurricane Andrew, on the 18th of August to be precise, a tropical wave that had emerged from western Africa moved almost unnoticed over the Atlantic crossing over Panama into the eastern Pacific basin where, on September 6, 1992, it was designated as tropical depression #18 packing sustained winds peaking at 45–50 kph. This system progressed to a tropical storm Iniki, which having reached hurricane strength made landfall in Kauai on September 11, 1992, traversing the island from south to north with maximum sustained winds of 225 kph gusting to 280 kph. The eye of the hurricane made landfall near Waimea Beach at 3:30 p.m., and 40 min later emerged once again over the open waters of the Pacific near Haena Beach. Close to 15,000 homes were damaged by Iniki in Kauai, including 1421 that were totally destroyed, of which 63 were demolished by the storm surge that hit the southern coast of the island. More than 5200 of the affected houses suffered major damage caused by the wind and the impact of flying debris, among which was Helena and Giovanni's beautiful new house where they and Marlene had taken shelter during the hurricane.

This is the true story of Marlene, who during the first 58 years of her life had only felt the winds of a weak hurricane crossing more than 100 km away, and then in 1992, in the short span of only 18 days survived the destruction of two houses belonging to her children, one by category 5 Hurricane Andrew and the other by category 4 Iniki in two tropical paradises separated by more than 8000 km. What are the probabilities of seeing this series of events repeated?

This is an example of a story that illustrates the human side of hurricane impacts, just one example among the millions of similar stories out there represented by each survivor of a hurricane. This is a story that invites us to reflect upon the lessons learned through the experiences of others.

The main lessons are the following:

- It only takes one impact. It does not matter if for 15 years the hurricanes we have experienced were no big deal. It does not matter either, if the current hurricane season is a slow one, or if the probability of impact from an approaching hurricane is low. As we have seen in the story of Marlene, one impact was more than enough to cause catastrophic damage, death, and human suffering, such as we saw during Hurricane Andrew.

Two Hurricanes in Three Weeks

- We must be prepared at all times. If a single impact is all it takes, and we do not know if such impact will happen during the current season or 50 years from now, we must always take very seriously the potential for damage of which hurricanes are capable.
- Mitigation is about damage reduction. Mitigation provides a solid foundation for good preparedness. Mitigation consists of those effective measures we implement continuously and over the long term, to reduce the potential for damage to our buildings, homes, and property from the impact of recurring hurricanes.
- Hurricane prediction, even with the continued improvements that have taken place over time, remains an inexact science. Although, in the story, very few details were given relative to how hurricanes David, Andrew, and Iniki were generated and how they intensified, it is clear that numerous interacting atmospheric and oceanic factors can influence the behavior of a hurricane. It is also clear that we depend on remote observations to secure the necessary data to forecast the trajectory, intensity, and area of landfall for any given hurricane. With the example of Hurricane David, we saw how the projected track and region of landfall followed one trajectory and at the last hour changed course, while on the other hand, a change of course that did not happen was predicted for Hurricane Andrew.
- The science of hurricane prediction has improved continuously and considerably over the past few years. We now have more and better remote-sensing instruments onboard satellites, better equipped hurricane-hunting aircrafts, as well as growing networks of surface sources of real-time data acquisition. There is also a suite of predictive models and available supercomputing power to process much more data much faster to feed the models. Gradually, the margin of error in track and landfall prediction has been reduced, but several uncertainties remain to be resolved specifically regarding the prediction of hurricane intensity. We must remain aware that the science of hurricane prediction remains inexact; it is therefore preferable to err on the side of being overcautious than incur failure for having taken undue risks.
- To underestimate is to fail. Many who have been through the impact of a minor hurricane or who have only experienced the peripheral impact of a major hurricane tracking at some distance may think that all hurricanes are the same and in general "are not that big a deal." How many may have thought that Hurricane Andrew (1992), or Hurricane Gilbert (1988), or Wilma (2005), or Sandy (2012) "would not be a big deal" and ended up paying dearly for having misjudged these hurricanes?

Every hurricane, regardless of how minor it might be, has the capability for causing serious to significant damage. Some hurricanes cause most of the damage with their strong winds; others do it with storm surge, and still others mainly with torrential rain and flooding, and the truly damaging use the full arsenal of damaging components to generate catastrophic results. Those who disregard an approaching hurricane as just a minor storm run the risk of tragic failure in their assessment of potential results from their impacts.

- Hurricane amnesia. After several years without a hurricane coming close, or when the impacts have been indirect or truly minor, many little by little tend to forget what it means to experience a hurricane hit. Those who have never endured such impacts easily forget what they saw or heard in the media about such events. Even in places that have suffered catastrophic impacts, after many years, the details become fuzzy and fodder for old folks. Lessons taught by nature are forgotten and the errors that contributed to increased damages are repeated. It is as if we suffer from amnesia, *hurricane amnesia* to be sure. It is this act of forgetting that can make us lose respect for nature with dire consequences the next time a hurricane approaches.
- Education must be constant. In the story of Marlene, two tourist paradises were mentioned, the Florida Sun Coast and the islands of Hawaii. Both of these are places where people from many other places, who may have little or no knowledge of what a hurricane is capable of doing, come to live. The vast majority of these *transplants* only acquire an idea about hurricanes by listening to the stories and opinions of their neighbors who may have, in some cases, directly suffered the impact of a tropical cyclone. Others, those of recent arrival or those who pay little attention to these storms, may at some point pay dearly for their ignorance or lack of attention.

In this respect, Quintana Roo is quite similar to Florida and Hawaii. These three places are quite alike in that they all are tourists' paradises, full of immigrants and visitors, with constantly growing populations and large numbers of residents with little or no practical knowledge about hurricanes.

- Let us learn from others. Every hurricane impact is an event full of lessons to be learned. The fact that our particular paradise might have gone several years without an impact does not mean we would have to wait until we suffer a direct impact to learn our lessons. We are allowed to learn from the experience of others. Hurricanes neither have nationality nor do they respect political borders; the same thing happens with successfully effective measures to prepare for and mitigate the impacts of hurricanes. If Cancun has been particularly successful in implementing preparedness and mitigation initiatives, communities in Florida and Hawaii must truly feel fortunate to learn and benefit from such best practices. On the other hand, if a given community has made considerable progress in adopting design criteria and construction methods to build hurricane-resistant buildings and infrastructure, those who are design professionals or developers anywhere must use all means at their disposal to adopt these solutions for their own projects. To copy the good is a virtue.
- Success is based on knowledge not on luck. With respect to hurricane impacts, success is measured in terms of damages avoided or prevented as a result of implementing preparedness and mitigation measures. It is highly important that we recognize that our success will take place in direct proportion to specific knowledge we have acquired and applied. Luck has

no bearing on success, and those who may believe otherwise are destined to discover the error of their thinking when they find themselves under the impact of a hurricane.

As we reflect about the experiences of Marlene, and her family and neighbors, we must ask ourselves: How many of us have lived through similar experiences? How many of us might have been undecided about what to do when confronted by an approaching hurricane and we may have heard from a neighbor or from someone "with experience" comments such as: "There is nothing to worry about. I have lived here for twenty years and nothing has ever happened"?

With which of the protagonists of the story do we identify the most? What will we do the next time a hurricane approaches? How educated do we feel or are we really knowledgeable when it comes to hurricanes?

I believe that if we continue to dig deeper, many more questions and lessons, both big and small and always useful, could be added to our list.

3 Hurricanes, Vulnerability, and Causes of Damage

Knowledge of hurricanes will allow us to separate myths and fiction from reality; it will help us ask the right questions to become better informed; and, above all, it will lead us to the adoption of preparedness and mitigation measures for the protection of human life and the reduction of potential damage to our property, housing, and buildings.

In this regard, a good point of departure in our journey of knowledge acquisition is to understand that hurricanes are the by-product of natural processes beyond any influence of human control, but which at the same time are necessary and of critical importance in nature and even for human life on Planet Earth. We have the responsibility of knowing our own vulnerability to hurricanes, starting with learning all that we possibly can about these natural hazards. To that end, it may help to search for meaning in the etymology, the roots, of specific words as follows.

HURRICANE

In scientific language, a hurricane is a *tropical cyclone.* The word *cyclone* comes from the Greek *kyklouma*, which means wheel, spiral, and in turn derives from the Greek verb *kykloum*, meaning to turn, to rotate, whose root is *kyklos*: circle. It is clear that we all see and hear the phonetic association between the words *kykloum* and *cyclone.* The important aspect, however, is not just the sound of the word, but its meaning, because it is from this that we are left with the clear image of something that rotates, that turns, that moves in a spiral around a central focal point, just as a hurricane does.

Equally or even more descriptive are the words *hurricane* and *typhoon.* The ancient and extinct people of the Caribbean gave the name *Hurakan* to the god of terrible winds. Such a name is the root for *huracán* in Spanish, and *hurricane* in English, words we use to designate a tropical cyclone. *Typhoon* is also a word that meets these criteria of providing the right image through sound and meaning as its root is the Chinese word *taa-fung*, meaning great wind.

In summary, even if we were to limit ourselves to only studying the origin and meaning of the words *cyclone, typhoon*, and *hurricane* together with the adjectives of *great* and *terrible* found in their roots, we would surely grasp the concept that a hurricane is a great and terrible wind that rotates in a spiral, which is capable of impacting us, causing *damage.*

We should be able to round up the concept linking the results of this etymological exercise with the description of natural processes presented in the previous chapter. On the basis of this, we can conclude that a hurricane is a *natural hazard*, defined as a *source of potential damage*, which results from a natural process beyond our control.

27

By continuing to apply this methodology, we could, step by step, learn at the same time we define in detail the many terms associated with hurricanes, but this is not the main intention. The use of such etymological exercise emphasizes that relative to hurricanes and the damage they can cause, it is extremely important that we get to the bottom of the details for it is only thus that we can prepare effectively in order to mitigate the impacts of these hazards.

Unfortunately, experience has shown that most of those who reside in vulnerable communities have, at best, some rather general knowledge about hurricanes, the main causes of damage, and what we must do to mitigate such damages. Relative to hurricanes, in general and irrespective of what country it is, most people live in a state of *peaceful ignorance*, even in this era of instant graphic news on television, satellites, digital communications, and social media.

There are several reasons for such a state of affairs. Many regions exposed to the impact of hurricanes, such as Florida and other coastal zones around the Gulf of Mexico and the Caribbean, are like magnets that attract thousands of individuals and families who want a better life, a better future, to improve their economic situation, or just to be in a nice environment with great climate and lots of sun, sand, and water.

It is not by chance that most of the same regions are also tourist destinations, where visitors flow from all over the world, generating demand for continuous investment in hotels and infrastructure, which in turn translates into jobs that attract even more people. All of this creates dynamics that once in motion are practically impossible to contain. Some of those who come to live and work in such paradises originate from other countries, states, or regions where they may have already experienced a hurricane and will have an idea of what that is like. Another large segment of the population, even those who may have resided in a vulnerable community for many years, may have never suffered a direct impact from a hurricane. And to reach the limit, there are those from somewhere else who may have been directly affected by a hurricane in the past and with the passage of the years, may already be suffering from *hurricane amnesia*.

Such is the reality of numerous hurricane-vulnerable communities in Florida, around the Gulf of Mexico, or up the Atlantic coastal region in the United States, the Caribbean, the Pacific Islands, or the Cancun–Cozumel–Maya Riviera complex, which in the short lapse of about 30 years has seen the permanent population grow by a factor of 1000%, while also becoming the principal tourist destination in Mexico. The same can be said about southeast Florida, where some 100+ years ago there were only mangroves and swamps and now it has become quite a large urban area with a permanent population nearing 7.0 million, which hosts tens of millions of tourists annually.

WE NEED TO BE EDUCATED

We must view such reality as a situation that requires a constant effort of education at all levels, including our own personal basis. The truth is that when it comes to hurricanes, we will always have something new to learn.

In this regard, it is important to recognize and give credit to initiatives and the continuing efforts undertaken by authorities and various organizations in

Hurricanes, Vulnerability, and Causes of Damage

the United States and other countries to inform, educate, and protect the general population and the built environment from the impacts of hurricanes. An example of such initiatives is enactment of the *Disaster Mitigation Act of 2000* (DMA 2000), a federal law (Public Law 106–390) enacted on October 30, 2000 that modified the Robert T. Stafford Disaster Relief and Emergency Assistance Act. DMA 2000 made the practice of *mitigation planning* for all states and their jurisdictions mandatory, taking a pioneering pilot program developed in Miami-Dade County known as the *Local Mitigation Strategy* (LMS) and making it a national requirement, a prerequisite for states to qualify for federal funding for hazard mitigation projects. In addition, DMA 2000 introduced the concept of *Predisaster Mitigation* as a funding program to foster the practice of hazard mitigation on a continuous basis across the nation. DMA 2000 has resulted in the creation of mitigation planning working groups in municipalities and counties throughout the country and in the investment of billions of dollars in federal, state, and local monies to implement a wide range of hazard mitigation measures to protect eligible facilities and infrastructure against the impacts of hurricanes and other natural hazards.

This push for mitigation triggered by DMA 2000 has been complemented by a host of equally positive and innovative initiatives by other agencies and sectors, including improvements in technology used by NOAA in hurricane-hunting methods, which has improved hurricane prediction on several levels, and the development of new public information tools to communicate the severity of storm surge in simpler easier-to-understand ways. In reviewing the positive outcomes of the initiatives mentioned above, an obvious conclusion would be that hurricane-vulnerable communities are better protected today, but actual hurricane events resulting in catastrophic damage, such as Sandy (2012), or the many years that have passed since the last hurricane event, 9 years and counting in Florida, quickly make us realize that not all is well, that several sectors have not kept pace with the need to practice mitigation. In summary, despite all of the concrete and positive mitigation efforts, it is clear much remains to be done as the vulnerability of our communities continues to increase.

Another good example is the work of authorities in Quintana Roo, Mexico, at the state and municipal levels, with widespread participation of both public and private institutions and NGOs, including the Red Cross, the University of Quintana Roo, and several professional associations engaged in a wide range of activities mainly related to tourism and protection of the general population. These efforts have mainly focused on emergency management through the practice of *civil protection*, resulting in the institutionalization of such an important practice by the state government in support of similar activities at the municipal level. Benefits of such endeavors were evident during the impact of Hurricane Wilma (2005) in Cancun and its surroundings. The timely activation of its emergency plan by the municipality of Benito Juarez, which included a mandatory evacuation order for coastal areas such as the hotel strip where numerous tourists still remained, activation of all hurricane shelters, and a supportive public information campaign were credited with having prevented loss of life under the impact of quite a destructive hazard that caused severe damage to buildings and infrastructure.

In contrast with the success achieved by the activation of the emergency plan in protecting human life, Hurricane Wilma made evident the many weaknesses that persist in the design and construction of buildings as well as in the integrity of the beaches. Much still remains to be done in Cancun and other similarly vulnerable places in this regard.

The challenge is clear for all of us who might have any kind of an interest in any of the communities in Florida or in Quintana Roo that have been mentioned, be it as investors assessing the feasibility of building a hotel, a restaurant or shop, or of investing in a given business in the region, or as design and construction professionals involved in one project or another, or those of us who may have a scientific or other type of professional perspective, or simply those of us who may only want to come and live here in search for new horizons, to work or in some other way be a part of all the natural beauty, the wellness, and the exciting future offered by this region.

The main challenge, however, is to recognize that the specific place in which we may be interested is vulnerable to hurricanes, that each year there is the risk of being hit by a hurricane, and that we are obligated to take action and to know as much as possible about hurricanes and the manner in which they cause damage, and about what alternatives we may have to mitigate the potential for damage and for protecting life and property the next time we might suffer an impact.

VULNERABILITY

As a first step, I recommend we familiarize ourselves with the concept of *vulnerability*. By returning to the etymological method, we will see that vulnerability comes from the Latin name *vulnus = wound* and the verb *vulnerare = to wound* or *to be wounded*; immediately, our mind will project an image of something painful.

For our specific purpose, it will suffice for us to learn that vulnerability results from the interaction of human activity with natural or anthropogenic hazards. Or if we were to simplify: *vulnerability = exposure to hazards*.

We have already identified a hurricane as a natural hazard, and have also defined hazard as a source of potential damage. In addition, we know of communities in Florida, Quintana Roo, and elsewhere that have suffered the impacts of hurricanes. From this, we can conclude that any one of those communities is vulnerable to hurricanes, and consequently any human activity taking place there is also vulnerable to hurricanes.

There are two classes of vulnerability: *absolute vulnerability* and *relative* or *specific vulnerability*.

Absolute vulnerability is a function of geographic location and the effects of natural processes, and it is beyond all possibility of human control. In absolute terms, Florida, Texas, Louisiana, Mississippi, North Carolina, Quintana Roo, the Philippines, Japan, etc. are all vulnerable to hurricanes.

Relative vulnerability is a function of the human or natural factors that may be capable of modifying the impact of a hurricane that hits a region or specific site. Because some of such modifying factors may have been built by humankind, there exists a possibility of having some degree of human control.

To illustrate the difference between absolute and relative vulnerability, let us consider the following example: in absolute terms, all of Florida is vulnerable to hurricanes; however, the coastal zone is relatively much more vulnerable than the interior

Hurricanes, Vulnerability, and Causes of Damage

of the state, because factors such as the sea are at play as is the damage that may be caused by storm surge generated by a hurricane.

Continuing with our illustrative example, we could also compare a site located on the coast where near-shore waters are quite shallow due to a gently sloping continental platform with another site where there are deep waters near the shore. In terms of relative vulnerability, we could say the first site described is more vulnerable to coastal flooding because local factors contribute to a storm surge that penetrates quite far inland, causing extended damage but in relative terms, the second site is more vulnerable to the damaging impacts of forces generated by hydrodynamic pressure and breaking wave impacts because local factors contribute to higher waves and faster flowing water but much less inland penetration by storm surge. In this comparison, it is clear that locally specific factors, such as depth of water, generate quite different storm surge impacts as long as both sites are basically similar in every other respect.

To all those who in one way or another are already involved, or who may have the intention of becoming involved in some activity in hurricane-vulnerable coastal regions, and more specifically in the design, retrofitting, and or construction of buildings, it is strongly recommended that you pay particular attention to the relative vulnerability of the specific site for your project.

DAMAGES

Damages are the adverse consequences of the impact of a hazard (hurricane). We are talking about all that is bad that may be caused by a hurricane impact, from loss of life and injuries to structural damage, damage to the interior of buildings and homes, damage to goods and property such as furniture, equipment, documents, and other contents, as well as the degradation or interruption of services, businesses, governance, and human activity in general.

In this regard, it is quite important we all realize that although physical and structural damages are the more obvious and easily seen in the aftermath of a hurricane, it is the interruption of function, commercial or of some other type, that may lead to catastrophic damage. The incidence of loss of jobs, bankruptcies, and of business closures as a consequence of a major hurricane impact is very high in the affected region. I do not have specific numbers on what happened in Cancun as a result of Hurricane Wilma (2005), but I have anecdotic information and was also able to personally observe how numerous hotels and businesses remained closed for many months after the impact. By the same token, it took more than 10 years for the City of Homestead, in Florida, to return to the level of economic activity and local employment that it had before it was devastated by Hurricane Andrew (1992).

Damaging Components

Before we can implement hurricane mitigation, we must first learn what the main causes of damage during the impact of a hurricane are. A hurricane is a *system* consisting of several components, which are ultimately capable of causing damage. Let us call these *damaging components*.

The main damaging components of a hurricane are the following:

Wind Pressure

Wind has the capability of rushing against and over a building, generating forces, or loads, that can push or pull on its exterior surfaces and create stresses in the supporting structure. These loads are the product of complex interaction between the wind and the surfaces of the building that interpose themselves into the wind field. This particular damaging component is known as *wind pressure*, and the force it generates can be quantified in terms of *newtons* using the International System of Units or "SI" for short.

Windborne Debris

The same wind pressure is capable of picking up or tearing off objects to propel them through the air converting them into veritable *missiles*. Such missiles vary considerably in their mass, shape, and aerodynamic properties. There are compact and rounded missiles; there are some that are larger in size that are elongated and shaped as rods; and there are still others that are quite flat and large shaped like sheets. Another important characteristic of missiles is that some are rigid while others are deformable.

Independently of their shape, size, and other characteristics, all wind-propelled missiles fall under the generic designation of *windborne debris* and are capable of causing considerable damage when impacting a building. The force of an impact by windborne debris may be quantified either on the basis of the *energy of impact* or their *impact momentum*. The energy of impact is quantified using the famous Einstein equation: $E = mc^2$, that is, energy = mass × the square of the velocity. Simply put, the energy at the moment of impact by a piece of flying debris, really its capacity for causing damage, depends principally on the mass of the missile and the velocity at which it is being driven by the wind. Clearly, the damage-causing capability also depends on the rigidity or deformability of a missile, as well as its shape.

Torrential Rain

Torrential rain commonly generated during a hurricane is capable of causing damage in two ways. It may penetrate a building causing damage to interior finishes and systems, such as electrical installations, and also to furniture and other contents in the building. Materials such as drywall, wood, carpeting, insulation material, suspended ceilings, electrical panels, communications, and computer systems are all susceptible to damage when they get wet or are submerged under water as a result of torrential rain penetrating a building.

Torrential or extended rain can also accumulate, resulting in flooding of the interior of a building damaged by a hurricane or an entire region, which usually results in considerable damage to buildings and infrastructure.

Torrential or extended rain can also result in consequential damages, which only become evident after a certain period of time. A typical example of such consequential damages is *mold* that grows in places that have been flooded or drenched by the rains. Mold is also the source for numerous health problems, some quite serious, for those exposed to it.

Next, I will share two examples to illustrate the large potential for damage caused by rain.

Hurricanes, Vulnerability, and Causes of Damage

The first example is of a 400-bed hospital located in Pensacola, Florida. The main building of this hospital is an eight-story structure that performed reasonably well under the impact of Hurricane Ivan (2004). It did not suffer structural damage, and its building envelope remained mostly whole except for a few windows that were broken. There was however some serious damage to the roof, which lost some of its covering under the suction of negative wind pressure, and as a result of roof-mounted pieces of equipment that were dislodged or torn off their supports or anchoring devices. This combination of damage was enough for leaks to develop on the roof, allowing water to penetrate the interior causing more damage, which eventually amounted to more than $30 million dollars.

The second example I will share with you is that of a public library hit by Hurricane Andrew in 1992. This two-story reinforced concrete building resisted winds in excess of 220+ kph quite well, but a large window was broken by the impact of flying debris, allowing wind and rain into the building. This resulted in more than $2.0 million dollars in damage by rain water to books and documents in the library collection that were damaged beyond any possible repair, even after implementing a restoration program using advanced techniques of freezing and drying to get rid of the mold, which was successful in restoring more than 30% of all the books that had been damaged.

Flooding

Hurricane impact carries a high probability of flooding mainly in low-lying areas such as the coastal zone. Extreme rain, rivers overtopping their embankments, and storm surge are all potential causes of flooding associated with hurricanes.

The topic of potential damage from flooding was already covered in the preceding section on torrential rain, so please refer to that should you need to refresh on the adverse consequences from this hazard.

I will only add that depending on a number of factors, there can be instances of prolonged flooding conditions in which standing or slow-flowing waters that remain over an area for several days also serve as transport for numerous contaminants, from fecal matter to chemical and toxic hazardous materials, which can have serious adverse consequences for human health and the natural environment. Often, flooding will lead to contamination of water supply systems and even aquifers, which are sources of potable water for the population, causing health problems and uncomfortable conditions.

Hydrodynamic Pressure from Storm Surge

When a hurricane advances over the ocean, the interaction of atmosphere and sea generate quite a variety of phenomena, one of which is the localized rise in sea level. The low central pressure, combined with the peripheral pressure of the overall tropical cyclone, create a somewhat flattened dome of water, which is pushed by the wind ahead of the core of the hurricane.

When these waters are pushed over the continental platform near the coast, the laws of physics come into play: as the waters press against the upward-sloping bottom of the sea near shore, a reaction force is generated that pushes the dome of water higher and higher as it gets nearer the beach.

Finally, the massive torrent of rushing water that is known as *storm surge* climbs over the beach rushing inland, hitting and dragging everything in its path, be it buildings, infrastructure, trees, or the beach itself.

When colliding with a building, storm surge exerts a force that pushes perpendicularly on the surface with which it comes in contact, except those that are oriented parallel to the direction of the flow; such a pushing force is known as *hydrodynamic pressure*, which can be quantified in terms of *newtons per square meter* (N/m^2) or kN/m^2 (one thousand newtons of kilo-newtons per square meter) or in *pascals*. The total value of hydrodynamic pressure is proportional to the square of the velocity of flow of storm surge.

In engineering practice, two types of storm surge flow are used to calculate the value of hydrodynamic pressure. Storm surge that flows at 3 m/s or less is designated as being of *slow velocity*, while storm surge flowing at velocity above 3 m/s is designated as of *high velocity*. From a practical standpoint, the difference between high-velocity and low-velocity storm surge flow allows for a simplified method to be used in calculating hydrodynamic pressure for the latter.

At this point, it is important to note that storm surge has the potential for attacking a building from two directions, first as it rushes inlands and then from the opposite direction when it returns to the sea.

Wave Impact

Independently from the storm surge generated by a hurricane, there will always be the *tides* and the *waves*; the tides driven by the gravitational pull of the moon and the sun on Earth, and the waves resulting from the transfer of energy from the wind to the water. When high tide coincides with the arrival of storm surge on shore, its impact will be much higher. On the other hand, waves are capable of exerting large dynamic loads as they break against the exterior of a building. Relative to this, it is of interest to note that salt water is roughly 1000 times denser than air at sea level, which makes the impact of surge on a building so much more damaging than that of wind (moving air). Anyone who has waded into the ocean and been hit by a breaking wave can attest to the tremendous force it generates. It is clearly much greater than the simple rush of the water. In fact a 0.60 m breaking wave can generate as much force as a 190 kph wind.

Hydrostatic Pressure due to Flooding

When flood waters, regardless of their source, surround a building, they will apply lateral pressure on the surface of exterior walls. Since these waters are basically at rest, in the sense that there is no rushing flow, the pressure generated is designated as *hydrostatic pressure* and it is quantified in *newtons per square meter* or *pascals*.

This is not all, however; flood waters will also penetrate the soil below, which depending on its permeability will have more or lesser capacity for becoming saturated or water logged. Water-logged soils have the capacity of exerting hydrostatic pressure to the underside of a building or to its foundations in a vertical direction from below as well as laterally.

Hurricanes, Vulnerability, and Causes of Damage

Floating Debris

Storm surge is capable of dragging or tearing off objects in its path, making them float and propelling them as *floating missiles*, more commonly known as floating debris.

Such debris, which can be classified by differences in type and size, applies an *impact load* when colliding with a building or other objects. These impact loads are capable of causing damage to the exterior of a building, as well as to its structure.

Looking back on the list of damage components that have been described herein, it becomes clear that when it comes to hurricanes, there are two main contributors to potential damage: the *wind* and the *water*.

In my experience, I have always benefited from learning as much as possible about specific subjects of study. Following such an effective practice, I shall go deeper into the characteristics of wind and water, their respective behaviors while driven by a hurricane, and the effects they can each have on buildings and infrastructure.

4 Wind and Water

AIR WE BREATHE

The atmosphere of our planet is a marvelous thing. That tenuous and almost imperceptible veil contains the air we breathe for life and is the shield that protects us from the sun's harmful radiation. The atmosphere regulates the temperature and the environment, allowing for life, human life, to exist on Earth (Figures 4.1 and 4.2).

Equally wonderful is the air than constitutes the atmosphere—*we do not see it, but we need it to live.* The air is a mixture of gases that includes nitrogen (N_2), representing 78% of the total volume; oxygen (O_2), which occupies 20.9% by volume; and argon (Ar), occupying 0.9%. The air also contains the so-called greenhouse gases, stratospheric ozone (O_3), carbon dioxide (CO_2), methane (CH_4), and water vapor (H_2O), which all together represent 0.03% (that is three-hundredth of 1%) of the total volume on the atmosphere. That miniscule aggregated volume of greenhouse gases is the shield against solar radiation and the thermostat that keeps atmospheric temperature within the range that allows human life on Earth. In addition, the air also contains trace amounts of neon (Ne), helium (He), krypton (Kr), hydrogen (H_2), nitrous oxide (N_2O), carbon monoxide (CO), xenon (Xe), tropospheric ozone (O_3), ammonia (NH_3), sulfur oxides (SO_x), and nitrogen oxides (NO_x).

Beyond its own chemical gaseous composition, the atmosphere contains a large number of solid microscopic particles of both organic and mineral origin. These particles include grains of dust, volcanic ashes, pollen, and many more that are by-products of human activity and natural processes. The atmosphere remains around our planet, held in place by gravity.

If we stop and think for a while about the many components of our atmosphere, we could imagine it as some kind of soup, a *multivitamin broth* that extends from the surface of the planet to about 600–700 km above mean sea level. For our purposes, as we share the topics of this book, it is important that we visualize air as a *fluid* and understand that it behaves as such.

Intuitively, we can also imagine that this broth that is the atmosphere, the air, is denser at its lower levels, near the surface of Earth, than at higher elevations. In fact, the atmosphere is divided into several clearly defined levels, each having its own characteristics.

The lower segment of the atmosphere, known as the *troposphere*, is where almost the totality of we humans will remain for our whole lives; it is the densest of all and it begins at the Earth's surface and ends at approximately 14,500 m above sea level. Almost all of what we call the *weather*, the storms, rain, hurricanes, etc., takes place here. Air temperature drops from an average of 17°C at the surface to −52°C at the start of the *tropopause* that separates it from the next layer known as the *stratosphere*.

FIGURE 4.1 Transparent layers of Earth's atmosphere right after sunset. (Adapted from NASA.)

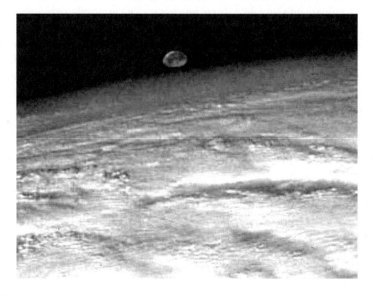

FIGURE 4.2 The moon as seen through the transparent layers of the atmosphere over Earth covered by clouds. (Adapted from NASA.)

Wind and Water

The stratosphere extends all the way to 50 km above sea level; it is dryer and less dense than the troposphere. The temperature in this atmospheric layer gradually rises from −52°C to −3°C because of the absorption of ultraviolet light from the sun. This is where the famous protective *layer of ozone*, which shields us from harmful solar radiation, is found. Approximately 99% of all the air in the atmosphere is contained within the troposphere and stratosphere.

The *stratopause* divides the stratosphere from the next layer known as the *mesosphere*, which reaches up to 85 km in elevation, where the *mesopause* separates it from the next layer, the *thermosphere*. The top layer of the atmosphere, the *thermosphere*, extends up to 600–700 km or so above sea level. The air in this layer is so rarified that there might only be less than 30 molecules per cubic meter, and as a consequence, chemical reactions occur quite rapidly while most of the incoming solar energy goes through uninterrupted to the middle layers of the atmosphere below. As a result, ambient temperature rises very rapidly to maxima above 927°C.

As it would be expected, there is no specific physical limit, a "pause," marking the "end" of the atmosphere. Measurements taken by highly sensitive instruments show there are still a few atoms, mainly hydrogen and helium, beyond this elevation. This region of the atmosphere, known as the *exosphere*, continues up to an undefined point where it merges with what is generally known as *interplanetary space*.

At this stage, I believe it is important to pause in order to describe certain aspects of the atmosphere in some detail, not only to gain an understanding of its complexity and breadth, but also to continue in the quest for education that we have initiated and to discuss one very important characteristic of this broth of air that surrounds us, *atmospheric pressure*.

Let us imagine that we can isolate a segment of the atmosphere in the shape of a tall column with a section of 1 m², which reaches from Earth's surface to the limit of the thermosphere at 600,000 m of elevation. Such a column would have a volume of 600,000 m³, and an incredibly large capacity to contain an unimaginable quantity of molecules of the elements that constitute the air. Each molecule has its own physical dimensions and mass even though we may not see it with the naked eye because it is so small. If we were to quantify the total number of molecules contained inside the column, based on the percentages discussed before, we could calculate the total mass of the air inside to be 10.2 metric tons. The weight of such mass pushing down on the terrestrial surface is what we know as *atmospheric pressure*.

If we were to change some of the parameters, for example, an atmosphere in motion rather than one at rest, or being at 2000 m above sea level rather than at sea level, we would see that the atmospheric pressure would also change in response.

Depending on the country and the system of measurements used, atmospheric pressure can be measured in *inches of mercury* (in Hg), in *pascals* or *kilopascals* or in *millibars*, this last unit being the one most used in the United States, Mexico, and internationally. The "average" *atmospheric pressure* at sea level is 1013.25 millibars.

Relative to atmospheric pressure, it is important to also consider the concept of *isotropy*. To explain it, let us consider that air, as a fluid that it is, obeys the laws of physics. Pressure exerted by a fluid is *isotropic*, meaning that its physical properties are independent of direction. Stated differently, the atmospheric pressure at a given elevation has the same value regardless of the direction chosen.

WIND

In the preceding section, we referred to a static atmosphere, that is, air without movement. In reality, in nature there is no air without movement. Under the influence of various factors, mainly changes in temperature and in atmospheric pressure, air is always in motion from regions of high pressure to regions of low pressure.

The *movement of air is the wind*. As the sun warms up the surface of Earth, heat is irradiated to the atmosphere. As the air heats up, it expands and becomes less dense, exerting less pressure on the surface as it also rises to higher elevations; as this happens, the space vacated by the warmer rising air is occupied by colder, denser air. Because the surface of the planet is not all heated up equally or at the same rate, there will always be regions that are colder or warmer than others, causing the air to be in constant movement. In summary, there will always be wind, at times calm and blowing almost imperceptibly, and with great velocity and violence on other occasions. These differences in temperature and pressure are the generators of winds.

Relative to the generation of winds and the prior discussion above, it is important to place it all within the context of the atmosphere and the fact that it is in contact and in constant interaction with the surface of the planet, which is close to 71% oceans. Consequently, this discussion must be placed within the context of such interaction, and in the case of the central topic of hurricanes, the proper context is what we refer to as the *coupled ocean–atmosphere* system. What this means is that we must consider both wind and water and their constant interaction. If we think of the weather as a product of such interaction, we could say that *wind is the engine* and *water is the fuel*.

For our purposes, the most important aspect is to study what happens when wind interacts with buildings, houses, and the infrastructure that are products of human activity.

What happens when hurricane winds encounter a building in their path? What can we learn from the interaction of wind with a building that will help us design and build hurricane-resistant edifices?

As a first step, I submit we need to become knowledgeable about certain *rules of wind behavior*. Wind obeys physical laws; it also modifies its behavior in response to changing conditions in the environment through which it flows. Wind blowing over the open sea or a plain will flow differently when it encounters topographic accidents, a forest, buildings, or cities. The wind flowing near the surface behaves differently from wind at some higher elevation.

WIND BEHAVIOR

Wind Speed Increases As It Flows at Higher Elevations above Ground

There are three reasons for the change in wind speed with elevation above ground: (a) the density of air diminishes as height above ground increases, making it lighter, allowing it to move faster; (b) the attraction of gravity also diminishes with height above ground; and (c) the effects of friction with the ground and topographic features, which affect the movement of wind, disappear as elevation above the ground increases. In the context of wind behavior and its interaction with the built

Wind and Water 41

environment, which is at the lowest level of the atmosphere, it is clear the dominant effect is friction with the ground and topographic features and the buildings themselves. Consequently, this is where our focus must be when dealing with the interaction of buildings with hurricanes. The increase of wind speed with elevation above ground may be of interest when rather tall buildings are involved; otherwise, it may be disregarded the same as the reduction in the force of gravity. On this basis, relative to this specific behavior of wind and its interaction with the built environment, our attention should be directed at what happens within the first 100–200 m of elevation above ground, where the vast majority of buildings and infrastructure will be located. Any building or structure that is higher can be addressed by exception in terms of what wind effects need to be considered.

Being aware of and understanding these wind effects becomes critically important for those of us who are interested in the design and construction of buildings, as project owners, developers, or design professionals, in Florida, the Gulf Coast, in Cancun, Cozumel, other coastal regions of Quintana Roo, or in any other hurricane-vulnerable region. This is even more so when the project involves a rather tall, multistory building because of the need to determine if, when hit by a hurricane, it may sustain much more intense winds at its top floors and roof than at its ground level. For example, it is possible that while surface winds are those of a category 2 hurricane, wind on the upper floors and roof are those of a category 3 hurricane.

Static Wind Pressure Diminishes As Its Velocity Increases and When Wind Encounters an Object in Its Path, It Increases Its Velocity to Surmount It

Because it is fluid, wind, the air in motion, obeys the laws of fluid mechanics, specifically those represented in what is known as *Bernoulli's equation for incompressible flow*, discovered by the well-known scientist Daniel Bernoulli (Dutch/Swiss, 1700–1782), which illustrates the relationship between *static pressure*, meaning the pressure exerted by the fluid (air) independently of its motion, *dynamic pressure*, which is a directional component of pressure in a moving fluid acting perpendicularly to the direction of flow, and *total pressure*, which is the sum of static and dynamic pressures. As per Bernoulli's law, the higher the velocity of the air (the fluid), the lower its static pressure, and vice versa. The typical example to illustrate this principle is that of the wing of an airplane, where its cross-sectional profile is designed in such a way that makes the wind flow at a higher velocity above the wing than underneath it, exerting, as a consequence, much lower static pressure on top than below the wing. The net result is *lift* on the wing, which allows the airplane to become airborne.

What is important for us is to consider that a building, especially a multistory building, may experience the impact of positive, inward-acting (pushing), wind pressures equal to the dynamic pressure of the wind on its windward face, while the acceleration of the wind around corners and over the top of the building generates large localized negative, outward-acting (suction) pressures. This results in large variations in wind pressures applied to various parts of the building. Visualizing these effects, we find a positive pressure pushing on the windward face of the building, and a negative pressure applying suction to the leeward face, while both the sides and the top of the building may be experiencing a combination of both negative and positive pressures. It is not difficult to also visualize how these wind pressure effects, acting simultaneously on a building, create conditions that may lead to damage. From the above, we may infer that, just as the lift on the wing of the airplane is generated by changes in speed and pressure, various parts of a building may also react differently under the influence of similar types of changes in speed and pressure during a hurricane. Furthermore, we can also visualize what happens in an urban setting where there are numerous buildings of various heights contributing to increased turbulence in the flow, which increases the variation of local pressures on the surfaces of any downstream building.

Characteristics of Wind Flow Will Change in Response to Changes in the Terrain over Which It Flows

In the previous discussion, we addressed how wind speed increases with elevation above ground and how, for the purposes of understanding the effects of the interaction between buildings and hurricane winds, we need to focus our attention on the behavior of wind in the region close to the surface of Earth up to an elevation of 100–200 m. Perhaps we could enhance our understanding of wind effects on buildings by looking at this from a different perspective. Instead of considering the increase in wind speed with elevation above ground, we should study what happens as wind approaches the surface of Earth, the so-called *atmospheric boundary layer*, and frictional forces associated with the roughness of the surface have an increasing influence on the moving air as the height above ground diminishes. Relative to this, it is important to note that surface roughness takes a range of forms, from waves and mist above the ocean surface to topographic features such as hills and escarpments, vegetation, and buildings of various heights above ground.

Careful analysis using the proposed top-down approach will show several important changes in wind behavior within the boundary layer. First, what is generally a horizontal flow of air at higher altitudes is affected by a wide range of nonhorizontal forces as the wind interacts with surface roughness increasing the gustiness or turbulent characteristics of the flow. Second, the mean wind speed is reduced by these frictional effects, which may also induce slight changes in direction. Lastly, the effects of the *Coriolis* force (an apparent force generated by the rotation of Earth that pushes the wind flow laterally, to the right of the direction of motion in the northern hemisphere) and the *pressure gradient* force (a force that has two components, a vertical one counteracting gravity and a horizontal one that pushes the air forward from a point of high pressure to one of low pressure) are considerably reduced as turbulence and friction become dominant within the surface layer. In summary, the mean speed of wind that interacts with buildings will show variations, from slower to faster, with height above ground in the boundary layer where most of the built environment is, which can be illustrated by a curve representing the *mean wind speed profile*, in reality, the wind shear or the rate of change in wind speed with height. Meteorologists and engineers have used a variety of methods and instruments for many years to measure these variations in wind shear with the help of mathematical expressions developed for this purpose. One such mathematical expression, which is preferred by meteorologists, is the *logarithmic law* or "log-law" for short. Engineers prefer to use what is called the *power law* mainly because it is an easier mathematical

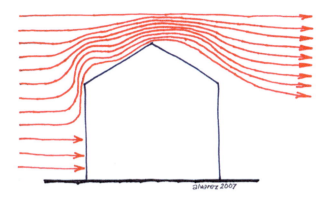

FIGURE 4.3 Graphic showing lines representing an idealized depiction of laminar wind flow. Note how the flow separates from the surface when it encounters an abrupt change in direction. These changes in direction are critical areas of a building, since frequently, the wind will apply positive pressure on one plane and negative on the one just around, which will cause deformation of the building, increasing the potential for damage during hurricanes.

expression to use than the log-law. A comparison of results from these two mathematical approaches shows a rather close match, indicating the power law is adequate as a basis for engineering. It is important to mention that measuring the mean wind speed profile in hurricanes has proven quite challenging for a number of reasons, including that most of the hurricane activity occurs over water, making it rather difficult to take measurements of the wind field near the surface, and also it is practically impossible to fly instrumented aircraft low enough to measure wind fields in the 100–200 m elevation that is of interest for studies of buildings. New instrumentation and methods, including the use of dropsondes released from hurricane-hunter aircrafts, the deployment of 10-m data-acquisition meteorological towers ahead of approaching hurricanes, instrumentation of houses along the coastline in hurricane-vulnerable regions, and the use of sonic radar have improved the acquisition of wind data near the surface, but this is still work in progress. On the other hand, however, the methodology for calculating wind loading of structures, such as is contained in the ASCE 7 standard of the American Society of Civil Engineers (ASCE), is well developed and quite useful for establishing building design criteria.

Building owners, project developers, and design professionals, especially architects, need to be well informed about these characteristics of wind flow and the need to address potential damaging effects through appropriate design criteria (Figure 4.3).

TURBULENT FLOW

Wind is almost always turbulent near the surface of Earth. However, it is especially turbulent in urban areas during a hurricane with frequent flow reversals as it swirls between buildings; it could be stated that hurricane surface winds in this case will have turbulent flow as a consequence of friction with the terrain and the *roughness* of the same, which includes natural and human-made features such as buildings.

In this regard, it is important to note that the turbulence intensity, its gustiness, is also directly related to the surface roughness. This means that the rougher the surface, the more intense the turbulence will be. In the case of an urban environment, the more varied the mix of buildings such as a combination of high-rise and medium-rise buildings that is found in a typical downtown area of a major city, the rougher the terrain becomes and the higher the magnitude of the turbulence. Generally, turbulence intensity increases closer to the ground, but it is important to note that the interaction of hurricane winds with a fully developed urban environment where numerous high-rise buildings exist makes for a rather complex wind regime, where case-specific studies would be required in order to assess the potential effects on individual structures. Another important consideration regarding this characteristic of wind flow is the height through which these effects are observed: about 250 m for open water and up to 500 m for cities are currently the generally accepted criteria.

The importance of understanding this issue of turbulence, gustiness, and turbulence intensity is so critical to understanding the potential for damage posed by the characteristics of wind flow that ASCE 7, the standard established and maintained by the ASCE to support design criteria for wind loading of structures, is based on a *basic wind speed* measured in terms of a 3-s *gust* of wind at 10 m above ground in open terrain (flat field with few obstructions). It then uses relationships between winds in different exposures to calculate wind loads for buildings located in various terrain exposures. At any given height below the top of the atmospheric boundary layer, the wind speeds (mean or maximum gust) will be greatest for an open water exposure than an open country exposure, and the open exposure winds will be greater than those at the same height for a built-up area. For a lay audience, this means that the wind loads on a building, both local peak pressures and overall wind loads, will generally be larger on the building in an open water exposure than for the same building in an open country exposure, and much larger than on the same building in a built-up environment. The difference will be greatest for mean or average pressures and overall wind loads and smaller for local peak pressures or wind loads on components. The fluctuations or changes in wind pressures with time will generally be larger in the built-up areas where the turbulence is highest. Consequently, project owners or developers, and design professionals, must educate themselves on this topic of turbulent flow in different exposures, to be aware of the risks inherent in building in hurricane-vulnerable regions, and of the need for mitigating the expected impacts.

I am sure many have experienced the effects of turbulence in an urban environment while walking among high-rise buildings in any big city, and suddenly being hit by a rather strong gust of wind seemingly out of nowhere. Now imagine the same condition during a hurricane event. Flow lines depicting turbulent flow will look like those shown in Figure 4.4.

WIND EFFECTS

To talk about wind behavior is, in a sense, like describing the temperament of a person, sometimes peaceful and sometimes turbulent. We also know that there are always consequences to pay from the type of conduct of an individual. We could say the same about wind.

Wind and Water 45

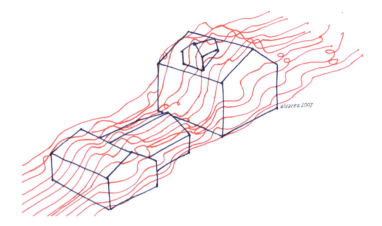

FIGURE 4.4 Graphic illustrating the turbulent flow of hurricane wind as it interacts with buildings. Note the effect of adjacent buildings on the flow itself and of one building over a neighboring one. When assessing the vulnerability of a building to the impact of a hurricane, it is important to consider the characteristics of the vicinity around it, including those of neighboring structures, that constitutes the environment surrounding the new or the existing building.

That said, it is important to consider the *effects* wind may have as a result of its behavior. Specifically, it is essential that we become knowledgeable about the effects of wind on buildings, houses, and infrastructure, if we want to design or build, or develop a project in a hurricane-vulnerable area. Before we explore the various kinds of effects hurricane winds can have on a building, there are some important aspects of which to be aware. In the context of the previous discussion about wind characteristics and pressure, reference has been made to generation of lift by wind acting on an airplane wing, and other similar examples. In this regard, it is critically important to recognize the difference between an airplane or airplane wing, which are considered aerodynamic or *streamlined* bodies, and buildings, which are generally boxy in shape and are anchored to the ground. Most buildings of interest for the purposes of this discussion are classified as *bluff* bodies (*Wind Loading of Structures* by John D. Holmes, 2003, Spon Press, London) with respect to their interaction with wind flow.

There are significant differences between what happens when wind flows around a streamlined body, such as the airplane wing, and when it flows around a bluff body, such as a boxy building. Wind flowing around an airplane wing, or other streamlined body, will closely hug the surface and follow the contours of the wing. As the wind streams around the wing, it is separated from it by a very thin smooth layer known as the *boundary layer* attached to the surface. Wind flow emerging past the rear end of the wing will form a rather narrow wake and quickly reattach downwind. In contrast, when wind encounters a building that is rectangular in horizontal cross section, the flow will separate as it hits the corners and it continues to flow along the sides of the building, where it will ride a layer of turbulent flow where vortices can form to roll toward the back of the building, where a wide wake is formed characterized by vortices shed downwind. These differences in wind flow around streamlined and bluff bodies are idealized in Figure 4.5.

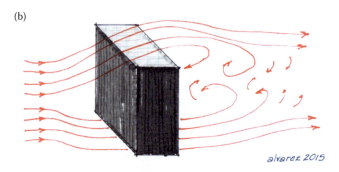

FIGURE 4.5 Wind flowing around a streamlined body (a) will hug the surfaces in what is known as the boundary layer, generating a rather narrow wake once past the body. In contrast, wind flow will separate around a blunt body (b), generating eddies that roll a turbulent layer on the sides of the body, which will flow into the void behind the leeward side, where a rather wide wake is created before the flow comes together again downwind.

Still on the topic of bluff bodies, the flow of wind around tall buildings will add other characteristics than those illustrated above in simplified fashion. This has to do with wind flow in the vertical plane of the building, where we will find that as the wind hits the windward face, there is a point of stagnation, located about 75% up the total height of the building, below which there is a downward rush of wind toward the ground, which can cause damage at street level. There are other characteristics of flow related to the sides and the back face of tall buildings that will be discussed later on.

Positive Pressure

We have previously established that air has mass, and that air in motion is wind. Consequently, wind is capable of *pushing* on buildings in its path. Said differently, the windward facade of a building will suffer the push of the wind, a pressure related to the dynamic pressure of the wind because the windward face of the building will momentarily stop the wind striking it, before diverting it horizontally and vertically to continue flowing around it. This push will be in the same direction as that of the wind flow, and because the pressure pushes on the face of the building toward its interior (Figure 4.6), most building codes and design standards designate it as a *positive* pressure and identify it by a " + " sign.

Wind and Water

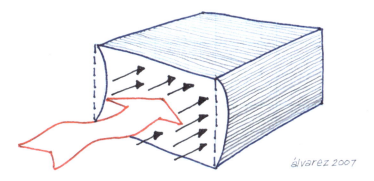

FIGURE 4.6 Hurricane winds will generate a force that pushes on the exterior wall, windward, of a building in its path. The effect of this force generated by wind pressure is known as positive pressure.

Suction

The effect of wind on the leeward face (that which is opposite the face suffering the push of the wind) of the building mentioned above would be one of *suction*, which is also called *negative pressure*, and it is identified by the minus " − " sign because it acts away from the interior of the building.

The leeward facade is not the only surface subjected to negative pressure. In general, any sector of the building where there are substantial changes in the direction of adjoining surfaces, such as in corners of exterior walls, or where the roof meets a wall, it is possible to have positive pressure on one surface and negative pressure on the adjoining surface. Figures 4.7 and 4.8 illustrate different cases where the suction effect is present.

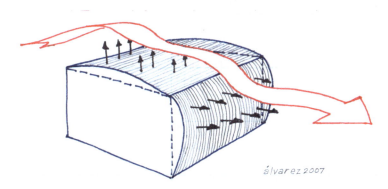

FIGURE 4.7 Following the laws of physics, wind flow (arrow) will increase its velocity as it surmounts a building (Bernoulli's effect), generating a negative, suction, force on the surface on the building. On building surfaces opposite, the leeward side, the flow of the wind will also sustain suction forces. This suction effect is known as negative pressure.

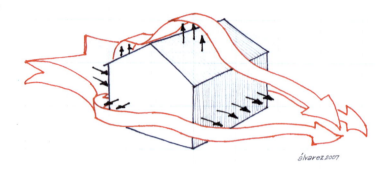

FIGURE 4.8 When hurricane winds flow around a building, wind pressure will exert a positive force that pushes against the windward wall while also generating a negative force, suction, pulling on the leeward wall on the opposite side. This interaction will generate suction forces on parts of the roof and the side walls of the building. This change from positive to negative force, typically takes place where there are changes in the direction of the plane of the building surface, as it happens at the corners of the building, or the peak of a sloping roof. This effect is known as suction.

Drag

When the turbulent wind flow described above interacts with a building, a bluff body, it exerts a force commonly known as *aerodynamic force*. In order to understand and assess what effect such aerodynamic force will have on a building, engineers resolve it into two main components or force coefficients, one acting along the mean wind direction designated as *drag*, and one acting cross-wind designated as *lift*. For purposes of analysis, engineers evaluate drag and lift as they align with two directions, one parallel and the other perpendicular to the mean wind direction, which are called *wind axes*, as opposed to parallel and perpendicular to the geometry of the building, which are called *building axes*. The wind axes and building axes are related in terms of the angle between them, known as the *angle of attack*, which represents the actual mean direction of the turbulent wind as it hits the building. The drag effect on buildings is mainly the result of wind pressure; for example, the positive pressure acting on the windward face of the building and the negative pressure on its leeward face both contribute to this aerodynamic drag, which is proportional to the shape and dimensions of the cross section of the building. Most people find it easier to visualize the drag effect on a moving vehicle, as the force the car has to exert to push the air out of its way as it speeds along the highway. In contrast, a building is stationary because it is anchored to the ground, and drag is the result of the wind having to go around the building, which "pushes" it in the mean wind direction. The effect of drag relates directly to the width and height of the projection of the building perpendicular to the direction of the wind, but is generally greatest when the wind is blowing roughly perpendicular to one of the faces of the building. Chamfered or stepped corners have been shown to reduce the magnitude of the mean drag on a building but may not reduce the fluctuating loads as much. Besides pressure, drag may also be influenced by friction, although this happens mainly with

Wind and Water

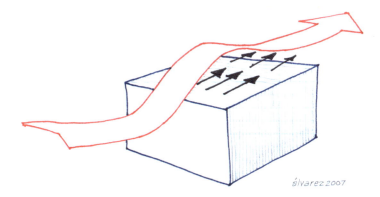

FIGURE 4.9 Because of friction, hurricane wind will have a dragging effect in the direction of flow as it interacts with a building. It is as if the wind is trying to carry the building with it as it flows around it. This effect is known as drag.

streamlined bodies and not with bluff bodies where the flow separates to go around the leading corners and along the sides of the building a number of phenomena occur such as the generation of eddies and the formation of a wide trailing wake downwind from the building. However, the effect of drag along the sides of the building is actually negligible in comparison with pressure drag associated with the windward and leeward faces of the building.

Regarding drag, it is important for project owners, developers, and designers to understand how the shape and cross section of a building contribute to drag, and to take appropriate design measures to manage its effects (Figure 4.9).

Shaking

It is practically impossible for wind direction and velocity to remain constant, especially during hurricanes and storms. On the contrary, the norm is for turbulence as the wind interacts with buildings and other obstacles near the surface, as well as gusts and frequent changes in direction to occur (Figure 4.10).

Under such wind behavior, it is common for exterior building surfaces to experience large fluctuation in wind loads that can cause them to heave in and out, shake, and, if loose, to flap around. Generally, such *shaking* effect is more intense when it involves somewhat flexible surfaces, such as tents or surfaces that cantilever as they are only anchored on one side.

Vibration

Buildings, especially tall ones, will move back and forth, vibrating not randomly but harmonically, under the influence of wind gusts that have the same frequency as the building. The lower the natural frequency of the building, the more likely it is for *vibration* to occur during a strong wind event. Vibration can be a big contributor to structural damage, and also to damage of some flexible cladding systems.

Buildings tend to shed vortices at regular intervals based on their size, overall dimensions, and on the wind speed. As these vortices travel downwind, they will

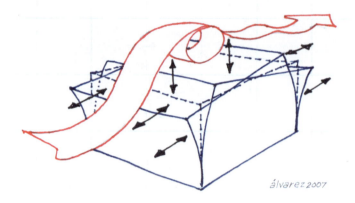

FIGURE 4.10 Turbulent wind flow (arrow) over a building cause a shaking effect, shown here in exaggerated fashion. Higher buildings will tend to shake more than lower ones, as will those with flexible rather than rigid main structures.

affect other buildings downstream, and if the vortex shedding frequency aligns with the natural frequency of a downstream building, its vibration can be greatly amplified increasing the potential for damage (Figure 4.11).

Vorticity

When the wind rushes against a building at an angle over a section where three different surfaces come together, such as a corner where two exterior walls and the roof coincide, vortices may develop (Figure 4.12).

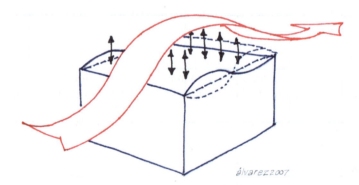

FIGURE 4.11 Depending on a range of factors, including the dimensions and types of materials used in the construction of the building, especially its structure, the flow of the wind may induce vibration, including harmonic vibration in the building structure. To visualize this effect, imagine the wave that "travels" along a rope by moving its end up and down while it lays flat on the floor. Flat roofs on buildings that are long and narrow will tend to vibrate when the wind flows over them and will have a higher probability of experiencing harmonic vibration.

Wind and Water

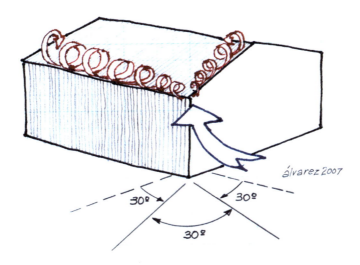

FIGURE 4.12 Figure showing what may happen when the wind hits the corner of a roof at a certain angle. Vortices may be generated at the corner and then propagate and expand along the edges of the roof. While these vortices may not cause structural damage, they can certainly damage the roof covering and underlayment, which may in some cases lead to extensive roof damage and possibly damage to the supporting structure.

Such vortices lead to extreme velocities as the wind behaves like a tornado and, as we have already discussed, static pressure will drop in proportion to the velocity squared, so these vortices can generate quite large localized negative pressures on the roof and walls of a building. These conditions often result in extensive damage to building components.

In the aftermath of a hurricane, examples of damage concentrated around roof corners are common, and are clearly the result of local vortices caused by the angle of attack of the wind and the geometry of the building.

Stagnation

Behaving as a fluid that it is, wind will try to fill every available space that it encounters in its path as it flows. There are cases where the geometry of a given free space is such that it causes the flow of the oncoming wind to momentarily come to rest resulting in a process of *wind stagnation*. This phenomenon traces back to the dynamic pressure of the wind. As the exterior surfaces of the building briefly stop the wind flow, a pressure about equal to the dynamic pressure of the wind is applied on the stagnation area.

Stagnation also occurs on the face of a building that is normal to the wind flow as the wind flow starts to divert to go around the top and the corners of the building to rush along the roof and the sides. The point of stagnation usually occurs near the center of the windward wall at a height of about two-thirds of the height of the wall for most buildings.

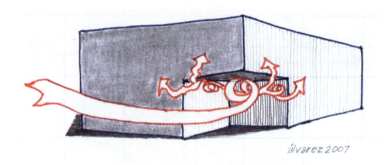

FIGURE 4.13 When interacting with a building, wind may encounter areas where its flow is interrupted due to the shape or geometry of the specific section. This figure shows a building with a "discontinuity" in its envelope. When the wind reaches that area, it becomes "trapped," resulting in a section where the flow generates strong turbulence. This effect is known as stagnation, and as illustrated in this figure, it has great capability for causing damage.

The zone where the underside of a roof overhang meets the top of an exterior wall, the junction of a cantilevered balcony and the exterior wall below, and other similar cases, are all examples of building zones where stagnation of the wind flow may occur (Figure 4.13).

Drift, Overturning, and Uplift

There are three additional effects resulting from the interaction of wind with buildings, which are illustrated in Figure 4.14.

Drift

As has been discussed, the speed of wind increases with elevation above the ground and, in consequence, the force it exerts increases over the higher zones of buildings. When subjected to lateral wind loads, a tall building will lean away from the vertical in an effect known as *drift*, even if the load did not increase with height, although it is clearly made worse by the increase in load with height. Clearly, such increase in wind load with height will increase the drift.

In almost all cases, the drift effect on tall buildings is temporary; however, if a building were underdesigned for wind to the extent that wind loads during a hurricane exceeded the elastic limits of structural members, there could be some permanent set of the drift after the storm. A tornado that struck a tall building in Lubbock, Texas resulted in this type of permanent deformation (Reinhold 2015, personal interview with Timothy Reinhold by the author). So, it is really more a question of design and elastic limits. In this respect, there are certain infrastructure elements such as posts used for public lighting, electrical distribution, or telephone service, or masts and flag poles that are much more susceptible to suffering permanent drift under the impact of a wind storm.

Overturning

When higher wind loads impact the upper zone of a building, the effect extends all the way to the bottom in the form of a total force, whose distribution by unit of

Wind and Water

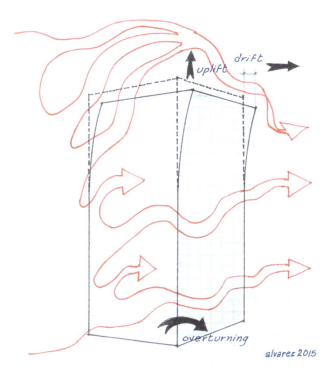

FIGURE 4.14 Drawing showing three effects of wind interaction (arrows) with a building, especially a tall one: drift, overturning, and uplift.

building surface gradually increases from the ground to the roof line. This total force actually takes advantage of the vertical length of the building, its height, as a lever arm with its fulcrum at ground level to try making the building rotate toward the horizontal. This effect is known as overturning.

There are a number of intervening factors that may increase the strength of the overturning effect. For example, the taller a building, the stronger the resulting overturning moment because the moment arm increases with its height. The overturning moment of force is also stronger when the surface of the face of the building perpendicular to the wind flow is not only very tall but is also quite wide when compared to the lateral walls aligned with the wind flow. Finally, as the building leans or drifts, the weight of the building also shifts in the direction of the lean as the masses of the floors and walls drift. This displacement of the weight of the building creates an increase in overturning moment and is commonly referred to as P-Delta effect.

Uplift
As previously discussed, the flow of wind over a building can cause suction or negative pressure; it is important to note however that such negative pressure is stronger when it acts over a flat roof, and even stronger when it is a flat roof atop a high-rise building.

54 Hurricane Mitigation for the Built Environment

When negative wind pressure applies suction to a roof, the resulting load is transmitted to the supporting structure, which in turn transfers it to other structural components, such as columns or load-bearing walls. Eventually, the totality of these loads is transferred to the building foundation.

The effect just described is known as *uplift*, which is so designated because in essence it is a force that is pulling on the roof and, in reality, on the whole building because of the transfer of loads and the combined work of the building envelope, the structure and the foundation. Consequences of this uplift effect could be quite adverse in the case of light buildings as a function of their total volume, or buildings with inadequate foundations.

Uplift is linked to the overturning effect discussed above, since overturning generates large uplift loads on the columns and foundation on the windward side of a tall building. In fact, uplift related to the overturning moment is the dominant form of uplift for tall buildings. In the case of low building roof, uplift is dominant.

Eddies

Just as a sailing ship cutting the water with its prow leaves a wake behind its stern, a building interacting with a hurricane causes the flow to separate as its windward face interferes with the wind that surrounds it, leaving a "wake" or a type of "elongated shadow," which extends from the leeward face over a certain distance downwind, after which the flow will tend to reunite. As the wind flow separates at the upwind corners of the building, eddies form in a region of high shear and vorticity along the sides of the building, and will expand and roll into the cavity behind the leeward face of the building where they will continue moving downwind. In a building with a long after body, it is possible for the separated flow to reattach to the side walls before reaching the back of the building, resulting in a smaller wake and turbulence effects downwind.

The wake projected by a building as it splits the wind flow creates a zone where negative pressure, suction, is generated. Frequently, in this wake zone, near the point where the flow separated by the building volume tends to come together again, fast rotating eddies are generated, which because of their turbulence and high rotational velocity have the potential for causing damage to buildings and structures they come in contact with (Figure 4.15).

Missiles

When speaking of wind as air in motion, it is important to underline that in addition to the various gaseous molecules that it contains, which have been previously described, it also includes several kinds of solid particles that it picks up as it flows. Grains of dust, ash, pollen, dead cells, and other similar materials are all part of the air in motion (Figure 4.16).

When the movement of air is very fast, as happens in a hurricane, the wind has the capacity of picking up larger and heavier pieces of material and objects, such as roofing components, roof tiles, sheets of metal, pieces of wood, tree branches, and many other objects, propelling them aloft within its flow until they eventually fall to the ground or crash against a building, house, or infrastructure components in their path. Let us think that all components of air in motion, from the gaseous

Wind and Water

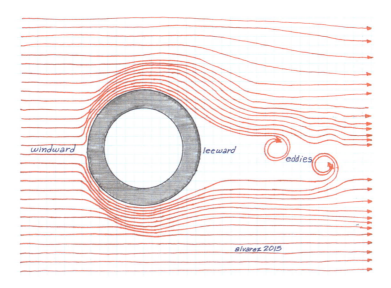

FIGURE 4.15 Wind flow, represented here by flow lines acting over a cylindrical object seen from above, separates when encircling a building. Depending on different factors such as shape and height of the building, the flow reunites itself again at certain distance from the leeward face of the building, creating a wake where turbulent eddies can develop with capacity to damage other buildings or infrastructure.

FIGURE 4.16 Example of the damaging capacity of windborne debris. The edge of this piece of plywood, 18 mm thick, one square meter in area, and 10 kg in weight, driven by Hurricane Andrew's winds (1992) impacted the trunk of a palm tree, 30 cm diameter cutting right through it.

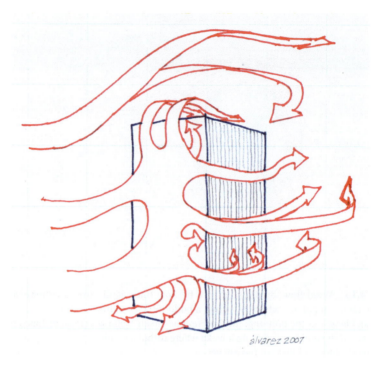

FIGURE 4.17 The wind flow around a large, tall building generates a complex interaction in which positive and negative pressures, drag, vibration, shaking, stagnation, overturning, drift, and uplift may all act simultaneously affecting different zones of the building.

molecules and microscopic particles as well as the much larger ones, are missiles propelled by the wind. It should be clear that the particle of a molecule of nitrogen or a particle of ash will go unnoticed, but the impact of a roofing tile or a piece of lumber will most probably cause plenty of damage as it crashes against a building or house.

In closing this section on the effects of wind, I believe it is important to emphasize that while each effect has been described individually and separately, in reality, all of these may occur simultaneously or in various combinations during a hurricane.

Finally, let us remember that it is the shape and volume of a building that to a large degree determines the various effects that the wind may cause as it interacts with it. A tall, large, and voluminous building will have a much more complicated interaction with wind than would a small building or a single family house (Figure 4.17).

WATER

We inhabit a water planet. Without water, there would be no life. Water is so abundant that 67% of the surface of Earth is covered by liquid water, and when we take into account the frozen water, ice, covering Antarctica, Greenland, and other regions, that percentage is close to 80%.

Wind and Water

The oceans contain 1.350 million cubic kilometers of water, a quantity so large that if Earth's surface were flat, without topographic accidents of any magnitude, it would cover the whole world with a layer of water 2500 m deep.

The energy of the sun warms up Earth's oceans, causing water to evaporate up into the atmosphere where it forms the clouds. At any given moment in time, there are more than 13,000 cubic kilometers of water in the atmosphere in the form of water vapor or as clouds. When atmospheric water finds temperatures that are sufficiently low, it condenses, and eventually it precipitates back to the surface in the form of rain, snow, or ice. This whole process is known as the *hydrologic cycle.*

Without a doubt, water together with solar energy are the two main factors influencing and determining changes in the atmosphere, and the climate, at large temporal scales.

For our own purposes of learning about hurricanes and their impacts, it is essential we consider salt water from the oceans and rain.

Water is a fluid that obeys physical laws and modifies its behavior in response to the environment in which it moves or changes in the atmosphere. The interaction of ocean and atmosphere is one of the most important factors in the formation of hurricanes.

Water has great capacity for causing damage during hurricanes, and as such it must be considered as a risk factor during such events.

WATER BEHAVIOR

In order to understand how water may cause damage during a hurricane, it is important that we first become familiar with its properties and its behavior. I consider the following as the most important aspects.

Water Is a Heavy and Incompressible Fluid

Water is a heavy liquid. Fresh water weighs 999.3 kilograms per cubic meter, and sea water, at an average, weighs 1024.8 kilograms per cubic meter, which is more than one metric ton. This is what we call the *specific weight of water.*

Water is a liquid that cannot be compressed. The combination of its density and incompressibility make water, especially sea water, an element capable of generating very large impact energy as it flows and great pressure even when at rest.

Water Pressure Increases with Depth

Water pressure can be measured in bars, with 1 bar being equivalent to 100,000 newtons per square meter at sea level. Once under the surface of the seawater, pressure increases at a rate of 1 bar per each 10 m in depth due to the weight of the water column above.

Characteristics of Water Flow Change in Response to the Characteristics of the Terrain over Which It Flows

Water in the ocean is always in motion under the influence of numerous factors. As a fluid in motion, water will react to changes in elevation in the terrain at the bottom of the sea over which it flows. When water is deep, the influence of the underwater

58 Hurricane Mitigation for the Built Environment

terrain is practically unnoticeable at the surface. However, as water flows closer to the continental platform and the underwater terrain near the shore, and dry land, the reaction of the water is easily detectable.

This specific characteristic of ocean water is rather important, as it is a key factor that directly influences the behavior of storm surge driven by a hurricane.

Sea Water Is Salty

Sea water is characterized by its *salinity* resulting from minerals that for millions of years have been dissolved as rain pounds the ground, to then be transported by run-off and rivers to the oceans. Such dissolved minerals are commonly called *salts*, although the correct term would be *ions* or charged particles of various elements.

As an average, sea water contains 35 mg of salt per liter (1000 mL), and for this reason, it is common to state that sea water contains salt at the rate of 35 ppm (parts per million) by volume.

When 10 L of sea water evaporate, pure fresh water will be converted into water vapor that will mix with the atmosphere, and at the same time, 353 mg of salts will be obtained. The most abundant component of sea water salts is *sodium chloride* ($NaCl$), representing 273 mg or 77.3% of the total, which is known as *common salt* and is used to season our food. Other components include 56 mg of magnesium salts (15.9% of the total), 15.4 mg of gypsum (or 4.4% of the total), and very small quantities of several other components such as *silvite* (potassium chloride) and *calcite* (calcium carbonate).

The fact that sea water contains all of these salts is significant because many of them are corrosive to various metals. These salts are additional *damaging components* of storm surge water during hurricanes as it comes overland and affects buildings, infrastructure, and many of the pieces of equipment and other components that are part of them.

Water in the Oceans Reacts to the Gravitational Attraction of Sun and Moon

The gravitational attraction between Earth and the moon generates two projections; in reality, two rather large domes of water, over the oceans that move from one end to the other under the influence of the rotation of Earth, creating, in turn, peaks and lows in the mean level of the waters. These changes in water level driven by gravitational attraction between Earth and its moon are known as *high* and *low tides*.

In most coastal zones, there are *semidiurnal* tides, which consist of two high and two low tides daily. In some coastal zones, however, there are other combinations of this daily pattern of tides.

Beyond the daily pattern of tides, there is a 28-day cycle related to the phases of the moon and how it aligns with the sun as it orbits Earth, which makes the tides much higher during *new* and *full* moon phases than during the *waxing* and *waning crescent* phases, which is when the sun and the moon are at an angle of 90° to one another with respect to Earth. In this respect, it must be noted that what has just been described is the global tide pattern, and it is necessary to assess the specific pattern that applies to each given coastal zone in order to characterize which pattern applies to the place. For this reason, it is essential to note that beyond the overall influence of the sun and the moon, there is a whole array of factors that influence and define the

Wind and Water

pattern and magnitude of tides in one specific place, such as the geomorphology of the shore, underwater topography, shape and slope of the continental platform under water, estuaries, and the mouths of rivers.

We must then evaluate local conditions in order to identify all factors, which are at play, and to know what the daily pattern is for tides in Miami Beach, Fort Lauderdale, Tampa, or in Cancun, or in Playa del Carmen, or in any other location of interest. Toward this end, it is recommended to conduct a review of historical records kept by local maritime authorities or by meteorological or oceanographic institutions at each location.

To those who might ask what is the relationship between the pattern of daily astronomical tides of a given place and the impact of hurricanes, I can say that the linkage between tides and hurricanes is a rather important connection. For example, if a land-falling hurricane coincides with high tide, the resulting storm surge generated by the tropical cyclone will be higher and will have a higher potential for causing damage.

The review of historical records on the pattern and level of tides for a specific place will provide us with essential data to project worst-case scenarios of the combination of high tide and storm surge for which we must prepare. Such information is rather useful in the process of designing and siting buildings and projects in the coastal region.

All of this is about assessing the relative vulnerability of a place in order to identify and implement the most effective mitigation measures possible.

Sea Surface Water Temperature Varies Considerably Depending on Latitude

The sun warms the water in the ocean up, which then stores the heat for future gradual release into the atmosphere contributing, in the process, to the modulation of the global climate.

The layer of surface water of the ocean, say up to a depth of 300 m, is the one that best reflects changes in temperature as a function of latitude on both sides of the equator. Tropical and subtropical surface waters, those within a band extending from latitudes 28° 30′N to 28° 30′ south, maintain an average temperature that is generally above 25°C. Temperate latitudes ranging to 50° north and south of the equator maintain an average temperature of 17°C during the summer and 10°C in winter. In the zones north or south of 50° of latitude ocean waters are rather cold.

Of special interest for us are the tropical waters of the Atlantic north of the equator, which is where hurricanes that may affect Florida and the Gulf and Atlantic coasts of the United States, the Caribbean, Central America, or the places of our field studies in Cancun, Playa del Carmen, Cozumel, and others in Quintana Roo originate. In this region, when surface water temperature reaches 27°C and continues to rise, one key condition for tropical cyclone generation becomes quite favorable.

For those of us interested, or residing, in hurricane-vulnerable places, it is recommended that we pay special attention to temperature variations in the surface waters of the Atlantic north of the equator. In fact, scientists now have the capability for issuing long-term forecasts on the temperature of oceanic surface waters, which together with other parameters are useful in assessing the annual probability of tropical cyclone activity in a given basin.

Water Effects

Given that water can be one of the main damage components during hurricane impacts on coastal regions, it is rather important to learn about its effects on buildings, infrastructure, and beaches.

Hydrostatic Pressure

Being the undeformable, incompressible fluid that it is, water exerts pressure perpendicularly to the surface of any object that it touches. Also, when water is at rest (*static*), such pressure will have the same value in any direction that is chosen (*isotropic*).

The pressure of water at rest, denominated *hydrostatic pressure*, varies in direct proportion to depth, and it is quantified in terms of *pascals or newtons per square meter (N/m)^2*.

Hydrostatic pressure will apply a load on surfaces below water, which will always be perpendicular (*normal*) to the submerged surface. Given these characteristics, three load patterns are possible:

1. In the case of a watertight building totally under water because of flooding, there will be a force acting downward on the roof and structural elements that support it. Such a force will be vertical when it acts on the horizontal plane of a submerged surface. It should be noted that if the building is flooded, then water pressures outside and inside will equalize (Figure 4.18).

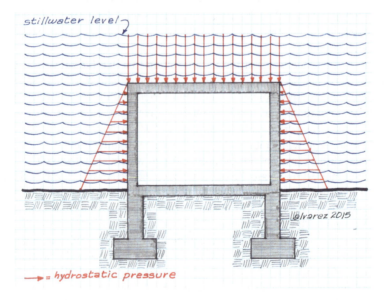

FIGURE 4.18 Diagram illustrating the hypothetical case of a watertight building submerged in flood or tide waters. The arrows show the action of the hydrostatic pressure on the top surface of the building (roof), which in this case is horizontal. If the said surface were sloping, the hydrostatic pressure would always act perpendicularly to the same.

Wind and Water 61

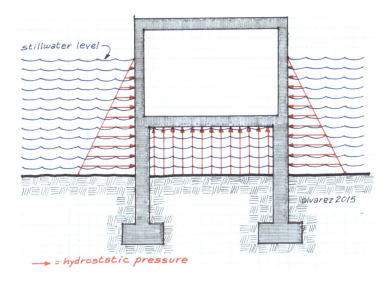

FIGURE 4.19 Diagram showing hydrostatic pressure applying a buoyancy force to the inferior (lower) surface of the building. This case shows a building elevated above the ground. Even if the building were not elevated, there is always the possibility of hydrostatic pressure pushing on the building from below, caused by saturated ground under the building.

2. When water is able to flood under a building, hydrostatic pressure will exert a force acting upward on the underside of floor slabs and structures, provided the interior of the building is not flooded. This specific kind of force is also known as *buoyancy* (Figure 4.19).
3. In cases when flood waters surround a building, without covering or getting underneath it, hydrostatic pressure will generate a horizontal load acting laterally on all exterior vertical surfaces or structural members, provided the inside of the building is not flooded. In this specific case, in order to quantify the total force acting on the building, it is assumed that the equivalent resultant force is applied at a point below the level of the water located at two-thirds of the total depth (Figure 4.20).

Relative to these types of loads, it is important to note that *saturated* soil is also capable of generating hydrostatic pressure, which results in external upward forces acting on the underside of the building or in lateral forces applied to those portions of the building that are below ground.

I want to emphasize the importance of conducting soil tests on the site where construction will take place; this is especially true in Florida, and the Maya Riviera and other places in Quinta Roo, where underground caves, and rivers, and potential sink holes exist that may undermine the foundations of buildings. This soil analysis is needed to determine the structural capacity of the soil, which is information that is critical for the design of foundations, and also to establish the water saturation capacity of the soil in case of flooding in order to calculate forces acting on a building that are generated by the saturated soil.

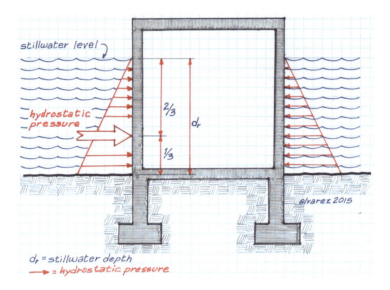

FIGURE 4.20 Diagram showing the effect of hydrostatic pressure on the walls of a building (vertical surfaces). The triangle represents the gradual increase in pressure with water depth. The total force acting horizontally is taken as if it is applied at a point two-thirds of the water depth below the level of the stillwater.

Hydrodynamic Pressure

When a hurricane impacts a coastal region, it is common to have water in motion, either from storm surge coming overland or from rivers overtopping their banks or some other similar hazard. Moving water is also capable of imposing loads on buildings and structures that interact with its flow. Such external loads can be of different types and are known by the generic designation of *hydrodynamic pressure*, which is measured in *newtons per square meter (N/m²) or pascals*.

Three different types of external loads can be generated when rushing water impacts a building:

1. A *frontal impact* load, the impact of water on the external building surface that first encounters the rushing waters. The magnitude of the resulting force will be equal to the product of the *hydrodynamic pressure*, in N/m², multiplied by the total area, in m², of the external building surface below the level of the incoming water flow. This load is considered as a *positive force*. Given the considerable specific weight of sea water, just above one ton per cubic meter, the positive force generated by hydrodynamic pressure, which is directly proportional to the square of the velocity of flow, as it impacts a building in the coastal region is capable of causing serious structural damage.
2. External building walls that are parallel to the flow of the rushing waters will be subjected to *friction drag forces*, which are the product of friction between the building and the water flow. Generally, this type of load is

Wind and Water

much smaller than drag caused by the difference between pressure on the upstream face and the downstream face of a building, and not really relevant when dealing with large massive buildings, but it has the capability for causing some damage to small and light buildings.

3. The external face of the building opposite that which takes the frontal impact of the rushing waters may be subjected to *negative forces*, as a result of the influence of eddies and vortices that will form downstream, as the flow of water is cut by the building itself as it interacts with the flow. These negative loads contribute to the overall drag, but they are smaller than the pressure on the upstream face.

Engineers generally use a couple of rather simple methods for calculating the loads generated by hydrodynamic pressure. In this regard, it is important to note that there is a general rule regarding which method to use to calculate these loads as follows:

1. A *simplified method* is used when the velocity of flow of the water is 3 m/s or less, which treats the loads as if they were caused by hydrostatic pressure (water at rest) except that it considers a higher depth of water.
2. A *detailed method* using basic concepts of fluid mechanics is used when the velocity of flow exceeds 3 m/s, to calculate the dynamic effects of the rushing water.

Tides

When assessing the vulnerability of the site where a project will be built or has been built already, it is important to take into account how the tides may contribute to potential damage caused by the impact of the waters.

Two factors must be considered relative to the tides:

1. What is the mean sea level at the site, and what is the average difference between mean high tide and mean low tide? Also, what has historically been the highest high water level during high tide at the site?
2. What would be the resulting *storm tide* (defined as storm surge plus the astronomical tide) depth when storm surge generated by a major hurricane (category 3 or higher in the Saffir–Simpson scale) approaching landfall coincides with high tide?

Waves

Wind generates waves as it transfers energy to the surface waters of the ocean. The stronger the wind blows, the bigger the waves will be. In the high seas, waves move in many directions and have what could be best described as chaotic behavior.

Closer to land, waves become more organized while their frequency acquires a repetitive pattern that is generally maintained up to the point, at the foot of the beach where waves break.

Regarding the waves, it must be made clear that waves do not transport water nor are they the result of water moving from one point to another. Waves only transport energy that is transferred by the wind to the ocean. Such energy will in turn be transferred to objects or features against which the waves break, such as a vessel or a reef, the beach itself, and buildings, roadways, and other infrastructure in the coastal region.

Because of the energy they carry, waves have the capacity for causing damage when they impact buildings in the coastal zone. In fact, waves apply an impact load as they crash against a building, which is in addition to the loads generated by the hydrodynamic pressure from storm surge.

It is also important to understand that waves never cease, even during a hurricane. In fact, waves become bigger and stronger during hurricanes as a result of the higher energy imparted by stronger winds. Waves continue to be generated above the storm surge pushed by the hurricane.

Given the capacity of waves for causing damage, it is important to estimate what size the waves that could impact a building in the coastal zone will be. Toward that end, it will be necessary to assess various factors, including how deep the storm surge waters will be above land at the point of impact with the specific building, as well as the amplitude, frequency, and height of the waves.

Without going into the details of the methodology for calculating wave height at a given point over specific terrain, it should suffice to keep in mind the *rule of thumb* that the height of waves will be equal to 0.78 times the *stillwater depth* of the surge at the location. Figure 4.21 describes the main components of waves, and should be studied carefully.

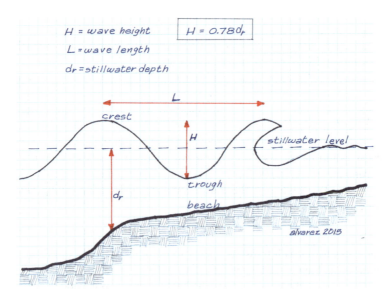

FIGURE 4.21 Diagram showing a schematic of waves and water levels that must be considered when evaluating the possible impact of storm surge. The level of stillwater is the level of the tide excluding the waves. When it is said that Hurricane Gilbert generated a 5-m storm surge, this refers to the stillwater level. To these levels, we must add the height of the astronomical tide that coincides with the storm surge.

Wind and Water

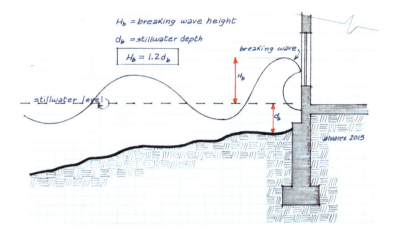

FIGURE 4.22 Schematic showing the profile of a breaking wave that rolls up against a building in the coastal region reaching a height equal to 120% of the stillwater depth at that point.

Relative to the impact of waves, the most important aspect is the height of a wave that breaks against a building or infrastructure near the beach. The same rule of thumb mentioned before establishes the height of a wave breaking against a building will be equal to 120% of the stillwater depth at the location (Figure 4.22).

Knowing the characteristics of waves in the specific coastal region of interest will allow engineers and design professionals to quantify the loads generated by the same as they impact a building. Once the magnitude of wave-induced loads has been calculated, we can then establish criteria for the design of structures and building envelope components that will be capable of resisting such forces with an adequate safety margin.

Storm Surge

During a hurricane, the combination of several factors, such as wind speed; low atmospheric pressure, which is central to a tropical cyclone; and the speed at which the whole system is moving, results in the phenomenon known as *storm surge*.

When atmospheric pressure drops, leading to the generation of a hurricane, the ocean expands and forms an area where the level of the water is higher than its surroundings, which is then propelled by the cyclone ahead of it, and following the same general trajectory as the total system.

While the hurricane travels over open ocean waters, the dome of higher water is barely noticeable, but as the system approaches land and begins to interact with the continental platform, it becomes progressively higher and higher until landfall when it rushes overland in a process known as *storm surge*.

Given the high density of sea water, about 800 times the density of air at sea level, storm surge has a high capacity for causing significant damage to buildings, infrastructure, the beach, and any other object or feature that it encounters in its paths as it rushes overland. The potential for damage will be a function of the velocity of flow

FIGURE 4.23 An example of the destructive power of storm surge: The wall shown was damaged by storm surge, which first eroded the beach and then undermined its foundation during Hurricane Wilma (2005). The dark line along the side of the wall marks the level of the sand before the impact, some 3 m above what is left of the beach shown here. Shown in this photo are my colleagues Timothy Reinhold and Hugh Gladwin who teamed up with me for this field trip to "ground zero" and Mario Stoute, a scientist with Office of Civil Protection in Cancun, Mexico.

of the rushing waters and the depth of the water over the terrain. Both of these factors will in turn change as functions of the slope of the beach and the inland coastal zone beyond it, and the submarine topography (*bathymetry*) near the beach over which the surge travels (Figure 4.23).

In low-sloped coastal zones and rather flat bathymetry, storm surge will generate small waves, but will have the capacity for penetrating far inland. In contrast, coastal zones with steep slopes and deep bathymetry off-shore will result in much higher waves, but much less inland penetration. Figures 4.24 and 4.25 illustrate both of these general conditions affecting the characteristics of storm surge.

The main causes of damage resulting from the impact of storm surge are

1. Hydrodynamic pressure
2. Wave impact
3. Floating debris
4. Erosion, scouring, and undermining

Flooding

A hurricane can cause flooding in a variety of ways. Intense rains that are often generated by a hurricane are capable of causing inundation. Take, for example, Hurricane Wilma, which in 2005 dropped more than 1500 mm of rain during a 24-h

Wind and Water

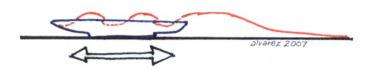

FIGURE 4.24 Figure showing a saucer with a liquid in it that will jump and fall far out from the edge of the saucer when you shake it as indicated by the double arrow. This saucer is representative of a coastal zone with a rather flat beach and shallow water offshore, and the experiment approximates how storm surge will behave under such conditions: not too high but extensive inland penetration.

period over Isla Mujeres and the northeastern region of the Yucatan Peninsula in Mexico, causing widespread flooding. Extreme rain can also increase the level and flow of lakes and rivers until they in some cases overtop their banks, flooding surrounding areas.

Storm surge also has the capability for causing inundation, but this will generally be limited to the coastal zone.

It is also possible for entire regions not in the direct path of a hurricane to suffer flooding when a tropical cyclone interacts with mountains. Because of cooler

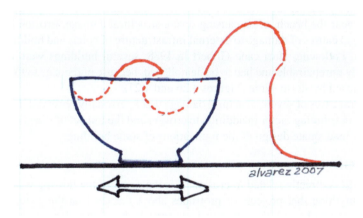

FIGURE 4.25 Figure showing an experiment that anybody can replicate to observe the influence of bathymetry over storm surge as it comes overland. The bowl containing a liquid represents a coastal zone with a rather inclined sloped beach and continental platform where there will be deep waters near shore. If we shake the bowl as indicated by the double arrow, the liquid inside will jump out and fall outside close to the edge of the bowl. The same happens with the storm surge in the coastal conditions described above; it will be high but will not penetrate too far inland.

68 Hurricane Mitigation for the Built Environment

temperatures at higher elevations than at sea level, such interaction often leads to heavy precipitation, mudslides, and instances of flash flooding. This type of inundation is particularly dangerous because it appears as a sudden hazard, with high velocity of flow, which contributes to the generation of higher loads from hydrodynamic pressure. This is because hydrodynamic pressure increases in direct proportion to the square of the velocity of flow. Examples of this are the several sudden flooding events generated by Hurricane Mitch as it interacted with mountains in Central America leaving more than 5000 deaths in three countries, most of them as a result of flooding.

The main causes of damage from flooding include

1. Hydrostatic pressure
2. Hydrodynamic pressure
3. Floating debris
4. Erosion, scouring, and undermining

Erosion

Both storm surge and fresh water flash flooding are capable of causing erosion in affected areas.

Clearly, beach erosion is one of the most obvious consequences of storm surge. Back in 1988 in Cancun, we all saw how Hurricane Gilbert caused severe erosion of the coastal zone, leading to the loss of 90% of some of the sandy beaches. This damage was repeated under the impact of Hurricane Wilma in 2005.

Erosion can be a problem even when a hurricane does not make landfall; the strong currents and waves of storm surge generated by a distant hurricane are often enough to cause damage to the beach.

Particularly dangerous is erosion that scours and undermines the foundations of buildings near the beach, often causing severe structural damage. Erosion is one of the principal causes of damage to external infrastructure of hotels and buildings near the beach. Following Hurricane Gilbert in 1988, several buildings were declared structurally unrepairable and had to be demolished, because of damage to their foundations caused by storm surge (Figures 4.26 and 4.27).

In several cases of severe structural damage that I personally observed in Cancun, a critical contributing factor in addition to erosion and the impact of storm surge was the totally inadequate design of the foundations of some buildings.

Leveling-Off

Leveling-off is directly related to erosion. It is the result of the flowing water trying to bring anything that projects or protrudes above the level on the ground or the external surface of a building, over and against which it flows, down to a common level. We find numerous and rather graphic examples of this effect in nature, in the form of rock formations whose surfaces have been leveled-off or molded by flowing water over the course of years and millennia.

The leveling-off results from the combination of several effects generated by flowing water, such as hydrodynamic pressure, erosion, and drag, when they all act almost simultaneously over an object or part of a building that project beyond the main surface of the same.

Wind and Water 69

FIGURE 4.26 During Hurricane Gilbert (1988), storm surge totally eroded the beach and undermined the foundations of this building that lacked a deep foundation, causing total structural failure to a wing of the building, requiring demolition.

In general terms, main buildings and major structures are not susceptible to suffering major damage from the leveling-off effect; however, nonstructural elements projecting beyond the external surfaces of a building may be damaged, or even destroyed, by such an effect. External signage on the grounds of a building site, ventilation hoods, external infrastructure, decorative nonstructural fences,

FIGURE 4.27 Erosion caused by storm surge during Hurricane Wilma (2005). Noticeable is the absence of deep foundations and poorly compacted soil under this building. The combination of inadequate foundation, poorly compacted soil, and storm surge often leads to serious structural damage.

landscaping, and other similar elements are highly susceptible to being damaged by the leveling-off effect.

Debris

During a hurricane, wind and water, its main damaging components, can cause considerable damage along the path of the cyclone, generating, in the process, debris of various sizes and types. Some of these pieces of debris are picked up by the wind and propelled as *flying debris*, while others are propelled by the rushing water as *floating debris*.

In order to design defenses against floating debris, these projectiles are classified on the basis of their anticipated impact, as follows:

1. *Normal impact:* This type of impact is generated by isolated, individual pieces of floating debris, such as tree branches or trunk fragments, or debris of various kinds, that may typically have a mass not exceeding of 500 kg, travel at the same speed as the velocity of flow, and impact one square foot of the surface of the building at a height above ground that is equal to the stillwater level or just below it. These pieces of floating debris can apply a strong concentrated impact load that is measured in newtons per square meter (Figures 4.28 and 4.29).
2. *Special impact:* Floating debris capable of generating a *special impact* consists either of large pieces capable of hitting a large area of the exterior surface of a building or a *conglomerate* or *aggregation* of smaller objects capable of generating a substantial load per lineal meter distributed across the full width of the building surface receiving the frontal impact of the

FIGURE 4.28 Interior view of a building in which storm surge and floating debris breached the building envelope, allowing wind and water to enter and practically destroy everything.

Wind and Water

FIGURE 4.29 Another example showing how floating debris driven by storm surge damaged the building envelope, allowing the rushing waters and floating debris inside the building.

water. Based on their individual sizes, these smaller pieces of floating debris might appear somewhat harmless, but in reality, because they act as a conglomerate of objects, they also tend to hit the same surface repeatedly, which increases the potential for damage.

Generally, this type of aggregation of pieces of floating debris is common during flash floods or flooding events caused by rivers overtopping their banks, which generate a large volume of rushing water through urban areas, where there is an abundance of sources of floating debris as damage to the built environment takes place and the flow of water carries loose objects found in its path and pieces of building materials. In Hurricanes Ike and Katrina, there were clear lines of debris accumulated inland along the end of the surge region, a common sight in many other hurricanes.

FIGURE 4.30 Storm surge from Hurricane Gilbert (1988) carried several boats inland. This one shown here is small compared with others. The impact against a grown tree destroyed part of its hull; however, a vessel this size can cause serious damages when impacting infrastructure or a building.

3. *Extreme impact:* There are cases of pieces of floating debris of very large sizes, such as boats and ships, damaged houses, or buildings torn off their foundations by wind or water, debris from port installations and piers, and other similar large objects, which when propelled by storm surge or the rushing waters of a river become floating missiles capable of causing considerable and even catastrophic damage to buildings and infrastructure. An example of this was documented (Reinhold 2005) during Ike when properly elevated houses along the coastline were knocked down by houses across the street that had been built to lesser standards of elevation and were torn off their foundation by the surge (Figure 4.30).

During both my visits to Cancun in the aftermath of Hurricane Gilbert (1988) and Hurricane Wilma (2005), I observed and documented several instances of large vessels that were carried far inland by storm surge, and at least one instance of a building that was damaged by the impact of a ship propelled by storm surge.

After the impact of Hurricane Katrina (2005) on the coastal regions of Louisiana, Mississippi, and Alabama, I documented several cases of large ships or other floating structures that became floating debris under the impact of storm surge, causing considerable damage on land (Figure 4.31).

Whirlpool

An additional cause of damage generated by water results from *vortices* that form downstream as the surge, or flash flood, encounters a building and flows around it.

Wind and Water 73

FIGURE 4.31 Hurricane Katrina (2005) caused catastrophic damages in Biloxi, Mississippi, mainly from storm surge. These images show the "before" (a) and "after" (b) in a coastal zone.

Frequently, the interaction between water flow and an obstacle, such as a building or structure, generates vortices when the current goes around it and actually separates from walls parallel to the flow and then unifies again downstream. Because of the strong rotation and whirlpool effect of these vortices, there is a considerable potential for damage to buildings, and structures, in the zone affected by them.

5 Hurricanes and the Built Environment

We are now at a point where we can and must use previously shared knowledge to assess what happens, or could happen, as the effects of wind and water are felt when interacting with buildings during a hurricane.

Let us now examine and evaluate the role and expected performance of each of the components, systems, subsystems, assemblies, and materials that compose a building, both singly and in complement with others, when a building interacts with a hurricane.

The key objective here is to answer questions such as the following: Why does one building sustain major damage during a hurricane while others near and around it emerge practically unscathed? Why does the structure or other components of a building fail under the impact of a hurricane?

I believe that in trying to answer the above questions, we will benefit and may even get to a point where we avoid a failed building or the repetition of damage the next time there is a hurricane event.

Because my research and field work on the impact of hurricanes in Quintana Roo has focused mainly on hotels, commercial buildings, and multistory residential buildings, I will focus my analysis in this chapter on those types of buildings. I will leave the rather important and very much-needed discussion on the impacts on houses and small residential buildings to a future book on the topic of hurricanes.

Before broaching this topic, I would like to emphasize the following: The study and assessment of how the various systems and components that form a building contribute to a successful or failed performance, under the impact of a hurricane, must be undertaken preferably during the design phase of a new building. However, the same type of analysis and assessment can benefit existing buildings through a process of retrofitting or restoration, for it is never too late to take measures to prevent building failure as it interacts with a hurricane.

It is equally beneficial to conduct the same type of studies on buildings that have already been damaged by the actual impact of a hurricane, as the damages we observe will provide evidence as to the actual causes. All of the knowledge thus acquired will help in answering the question: Why did this building fail under the impact of this hurricane?

Regarding the subject matter of this chapter, I propose we itemize the various systems and components of a building to concentrate our attention on the following:

- Foundation
- Structure
- Building envelope
- External infrastructure

FOUNDATION

The structure, including the foundation, constitutes the main load-resisting system for a building, which must be capable of carrying the combination of all forces acting on the building both from internal and external sources. These include loads generated by the effect of the wind and the water, which have been already mentioned.

In other words, the structure and the foundation are the support of the building. The main functions of the foundation are

To support the total weight of the building, its occupants, equipment and contents, plus all loads exerted by external sources, including hurricanes: Loads acting on a building accumulate from the top all the way down to the foundation. Because of this, it is essential for the structure–foundation system to have continuity from top to bottom, to guarantee that all loads applied to the building can be transferred all the way down to the foundation.

To transfer the weight of the building and all additional loads to the ground: The total accumulated load transferred to the foundation is transmitted to the ground around it and distributed throughout the same. In view of this, it is absolutely critical to ensure that the ground where the building is anchored has the capacity to safely support the weight of the building and all loads applied to it.

The best way to ensure the ground that will support the building has the necessary structural capacity and integrity is by way of a soil study to be completed prior to the design of the building.

I emphasize how essential such soil studies are for buildings to be constructed in the coastal zone, near the beach, or in regions where there are caverns, underground rivers, or which have a history of sink holes, or where soils are generally sandy or consist of poorly compacted sediment layers that are also subject to the effects of moving water, such as erosion or saturation, making them generally unfit to support the weight and loads of a building.

To fulfill its function, especially when building near the beach, the foundation must have enough depth to reach soil layers with enough integrity and structural capacity. As a general rule, when building in coastal regions with sandy soils, or for that matter in any location where the top layers of the ground lack the required structural integrity and load-carrying capacity, the recommended approach is to use *pilings*. These structural members are driven into the ground by powerful mechanical hammers until they reach the required levels.

To anchor the building to the ground that supports it. The same as the roots of a tree, the foundation has the function of firmly anchoring the building to the ground, even when it is subjected to external loads such as those generated by a hurricane.

As has been explained, loads generated by the wind and the water during a hurricane act mainly along a horizontal plane, resulting in forces that push or pull perpendicularly on the external vertical surfaces of a building.

Hurricanes and the Built Environment

By visualizing the winds of a hurricane pushing on the topmost levels of a building with strong pressure, we could also visualize how this force uses the height of the building as a lever trying to make it rotate in the same direction in which the wind is blowing. When this happens, it is the ground surrounding the foundation that counteracts such force.

When the wind field of a hurricane encounters a building in its path, it flows around and over it, and in doing so it generates suction on the roof of the building, especially if it is a flat roof. In reality, this suction is due to a vertical force generated by the wind known as *uplift*, which tries to pull the building off the ground. When this happens, it is clear that the mass of the building and foundation will generate an opposite reaction to the uplift force, but in extreme cases, it is the holding capacity of the ground, by way of friction with the pilings, which keeps the building in place.

In order to function effectively, the foundation must reach a depth that ensures the mechanical connection, by way of friction, with the ground is strong enough to anchor the building with plenty of safety margin to resist extreme loading conditions. The use of pilings driven to depths that ensure these structural strength conditions are met is recommended in all such cases.

STRUCTURE

The structure is the *skeleton* of a building consisting of interconnected principal and secondary members that resist their own weight, plus the weight of the building, its occupants, equipment, and contents, as well as all external forces such as those exerted by a hurricane.

The main function of the structure, in addition to resisting the combination of loads already mentioned, is to provide a continuous path for all loads to be transferred from the top and periphery to the building foundation and the ground.

There are three important requirements the building structure must meet in order to effectively fulfill its functions as described below.

CONNECTIONS

The key for the effective performance of the structure, especially when the building is sustaining the impact of a hurricane, is how good the connections are. The connections are important because they are the points where loads carried by one structural member are transferred to another, as well as keys to developing a continuous load path.

Connections are of critical importance, so much so that even when individual columns and beams in the structure have ample capacity to carry the loads on the building, a bad connection between two or more members is all it may take to cause failure of the whole system.

REDUNDANCY

The structure must have capacity to carry out its function even when some individual members fail, without this leading to total structural failure. By way of example, it may happen that some extreme load exceeds the capacity of an individual structural member, causing it to fail, but even when this happens, the structure must be capable of having other members absorb the load no longer being carried by the failed element, and at the same time be able to reroute the load path to ensure its continuity all the way to the foundation. This is what we call *structural redundancy*.

OVERCAPACITY

The structure must have enough carrying capacity to resist the accumulation of all combined internal and external loads acting on the building, including some extreme load that may exceed design criteria, without reaching, let alone surpass, the capacity of individual members or the total capacity of the whole system. In other words, the structure must have an *overcapacity* to resist extreme loads. This is what we call *margin of safety*.

BUILDING ENVELOPE

The building envelope covers the structure and protects the building interior from the elements, the same as the skin does for the human body.

The building envelope consists of the roof, the exterior walls or cladding, and all of the elements that are part of them. Windows, doors, ventilation louvers, skylights, ventilation hoods, and other similar devices are all part of the building envelope.

The main functions of the building envelope are the following:

Protect the interior of the building, its contents, and its occupants, from the elements: The building envelope insulates its interior from the sun, wind, rain, heat, cold, dust, noise, thunderstorms, hurricanes, etc.

The protective function of the building envelope not only benefits the occupants, equipment, and contents of the building, but it may also have an important and positive effect on the building's energy, air conditioning, and maintenance costs.

Resist and transfer external loads to the building structure: Loads generated by the wind and water during a hurricane are first applied to the various surfaces of the building envelope, which then transfer them to the structural members that support them.

Regarding this specific function, it is important to keep in mind that the capacity of the building envelope to transfer loads to the structure, and the effectiveness with which it does it depends first on the strength and integrity of the cladding and components, but mainly on the connections between the envelope and its supporting structural members.

It is of little use to have a highly resistant structure and a strong building envelope if it is the connections between them that fail.

Be an architectural element that contributes to the "personality" of the building: The envelope is an important element in the architectural design of the building, as the materials used in its construction, the finishes, paint, and the shape of the envelope itself give the building a particular look that makes it different from other nearby buildings.

Hurricanes and the Built Environment

Relative to the building envelope, it is imperative that we learn about and emphasize the following two criteria:

- *The building envelope is as resistant (as strong) as the weakest of its components.* While some may consider this to be something obvious, I have, however, seen many instances where totally inadequate materials have been used to construct the building envelope relative to the hazards or the loads that it may encounter, which is why I consider it critical to emphasize this here. To illustrate this point, imagine a building envelope consisting of a built-up roof over a reinforced concrete deck, reinforced concrete exterior walls, aluminum and glass windows, aluminum ventilation louvers, and sheet-metal ventilation hoods mounted on the walls and roof. It is clear that the windows, louvers, and ventilation hoods are the weakest components of such a building envelope with much lesser capabilities for resisting the impact of wind and water during hurricanes.
- Preserving the integrity of the building envelope under the impact of a hurricane is absolutely critical because any breach of the same, even a relatively minor one, may lead to catastrophic damage. Damage to the building envelope caused by loads generated by positive or negative wind pressure, the impact of flying debris, hydrodynamic pressure from storm surge, wave impact, the impact of floating debris, or by hydrostatic pressure due to flooding during a hurricane, may lead to breaching of the envelope allowing wind and water to penetrate the interior of the building causing plenty of damage to finishes and contents, and even death or injury to occupants, and structural damage.

In some cases, breaching of the building envelope will generate loads inside a building that when combined with external loads will effectively amplify total forces acting on given sectors of the building, which in some cases could lead to catastrophic damage and structural failure.

By way of example, let us consider the case of an unprotected window that is broken by the impact of flying debris during a hurricane. This broken window, a breach in the building envelope, allows creation of an internal pressure equal to the pressure that would have occurred on the failed element. However, this pressure acts equally and somewhat uniformly on all interior surfaces. Consequently, the loads generated by the internal pressure can be much greater than the average of the loads on the exterior surface because, as we have discussed, external pressures are highly variable over the surface of the building. These internal pressures apply forces to the underside (the interior) of the roof at the same time that this component of the envelope is resisting an exterior uplift load from the wind flowing above it. Because the internal pressure is so uniform over the surface, it can actually double the net uplift on the roof when the envelope is breached on the windward face of the building. This creates a critical loading condition where both the interior and exterior loads combine into a much larger force, which could easily exceed the capability of the roof and its supporting structure to resist it, resulting in catastrophic damage to the roof itself and possibly structural failure as well.

Granted the example above describes a catastrophic occurrence, which should be considered extreme and of low probability. However, even in cases when the breaching of the building envelope does not result in significant structural damage, a high probability remains that penetration by wind and water will cause considerable damage to the interior finishes, furniture, equipment, and to other content that may have great economic or intellectual value to the building owners or occupants.

The final result could very well be a structure that survives the hurricane impact without major structural damage, but the interior finishes, contents, and equipment can still suffer extensive damage to the extent that they are considered a total loss, plus the even worse possibility of loss of life and/or injury to occupants of the building. I am quite sure none of us would like to confront such dire consequences resulting from a breaching of the building envelope.

Talking about protecting the integrity of the building envelope makes it necessary to address a recurring topic that has come up in most, if not all, of the hurricane-vulnerable communities that I have visited.

I am referring to a debate about what may be the best course of action: (a) to totally protect and seal the building envelope in order to avoid breaching under hurricane forces or (b) to leave some windows semiopen around the building to allow external and internal pressures to balance in order to prevent development of large internal pressures, which occurs when there is a breach of a sealed building envelope.

Relative to this interesting topic, based on many years of studying the causes of hurricane damage, I am of the opinion that while semiopen windows may to a degree contribute to an equalization of the external and internal wind pressures, and this in turn contributes to a reduction in internal pressurization, it fosters the flow of wind and rain through the building causing tremendous internal damage. Furthermore, if a door closes on an interior wall, the pressure will build up on that interior wall to such a degree that it may very well cause it to fail. Here, we must keep in mind that interior walls are usually weaker than exterior ones, so allowing hurricane winds inside can result in a gutted building by the storm effects. While this also creates the possibility of structural damage, it is the interior destruction of content and finishes that is the greatest risk.

The biggest problem I see in keeping some windows semiopen during a hurricane is that this allows winds that could range from 120 kph to more than 240 kph into the building, together with wind-driven rain and possibly windborne debris. We definitely do not want to have the impact of extreme wind, rain, and flying debris inside our houses and buildings. The resulting forces would act directly on the contents of the building, including furniture, art objects, finishes, office equipment, documents, and in summary on everything contained inside an office, commercial establishment, museum, factory, or a home, which have not been designed or made to resist such impacts, more often than not with catastrophic results.

The most effective line of defense against wind and flying debris, the *perimeter*, to use military terminology, is the building envelope. To the degree that we can preserve the integrity of the building envelope under such impacts, there is a high

Hurricanes and the Built Environment 81

FIGURE 5.1 Blades of this ceiling fan were totally destroyed by the wind after the building envelope was breached. A clear example of the need to prevent wind from penetrating the interior of the building where it can cause extreme damage to finishes and contents.

probability that the building will resist the impact, and continue to function in the aftermath of a hurricane.

Figures 5.1 and 5.2 illustrate some of the kinds of damage wind can cause inside a building, which can be avoided in most cases by protecting the integrity of the building envelope.

FIGURE 5.2 Photo showing what is left of an air-conditioned duct, manufactured with thin aluminum sheet reinforced with wires, that did not resist the turbulent wind pressure inside the building. Damage occurred after the failure of the building envelope. It is important to consider that the vast majority of materials, equipment, finishes, and furniture inside a building or a home have not been designed to withstand the force of hurricane winds.

EXTERIOR INFRASTRUCTURE

Exterior infrastructure includes all of those items installed or built above or outside a building to fulfill some of the following functions:

1. Items that are required for the functioning, the operation, of a building. These include, among others, mechanical equipment installed on top of or outside the building, water tanks, fuel tanks, emergency power generators, air conditioning equipment, electrical, water, or similar main supply points, which connect the building with municipal services.
2. Items that are independent of the building, but which are part of the grounds or a complex where the building itself is one of the components. These include landscaping and gardens, outdoor terraces, swimming pools, recreational installations such as game courts, light posts, paved roadways, walkways, signage, and others (Figures 5.3 and 5.4).

Each of the components of the external infrastructure must be treated as an individual and independent element, which merits its own assessment of vulnerability and mitigation measures to reduce the potential for damage under the impact of a hurricane.

Relative to this, it is important to note that the priority must always be those pieces of external infrastructure that are critical or essential for the building to operate, and which ensure the continuity of function and/or provision of services from within the building (Figure 5.5).

Special attention must be paid to the external infrastructure that connects the building to municipal or other external services provided by third parties, which in some cases might be private entities, such as electric power, water, sewer, telephone, other means of communication, etc. In this regard, it is recommended to

FIGURE 5.3 Example of external infrastructure. Cooling tower for AC installed on the roof, needed for the functioning of the building.

Hurricanes and the Built Environment

FIGURE 5.4 Example of external infrastructure. Light construction metal building sheltering main electrical supply and associated switchgear and controls from the electrical utility.

install alternate sources of supply and also develop redundancy of supply, in order to ensure continuity of function in cases when the primary source of supply might be interrupted.

Examples of the above may include the installation of emergency power generators that ensure electrical supply when service from the utility might be interrupted, installation of cisterns or potable water tanks to ensure the availability of water for various purposes should the public supply be interrupted because of damage from a hurricane.

FIGURE 5.5 Example of external infrastructure, which is not an essential component for the continuity of operation of the hotel itself but which complements the design of a hotel complex that provides recreational amenities for hotel guests.

SAILS, WIND-CATCHERS, AND WIND TUNNELS

Any surface that interferes with the flow of wind, the same as the *sail* of a ship does, catches the force of the same either as a push or a pull (suction). What this means is that external walls in a building act as *sails* during a hurricane.

Those "sails" that may require special attention because of the potential for damage are those items that are integral components of a building lacking major structural support or those pieces of external infrastructure that because of their specific functions must be built or installed under conditions of total exposure to the elements (Figures 5.6 through 5.8).

Other components that are susceptible to being damaged are those that, because of their shape or geometry, tend to "capture the wind" focusing or concentrating it in a way that focuses or increases the force resulting in higher loads. Similar conditions develop when the shape of the building itself creates nooks, crannies, or zones where wind will penetrate, becoming stagnant or turbulent, increasing the potential for damage. These are the components we generally designate as *wind-catchers* (Figure 5.9).

Frequently, wind-catchers are integral parts of the original design of the building, which means both their potential loading conditions and method of installation were part of the design criteria before construction took place. In other cases, however, and I say this based on experience, often a specific wind-catcher is added to an existing building, which results in new or changed loading conditions and potential for damage on the building structure.

Often, rather than separate pieces that are added or installed, it is the shape of the building itself that creates wind-catchers. That which could be considered an

FIGURE 5.6 Billboards and outdoor signs of various types, including traffic signals, advertising, etc., are typical examples of "sails." This traffic signal around Puerto Morelos, near Cancun, sustained wind pressures that exceeded the structural capability of the post. The combination of positive, overturning, and uplift loads ended up demolishing the entire assembly of sign and post.

Hurricanes and the Built Environment

FIGURE 5.7 Solar water heaters installed on roofs and terraces in several hotels and other buildings in Cancun are other types of "sails" that are generally damaged by the uplift forces. In the specific case of solar water heaters, the problem is more complex since the installation method is generally insufficient to withstand negative loads. Consequently, they are detached from their supporting frames, becoming windborne debris with great potential to damage neighboring buildings.

FIGURE 5.8 Another building component that acts as a "sail" and has a high incidence of damage from hurricane impacts is the metal rollup door shown here. Owing to their design and method of installation, these doors, which are flexible elements gliding in steel guides, can be damaged or sucked right out of the building by negative pressures exerted by hurricane winds. Something similar occurs with garage doors.

FIGURE 5.9 Typical examples of wind-catchers are the parabolic dishes that are quite common now. Their concave shape catches and concentrates the wind; in turn, the wind pushes with strong loads that shake and may overturn them. The loads are transmitted to the supporting structures and depending on the installation type, to the roof and structure that could be damaged. This specific example shows other possible causes of damage, in the paint cans and other loose materials left on the roof. Those can easily become flying debris.

interesting architectural design element becomes a wind-catcher, and a source of problems and potential damage when the building interacts with a hurricane (Figures 5.10 and 5.11).

I would like to mention yet one additional possible contributor to potential damage during a hurricane; it is what I refer to as a *wind tunnel*.

There are two typical cases of wind tunnels. The first one is when two or more buildings, most probably built at different times, end up in close proximity to one another. Such close proximity may result in "passages" between buildings through which extreme winds must flow during hurricanes. The narrowness of the passage creates a contraction, which requires the hurricane wind field to increase its velocity in order to traverse the resulting *wind tunnel*. Following the laws of physics, such increased velocity results in a decrease in wind pressure, which is often accompanied by turbulent flow, shaking, and loading conditions resulting from the combined effects of drag and leveling-off that may generate a high potential for damage.

The second type of wind tunnel results from the shape and design of the building itself, without adjacent buildings being involved (Figures 5.12 through 5.14).

SYMMETRY, CONTINUITY, CENTRICITY, AERODYNAMICS, AND HYDRODYNAMICS

When speaking of the effects of wind on buildings, I have often referred to this as the *interaction* between the wind and a building. By definition, interaction involves a

Hurricanes and the Built Environment 87

FIGURE 5.10 Example of a building whose shape, especially discontinuity of its building envelope, has created wind-catchers, the lines simulate wind flowing trying to occupy all available space. Owing to the multiple changes in direction, the flow turns turbulent and generates complex loads affecting nonstructural elements, such as the external ceiling.

FIGURE 5.11 Example of an architectural design that results in a complex geometry, creating adjacent wind-catchers. The lines of flow simulate the possible flow patterns when the building interacts with hurricane winds. It is easy to imagine the turbulence as the wind enters and becomes stagnant to then accelerate and escape the wind-catcher. Discontinuities introduced in the enclosure by the architectural design are possible contributors to the damage potential. In this specific case, there is a nonstructural external ceiling that will be affected by the wind during a hurricane. The damage potential is high due to the wind-catchers.

FIGURE 5.12 Wind tunnel created when the building on the left was built in 1976, very close to the building on the right, built in 1927. Here, it is important to visualize the wind flowing through it, accelerating and generating areas of turbulence between the two buildings. The building on the right has windows facing the wind tunnel in all of its floors, and those windows are very old and not impact-resistant, and were not designed or installed to withstand hurricane forces, which will be increased by the influence of the wind tunnel. On the other hand, the building to the left has a solid wall on the side of the wind tunnel. It may be concluded that the design group ignored the wind tunnel created by their design, as well as the possibility of damages caused by the same on the 1927 building.

FIGURE 5.13 A wind tunnel created by the building design; a semiopen space through which hurricane winds will circulate. This image helps visualize the different wind effects described earlier (Chapter 4), such as push, stagnation, and drag. It is easy to see the damage potential for the nonstructural external ceiling in the tunnel.

Hurricanes and the Built Environment

FIGURE 5.14 Another example of a wind tunnel created by building design. The external ceiling is highly susceptible to damage by the effects of wind pressure, the same as in the previous figure.

mode of *reciprocity* between the parts that interact, in this case, a building or house or piece of infrastructure and the wind field of a hurricane.

Because of such required environment of interaction, we may conclude that just as the wind can have given effects on a building as a result of complying with the natural laws of physics, the building itself will also have an effect on the flow of wind as a result of its external shape and other important design characteristics.

If we are interested in the development of projects or in building in any hurricane-vulnerable place, be it in Florida, the Gulf Coast, the Caribbean, Taiwan, the Philippines, Cancun, or other vulnerable zones in Quintana Roo, it behooves us, in reality it is imperative that we do, to become familiar with those building design characteristics that may have a significant influence on the behavior of wind flow as it interacts with those structures.

In my opinion, there are five important characteristics that we must pay attention to.

- Symmetry
- Centricity
- Continuity
- Aerodynamics
- Hydrodynamics

A detailed study of these characteristics, and especially of the analytical methodology to assess how each one may affect the flow of wind or water, is beyond the scope of this book, but it would be of benefit to complete a conceptual review of these five characteristics.

To set the context for such review, we must consider any building as a tridimensional geometric body, a volume, which interacts with the wind and water: the two principal damaging components in a hurricane.

Symmetry

Every geometric body has a *centroid*, also known as *center of mass* or *center of gravity*. Without using technical terminology or a full dissertation to define the term, imagine that when we use the center of mass to support a geometric body, it will be in perfect equilibrium.

Visualizing our building, which we want to design and build in a hurricane-vulnerable coastal zone, observing the dictum of *form follows function*, let us imagine its shape, volume, and proportions as being evenly distributed around its centroid. Let us also imagine that a simple visual inspection reveals balance and harmony of the whole around the centroid. From these results we can conclude there is *symmetry* in our building.

To the degree that we achieve a symmetric design, this promotes an efficient interaction between the building, in terms of its shape only, and hurricane winds. In this respect, let it be clear that we are, as a starting point, speaking strictly only about the shape, the form, of the building without regard to any other aspects, such as the structure, the details of the building envelope, or the materials of construction. Perhaps more importantly in terms of interaction with hurricanes, it should also be clear that at this stage, we are not even considering the lateral load-resisting structure, even though symmetry of form is often associated with an important degree of structural symmetry, but not always.

In designing a building, the distribution of space and its supporting structure are the result of several criteria, including the specific functions to be sheltered by the building, site characteristics, cost of construction, etc., and it is not always possible to achieve perfect symmetry. It is necessary then, as much as possible and after considering all pertinent factors, to aim for the best combination of symmetry, harmony, and balance in the design of a building.

A good starting point in seeking the *best possible symmetry* is to draw two perpendicular axes on a sheet of drafting paper, respectively, designated as *longitudinal* and *transversal axis*. The point where both axes cross identifies the centroid of the future building as seen in plan view (from above) over the horizontal plane of the site where it will be built. By using this simple tool, we should be able to develop the preliminary concept for the design of the building, assigning approximate areas for the various functions to be housed in the ground floor of the building. We would then repeat the process for other levels in the case of a multistory building (Figure 5.15).

The main objective of this exercise is to define the approximate shape and dimensions, the *footprint* if you will, the building will have when viewed in plan view taking into account the characteristics and limitations of the site and the search for symmetry. Upon completing this initial exercise, we can then start establishing initial criteria for the structural concept that will be required to support the building and resist external loads acting on it such as those generated by a hurricane or storm surge, while taking into account space distribution, area requirements and the relationship, interdependencies and overall shape of the aggregation of elements.

In assessing the symmetry of a building, we are also defining the horizontal profile it will present to the flow of wind or water, to lateral loads in general, at a given time. I recommend taking advantage of the described exercise to also identify

Hurricanes and the Built Environment

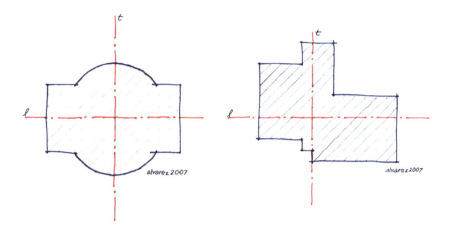

FIGURE 5.15 Illustration of the methods described in this chapter. The area in both the figures is the same; however, note the distribution with respect to the axes. The figure on the left is symmetrical and the one on the right is asymmetrical.

potential wind-catchers, wind tunnels, and sails, so that appropriate corrective measures may be taken on a timely basis, meaning during the design phase before the building is built. Evaluating symmetry is not only needed and recommended for the design of new buildings, but it is equally beneficial in the case of existing buildings as this will help assess their vulnerability to hurricanes, which will allow us to identify mitigation measures to be incorporated through a retrofit process that effectively reduces the potential for damage.

In summary, this is about the importance of shape, the *wind silhouette*, in helping determine how a building will perform under the impact of a hurricane. This critical importance is highlighted by the fact that post hurricane damage assessment and field inspections of hurricane damaged buildings, in which I and others have engaged numerous times, often reveal a causal relationship between building shape and type and amount of damage. Project owners, developers, and design professionals need to ensure the shape of a new building will contribute to optimal performance during hurricane events.

Centricity

Important as the shape of a building is, when it comes to performance under hurricane conditions, the most critical element is the structure of the building, with an emphasis on the *main wind-force resisting system* (MWFRS). The structure manages all dead and live loads as well as external environmental loads, such as those generated by the impact of a hurricane and storm surge, while also ensuring the integrity of the building envelope through effective connections.

Similar to the concept of symmetry with respect to the form of the building, the effective performance of the structure, especially relative to lateral loads and the various effects of drag, lift, drift, and others generated by hurricanes, may depend in good measure on the concept of *centricity*. In this regard, the building design team needs to consider the following three aspects: the *center of mass*, *center of stiffness* or *rigidity*, and the *aerodynamic center*. Structural centricity is achieved when the center of mass and center of stiffness coincide, which, while not always possible, should always be an aim of the design team. What is critically important here is to recognize the need to design for the eccentric loading (torsion) that will result as the wind attacks from different directions. In summary, if the building is neither symmetrical in terms of its shape (wind silhouette) nor symmetrical in terms of its center of stiffness (the centroid of its MWFRS), there is a misalignment between the axes, which will cause an uneven distribution of loads under hurricane conditions that in turn produces a twisting effect in the building. To this we must add the fact that the aerodynamic center will move as the wind may attack the building from any direction. From the above, it is clear how difficult it is to achieve structural centricity.

In the context of the above, but realizing that aiming for structural centricity is a positive thing that may reduce extreme torsional effects and eccentric loading, it is important for project owners and design professionals to learn more about this concept. The discussion that follows should be helpful in this regard. Centricity is directly related to the structure of the building and how it works, with emphasis on the load paths that transfer forces acting on the building from the periphery and the top to the foundation, and then the ground. In pursuing centricity, the main objective is to attain a *centric* structure in the sense that, to the degree possible on the basis of the architectural design, the main supporting elements of the building will be evenly distributed around the centroid (as marked by the intersection of both axes) of the same (Figure 5.16).

By achieving a centric structure, we try to avoid having a building where principal structural members might be concentrated in one sector, which in structural terms would make the building more rigid in one sector and rather flexible in another, which will affect its performance when interacting with a hurricane.

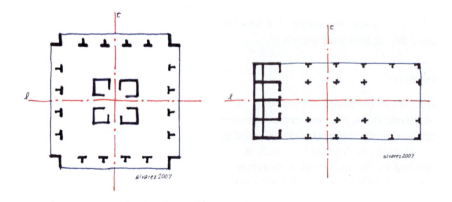

FIGURE 5.16 Floor plans of two buildings of similar area, and the main structural members. On the left, a centric structure, and on the right, an eccentric one.

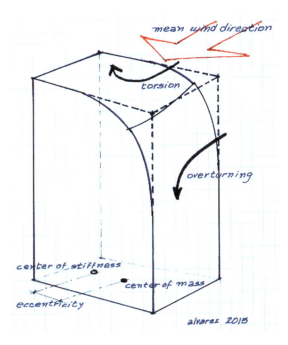

FIGURE 5.17 Combined effects of torsion and overturning when wind hits the face of a tall building with an eccentric structure, one where the center of stiffness does not coincide with the center of mass. Such loading conditions carry a high potential for damage during hurricanes.

Figure 5.16 illustrates this point. When observing the *eccentric* structure, the one on the right in the figure, we can imagine that when it is subjected to hurricane winds acting perpendicularly to the longitudinal axis, the left side of the building is much more rigid than the right side; consequently, this structural condition will be reflected in how the building reacts to the wind loads (Figure 5.17).

Continuity

Just as with structural continuity, which we have discussed before, the *continuity of the building envelope* is a rather critical characteristic relative to the interaction of the building with a hurricane.

Continuity of the building envelope exists when the surface of each of the external walls is in one plane, and there are no or very few projecting elements, no wind-catchers, and no intervening wind tunnels on them, and the changes in direction from one face of the building to another are achieved by way of stepped or chamfered corners. The same criteria of continuity also apply to the roof of the building as it is the integral element of the building envelope.

A continuous building envelope contributes to a reduction of loads on the main wind-resisting system as well as on cladding and components, by promoting a better distribution of loads through a less turbulent flow and fewer extreme pressure hot

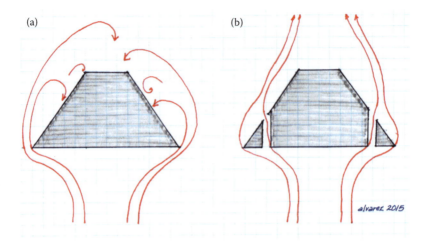

FIGURE 5.18 Schematic showing (a) how the wind flow around the corners of a building will cause separation and the generation of eddies rolling down the sides and behind the leeward face, and how such turbulent flow can be modified (b) by introducing some discontinuities in the envelope near the corners that allow the wind to "bleed through," resulting in a comparatively streamlined flow that reduces loads acting on the structure.

spots when it interacts with the wind, while also reducing other potentially adverse effects such as have been discussed previously. In summary, a continuous building envelope simplifies the pattern of external loads applied to the building during a hurricane, consequently limiting the potential for damage.

In this regard, it is essential that the design team consider the continuity of the envelope as a *critical factor* in the behavior and performance of the building under the impact of future hurricanes. It is we, the architects in charge of design, who must respect the power of the wind and the water by incorporating continuity into the envelope and other equally important characteristics in the design of our buildings, while also instilling in them that special "personality" that distinguishes one from the others (Figure 5.18).

Also on this topic of continuity, in the interest of enriching the discussion and of contributing contrasting points of view, it is important to note that there are many respected professionals in the field of wind engineering and hurricane research that can offer findings from their own work that argue some lack of continuity may offer tangible benefits. For example, the placement of balconies at corners has been shown to reduce component and cladding loads when compared with smooth continuous building surfaces. Also, some discontinuities are purposely introduced at the corners of tall buildings to "bleed the air" as the wind flows around corners, which helps reduce vortex shedding and loads on the MWFRS. There are also wind engineers that argue a complex building envelope actually reduces local extreme negative pressures by contributing to a well-mixed wind flow. They also argue a complex building surface tends to break up the vortices that generate some extreme cladding loads, while recognizing that the same complexity may still leave some localized hot spots where extreme loads prevail (Figure 5.19).

Hurricanes and the Built Environment

FIGURE 5.19 Two pictures at the top show building envelopes that are continuous. The building on the right has a tridimensional character and continuity in its building envelope. The buildings in the bottom pictures have discontinuous building envelopes. Let us try to imagine both types of covers interacting with hurricane winds.

From this, it appears continuity is generally a good thing, especially for low buildings, but for tall buildings or those that deviate from the boxy wind silhouette of codes, some level of discontinuity can help reduce turbulence and other effects as well as loads on cladding and components. This illustrates the benefits of wind tunnel studies when designing tall or unusual form buildings.

Aerodynamics

I believe criteria such as symmetry, centricity, and continuity share the common objective of facilitating and making more efficient the interaction of the building with hurricane winds. In this regard, we could say that all these characteristics contribute to the *aerodynamics* of the building.

It is a fact that we all consider an airplane to be, or that because of its function it should be, aerodynamic. In this regard, at times, we may also refer to an automobile in terms of its aerodynamics. Surely, many of us have seen television ads showing a car being tested in a large wind tunnel, with flow lines marked by white smoke streamlining around it as a demonstration of how aerodynamic it is when interacting with wind.

We use the term *aerodynamic* to refer to the capability of an airplane or an automobile of *flying,* of moving *rapidly* and *fluidly* through the air. The characteristic of aerodynamics is viewed by most as something good and positive in an airplane and also in a car.

I propose that we also consider *aerodynamics* as something good and positive when we refer to desirable characteristics in a building, because even though a building can neither fly nor move from one place to another as a result of being anchored to the ground, it nevertheless must interact with the flow of wind and it must respond to it. What we seek is an aerodynamic quality similar to that of an automobile not an airplane, because we do not want the building to fly, but to streamline through the flow of a wind field with the least amount of effort and turbulence possible.

Although *symmetry* as well as *continuity* both contribute to facilitating passage of a building through a wind field, its true aerodynamic quality results from its shape and geometry. In this regard, the design team, led by the architect, must strive to achieve as streamlined a shape as possible for the building that is put in service. Our previous discussion on continuity offered examples of measures, such as the use of chamfered or stepped corners, to introduce some level of beneficial streamlining to what will remain a bluff body. What is most important in this regard is for everyone involved with a project in a hurricane-vulnerable region, especially the design professionals, to understand how the specific building shape will perform under hurricane conditions and to design for the effects of winds on that shape. The more the shape deviates from the rather basic box shape used in building codes as the basis for establishing load criteria, the more the need for using wind tunnel tests to understand wind interaction, shape performance, and loading criteria.

HYDRODYNAMICS

In hurricane-vulnerable coastal regions, there is a high probability that at some point, a building near the beach may be impacted by storm surge generated by a hurricane.

Relative to storm surge, protective measures need to be taken to prevent the direct impact from the rushing waters or from pieces of floating debris on the building. However, even when this objective is met, there is always a possibility that water will flow around the building. In anticipation of such eventuality, it is always a good practice to endow the building with hydrodynamic resistant characteristics in order to mitigate the impact of water flow as much as possible and also to avoid or minimize problems associated with the damaging effects of drag or leveling-off and eddies caused by the rushing water. Another alternative is to concede the ground floor to the water by using it for parking or storage and other noncritical uses using sacrificial walls that will fail under the impact of storm surge, allowing water to rush through without losing the structural members that support the building and provide the required lateral support. This approach has been used in hurricane-vulnerable coastal regions in Florida with good results.

STRUCTURAL INTEGRITY

Logically, none of the beneficial characteristics described before would be of much use if damage and failure result because the materials and/or methods of construction, or the connections and anchors used in the building cannot resist the forces of a hurricane. In this regard, it is essential to emphasize that the most important characteristic is the *structural integrity* of the building.

Structural integrity refers to the aggregation of structural elements working together as a system to support the building and its loads. Structural integrity depends not only on the principal load-carrying system and its ability to transfer loads to the foundation and the ground, but it also involves the building envelope as a key building element, which is the first to receive the impact of forces generated by the wind or water to then transfer them to the structure itself.

Should the materials used in the construction of the building envelope prove incapable of resisting the anticipated loads generated by the impact of a hurricane, or if the connections between it and the structure cannot transfer loads without failing, then the reality is that there is no structural integrity.

I dwell upon this point, because in my long experience evaluating the performance of buildings under the impact of hurricanes I have found, and continue to find, cases where the envelope and the structure of given buildings have been treated as if they were two totally separate and independent elements. Often, the consequence of this approach is that cladding and components fail leading to heavy interior and content damage, while the structure remains standing with little or no damage.

Part of the problem stems from a design process where a structural engineer is responsible for designing the structure, while others are responsible for choosing materials for the envelope and the methods of installation. In some cases, some of the components of the envelope do not receive specific and detailed attention, being treated instead as systems or materials supplied by others or to be installed in accordance with manufacturer specifications. Some examples of this approach are windows, doors, and other cladding components.

Beyond the design criteria used, it is the actual process of construction that determines the structural integrity of the building. If we are in agreement regarding the premise that the building envelope is as strong as its weakest component and we are evaluating the construction of a hotel that will have 1000 windows, just to give a number, a critically important question is: How can we guarantee that each of those windows will be installed in such a way that it will work effectively in conjunction with the rest of the envelope? This is really a critical core issue, as it may only take one window that fails during a hurricane to generate a breach in the envelope, which allows wind and wind-driven rain as well as flying debris to cause catastrophic damage to the building interior and contents, which might even lead to structural damage.

The most effective method, that I know of, to ensure optimum quality during the construction process and to obtain the desired structural integrity, is by way of a process of *in situ* (on-site) inspection. In the case of components of the building envelope, such as the already-mentioned windows, this process must be continuous and cover each individual component.

Hurricane Mitigation for the Built Environment

This issue of structural integrity and the problems mentioned become one more challenge, a *charge*, for the design teams that will be responsible for so many future projects in Florida, in Cancun, or in any of the many hurricane-vulnerable regions throughout the world.

ONE HURRICANE IS ALL IT TAKES

In closing this discussion, I find it appropriate to return to the saying: When it comes to damage, even catastrophic ones, one hurricane is all it takes! Every year I meet individuals who ask: What will the hurricane season be like this year? News media anxiously wait for hurricane season forecast issued by the well-known researchers at Colorado State University, or those from the National Hurricane Center, so that they may in turn alert the public regarding the probability that one hurricane will make

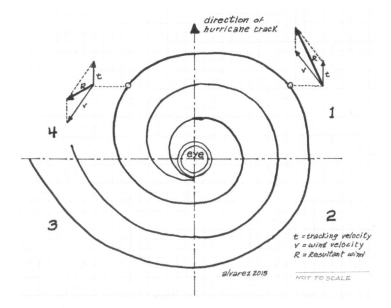

FIGURE 5.20 Simplified schematic of a tropical cyclone in the northern hemisphere. The vertical axis with the arrow pointing up indicates the direction of the hurricane track. The numbers 1, 2, 3, and 4 indicate the four quadrants of the hurricane, starting with 1 forward and to the right of the track axis, and then, clockwise, quadrants 2, 3, and 4. Quadrant 1 is definitely the worse case since the rotating wind and the forward motion speeds add up to produce the strongest winds of the system. This point is illustrated by the small force diagram to the right of quadrant 1, which represents the speed vectors at the point. The force diagram to the left of quadrant 4, is in contrast, showing that the resulting speed is lower than that in quadrant 1. It is important to clarify that the worse case is when the building is located within quadrant 1 and the eye of the storm passes over it, since this will subject it to wind forces from the opposite direction after the eye of the hurricane passes. For southern hemisphere tropical cyclones the diagram would be reversed, with quadrant 1 forward and to the left of the track axis, and quadrants 2, 3, and 4 following progressively counterclockwise.

Hurricanes and the Built Environment 99

landfall, or that there will be 17 tropical cyclones in the Atlantic basin, and that five of those may become major hurricanes.

These forecasts and the scientific research behind them, as well as the probability that there may be a specific number of tropical cyclones in a given year in the Atlantic basin, make for interesting and useful information. Actuarial experts use it to evaluate risk, emergency management professionals use it to plan and manage their resources, and many more use it to worry about what might happen.

In my opinion, we do not need these annual forecasts to be prepared. We must always be prepared. Knowing that we inhabit a region that is vulnerable to hurricanes is all that we need in order to practice mitigation in the design and construction of our projects; annual projections and probabilities make for interesting and somewhat useful information, but that is all. We must be prepared for a worst-case scenario with each new annual hurricane season, as it may only take one impact during what could otherwise be a rather slow and low-activity season to cause catastrophic damage.

Being prepared is a mindset that commences as soon as we make a decision to design and build in a hurricane-vulnerable region. It is at that point when together with our design team, we must assess the relative vulnerability of the specific site chosen for the project. It is then, based on our findings relative to the vulnerability of the project site and its surrounding region, that we, in conjunction with our design team, must identify the design criteria for the shape and the structure to ensure the required structural integrity.

Our challenge is to determine what the *worst expected impact* might be at the specific site selected for our project. Figure 5.20 should be helpful in determining what such worst impact might be from the perspective of the trajectory of a hurricane as it makes landfall and its relationship to the location of the building or project that interests us.

6 Cancun
A Mexican Gate to the Caribbean

Because most of the actual examples of hurricane impacts and building damage in this book are based on my work in the Cancun area, I believe it is important to provide context, and to support the argument that hurricane damage respects no frontiers and that we can all learn and benefit from the experiences of others, by discussing the characteristics of Cancun as a hurricane-vulnerable area so similar to many here in Florida, the Gulf of Mexico, or elsewhere along our coastal regions in the United States.

Toward the end of the decade of the 1970s, the Government of Mexico launched an ambitious project to impel even more what was already an important tourism industry by way of developing new world-class tourist resorts on both coasts of the country.

One of the main objectives of this initiative was the opening of a gate to the Caribbean at a place know as Cancun, with the goal of participating in the growing international tourism trade already attracted by the wonderful and beautiful beaches and seas of the region.

This project, started in 1970, took advantage of the Island of Cancun located 3–5 km from the northeastern coast of the state of Quintana Roo to develop a first-class resort fronting on the Caribbean Sea.

The initial phase of Project Cancun included the following elements: (a) the construction of an international airport; (b) the development and construction of a small city, for future resort workers, for a planned future maximum population of 100,000; (c) construction of a major civil works project to link both the southern and northern ends of the island to the mainland by way of land bridges; and (d) development and construction of all the necessary major infrastructure to support what would be a future hotel strip fronting on the beach, consisting of paved streets and roadways, public lighting, potable water, sewer, storm drainage, and others, which needed to be in place before the construction of hotels could commence on the former island. This initial phase was actually completed by 1974 (Figure 6.1).

MY FIRST VISIT TO CANCUN

I paid my first visit to Cancun in November 1979, having taken an early morning flight from Miami that barely lasted one hour. I had reservations at the Hotel Presidente located in Punta Cancun, the northern extreme of the former island, where I was able to enjoy the magnificent white-sand beach. I also took time to tour the full extent of the hotel strip as well as the City of Cancun proper to learn more about what I considered as a modern, ambitious, and rather interesting city planning and resort development project.

FIGURE 6.1 Picture taken from space showing Cancun "isle," Ciudad Cancun, and Isla Mujeres. (Adapted from NASA ref# ISSO 12ED7804.)

At the time of my visit, there were already five or six hotels fronting on the beach, and perhaps 3000 hotel rooms in the whole complex, as well as a convention center and an open plaza featuring typical Mexican entertainment, with plenty of dance, music, and song, and rather interesting shows such as the "Papantla Flyers." Cancun City, on the mainland, had already reached 25,000 inhabitants: I remember the city as happy, boisterous, animated, and noisy, and with all the vigor and bravado of the new frontier with plenty of opportunities for everyone.

During that visit, a Mexican friend mentioned that the construction of all of the existing hotels had been financed by the Mexican government. Despite its obvious and contagious energy, it was clear the "Cancun Project" was still in its infancy and in its initial development phase, still trying to attract major international tourism and hotel operators. Despite all the enthusiasm, it was clear that some uncertainty remained regarding the viability of such a huge undertaking.

In spite of this, or perhaps because of it, I did however return from my trip fully convinced of the brilliant future that awaited Cancun even then, when it only was a promise of what it has now become.

1979 ATLANTIC HURRICANE SEASON

There were a total of nine tropical cyclones in the Atlantic in 1979. These included Hurricane Henri, which generated near Cozumel and Cancun and made a brief landfall as a tropical storm before moving on beyond the Yucatan coastline to become a category 1 hurricane in the Gulf of Mexico. There were two additional hurricanes, Bob and Elena, both of category 1, that were generated near the Yucatan peninsula, but on the Gulf side posing no major threat or adverse effect to Cancun and Quintana Roo.

Success was immediate. Cancun saw tremendous growth both in the number of hotels and in the population of the city. By 1988, there were already 8000–9000 hotel rooms, timeshare properties were already being promoted among those vacationing in Cancun, while the construction of houses and other residential projects in the resort itself was growing rapidly. Cancun City had exceeded its original maximum population plan, having already reached 250,000 permanent residents who supported quite an active commercial enterprise generated by its population.

1988 ATLANTIC HURRICANE SEASON

In 1988, the Atlantic hurricane season saw higher than average activity when 12 tropical cyclones were generated. Two of these tropical cyclones, Gilbert and Keith, hit Cancun. Keith was a tropical storm with maximum winds around 100 kph, but Gilbert, which at one point became a monster of a storm more than 950 km in diameter and a category 5 hurricane with sustained winds in the 270–280 kph range and gusts above 300 kph, impacted Cozumel and Cancun, causing catastrophic damage.

Two other hurricanes during the 1988 Atlantic season, Debby and Florence, both of them category 1, developed in the Gulf of Mexico near the Yucatan peninsula, but had only little effect on Cancun.

In the aftermath of the disaster caused by Hurricane Gilbert, driven by the economic engine of tourism in Cancun, the entire northeastern coastal region of Quintana Roo, including Isla Mujeres and Cozumel, experienced tremendous development (Figure 6.2) with numerous new tourism projects, including the construction of new hotels, shopping centers, restaurants, parks, and entertainment centers, as well as several ecotourism projects. Today, the boom continues and now includes several new areas and resorts, such as Playa del Carmen, Xcaret, which blends world-class tourist accommodations with wonderful ecological and archeological treasures, Puerto Aventuras, and several places of great natural beauty and ecological wealth, such as Xpu-ha, Xaac, Akumal, Xel-ha, and the magnificent Maya archeological site in Tulum.

While admiring the great success achieved in just over 30 years in the economic and touristic development of the paradise comprising Cancun and the Mayan Riviera, we should not for a moment lose sight of the vulnerability of the region to hurricanes. Just as this region may go several years without the impact of a hurricane, as it happened during most of the decade of the 1980s, just like that, a new cycle began and a major hurricane Gilbert was generated, bringing destruction and human suffering. It just goes to show that one hit is enough to cause a disaster.

2005 ATLANTIC HURRICANE SEASON

The 2005 Atlantic hurricane season confirms what was just stated above. During a period of 16 years after the impact of Gilbert in 1988, all was quiet along the coastal regions of Quintana Roo in terms of cyclonic activity, except for a couple of storms and tropical depressions that had no real consequences.

All of this changed in 2005, a year when the northeastern coast of Quintana Roo was impacted by four hurricanes: Cindy on 3 July, Emily on 17 July, Stan on

FIGURE 6.2 View of the hotel and commercial zone in Punta Cancun, at the north end of the resort, showing the enormous development and recovery achieved after Hurricane Gilbert in 1988.

1 October, and finally Wilma, which hit Cozumel on 21 October and then made a second landfall between Puerto Morelos and Cancun on 22 October as a category 4 hurricane, causing death and enormous destruction in the region. Hurricane Wilma was basically a repetition of the disaster caused by Hurricane Gilbert 17 years before. Although preparedness and a superb job of emergency management by civil protection authorities, in the several municipalities affected, were a clear and vast improvement over what took place in 1988, damage to buildings, infrastructure, and the beaches, on the other hand, were far greater in 2005.

Without a doubt, Cancun and the Mayan Riviera, and for that matter the entire littoral of Quintana Roo, are a Mexican gate to the Caribbean, but they are also a gate to the hurricanes that are generated annually in the larger Atlantic basin. Let hurricanes Gilbert (1988) and Wilma (2005) be a wake-up call for all of us who may have an interest in developing activities of various kinds in Cancun or other vulnerable zones in Quintana Roo.

Let the disasters generated by these hurricanes be lessons to be learned by all of us, to keep always in mind, and to translate into good practices when we build or come to reside in this paradise.

PARADISE

The vulnerability of the coastal region of Quintana Roo to hurricanes and its associated risk coexist with plenty of natural beauty and a privileged geographic location with respect to sources and routes of international tourism. To this, we must add the prominent national economic importance of the state as a generator of foreign income.

Such combination of natural beauty, economic importance, vigorous development, and the attractive business opportunities that derive from these make Cancun, the Maya Riviera, and that entire region a true paradise.

Vulnerability to hurricanes does not in any way diminish the paradise designation given to the region, but it does alert us to what we must do to be able to enjoy it while we also ensure the protection and continuity of our projects and investments.

The knowledge and methods to design and build hurricane-resistant projects already exist. All we need to do is to access and integrate them into the planning and design of our projects, while we also convert them into effective tools to be used in the daily practice of our chosen professions.

7 Cyclones of Quintana Roo

A brief statistical review of the data contained in Figure 7.1 shows the following results. During the 121-year period reflected on the map, Quintana Roo was impacted by tropical cyclones in 82 of those years. On the basis of this, we may conclude that Quintana Roo as a whole has an annual probability of 67.8% of being affected, in some way, by a tropical cyclone. This is more than 34% above the traditional 50/50 chance that begs for indifference or, put in a different way, Quintana Roo is definitely vulnerable to hurricanes. Relative to this, when we take the 183 tropical cyclones over the 121-year period depicted in the map, we can say that the state of Quintana Roo has an annual probability of being affected by 1.5 tropical cyclones, of any category, on a regional basis.

While I researched the vulnerability of Cancun and Quintana Roo to hurricanes, I had the opportunity to consult quite an interesting and unique source of information. I am referring to the "Re-Analysis Project" conducted by scientists in the Hurricane Research Division of the National Oceanographic and Atmospheric Administration[*] of the United States, where I found data on the annual Atlantic hurricane seasons going back to 1851 (Figure 7.2).

The "Re-Analysis Project" offered me an additional 35-year period (1851–1885) of Atlantic basin hurricane activity to add to that (1886–2006) used to construct the map in Figure 7.1, giving me a total of 156 years of information on the Atlantic basin hurricane seasons to use in assessing the vulnerability of Quintana Roo.

From 1851 through 1885, there were 15 annual hurricane seasons during which Quintana Roo was impacted by a total of 19 tropical cyclones, including 17 hurricanes, of which three were major hurricanes (category 3 or higher in the Saffir–Simpson scale), and two tropical storms. There were a total of 202 tropical cyclones affecting Quintana Roo during the 156 years from 1851 through 2006.

By applying the same basic statistical approach to the entire 156-year period, we find that the probability that Quintana Roo would be hit by a hurricane during any given year was 62.6%. The annual probability was 1.3 cyclones per year. While the annual probability of impact based on the 156 years was somewhat lower than that for the original shorter period, from 1886 to 2006, it still qualifies Quintana Roo as highly vulnerable to the impact of tropical cyclones.

Caution is recommended when using statistical data as a basis for decision making. Although statistics are valuable in the assessment of trends, in the specific case

---

[*] NOAA (National Oceanographic and Atmospheric Administration) Hurricane Research Division: 1851–1914 Re-Analysis Project.

108 Hurricane Mitigation for the Built Environment

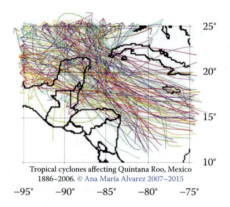

FIGURE 7.1 Map, created especially for this book, that includes the tracks of all hurricanes that made landfall or passed within 150 km from Quintana Roo's coast or boundaries between 1886 and 2006. The main reason to include cyclones not touching land is because even at a distance, the winds, torrential rains, flooding, and storm surge often cause damage. On the other hand, the map shows the tracks of the eye of these hurricanes, but it should be considered that individual systems may have been 300/400 up to 900/1000 km in diameter. A total of 183 cyclonic tracks are in this map. During the 121 years represented here, Quintana Roo was affected by at least one cyclone per year during 82 of the hurricane seasons and was free from impacts during 39 seasons. On four occasions, 5 cyclones hit Quintana Roo in a single season; in 9 seasons, the state suffered 4 cyclones in one year. (By Ana-Maria Alvarez Rivas, based on data by the National Hurricane Center, United States National Oceanographic and Atmospheric Administration.)

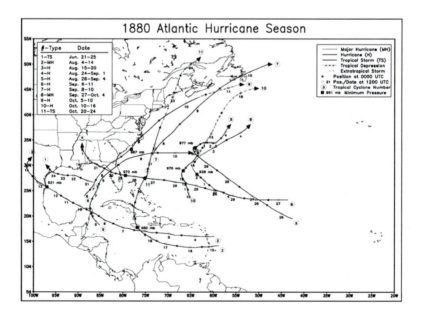

FIGURE 7.2 Map of the 1880 Atlantic hurricane season. (Adapted from NOAA—1851–1914 Re-Analysis Project.)

Cyclones of Quintana Roo

of Quintana Roo and its 156-year record of tropical cyclone impacts, it is equally important to also consider the following:

1. The 156-year period may appear long in terms of human life, but for statistical purposes of calculating probability of impact, it is rather short and the margin of error is high.
2. It has only been a bit more than 50 years since we have been using aerial reconnaissance or satellite observations to identify and track tropical cyclones over the Atlantic; consequently, it is entirely possible that records for annual hurricane seasons prior to 1950 may not account for the total number of tropical cyclones. For this reason, it is probable that the actual

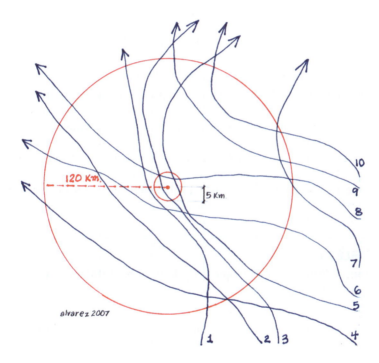

FIGURE 7.3 The dot in the middle of the figure represents the specific site of the building of interest. The small circle represents a 5 km radius around the building. The big circle represents the region around the building within a 120 km radius. Lines with arrows represent 10 cyclones affecting the region on a given year. Note that only three hurricanes crossed the small circle. If we collected this type of information for many years, the total number of cyclones would help us calculate the annual regional probability, and the number of cyclones crossing the small circle would help figure the annual probability on a site-specific basis. Another way of viewing this is as if it were target practice: the circles represent the target, and the cyclones the arrows. It is much easier to hit the large circle than the small one; therefore, the probability of hitting the large circle is greater than hitting the small one. The same applies to the probability of hurricane impact.

number of tropical cyclones during the period is higher than that obtained from available records.

3. There is considerable difference between *regional* and *site-specific* probabilities of impact. Probabilities derived from the 156-year record are regional. If the objective is to build a hotel or to develop a piece of property in the coastal zone of Quintana Roo, it will be necessary to use annual site-specific probabilities of impact to assess the vulnerability of the project and for decision making; otherwise, the use of regional probabilities would inflate the risk and lead to erroneous decisions.

4. A particular kind of analysis, which is beyond the scope of this book, is required to calculate the site-specific probability of impact by a tropical cyclone. Even without such an analysis, and in rather general terms, it could be concluded that the annual probability of impact on a site-specific basis would be a fraction of the regional probability. Figure 7.3 graphically illustrates this point.

5. To assess the risk of damage to a building or project from the impact of hurricanes, it is necessary to first establish the site-specific annual probability of occurrence for each category of tropical cyclones. There are two main reasons for this: On the one hand, each impact by a tropical cyclone regardless of its intensity has the potential for causing damage, and in fact the cumulative effect of impacts by minor hurricanes can eventually add up to copious aggregated damages. On the other hand, however, and everything else being equal, a major hurricane such as a category 4 or 5 has the potential for causing damages that are exponentially larger than those caused by a category 1 or 2 hurricane. When a sufficiently lengthy historical record of hurricane tracks is available for a given region, it is entirely possible

---

TABLE 7.1

Annual Probability of Tropical Cyclone Impact (Miami-Dade County, Florida)

Category (Saffir–Simpson Scale)	Regional % 120 km Radius	Regional % 80 km Radius	Site-Specific % 5 km Radius
Tropical storm 54–117 kph	43.5	37.0	31.1
1 118–152 kph	28.6	18.2	11.9
2 153–176 kph	16.7	11.1	2.5
3 177–208 kph	12.5	7.9	1.0
4 209–248 kph	7.1	4.1	0.1
5 249+ kph	3.3	2.1	0.018

to complete an analysis of regional and site-specific probabilities. In this regard, it is important to mention that the science of hurricane risk modeling has progressed to the point where models are widely used throughout the world, and it would be of benefit to those planning to develop new projects in hurricane-vulnerable regions to explore who is doing this kind of work, and what is available for the specific basin where the project will take place. In the absence of such a study for Cancun or other regions of Quintana Roo at the time I was conducting field work there, Table 7.1 shows such annual probabilities for the County of Miami-Dade in Florida.

8 Hurricane Gilbert—1988

As it often happens during summer in the northern hemisphere, an atmospheric disturbance, what we call a *tropical wave*, developed on September 3, 1988 over the eastern Atlantic Ocean off the northwestern coast of Africa approximately 5° north of the equator and began to move west by northwest aiming for the Windward Islands. On 9 September, this strengthening tropical wave was located 600 km east of Barbados and was categorized as the 12th *tropical depression* of the 1988 Atlantic hurricane season (Figure 8.1).

Still moving to the WNW at 28 kph, the tropical depression continued to strengthen and became better organized as it crossed over the Lesser Antilles, entering the Caribbean in the late afternoon of 9 September, where it became *Tropical Storm Gilbert* with maximum sustained winds of 63 kph, continuing to strengthen rapidly as it advanced over the Caribbean Sea.

Barely a day later, on 10 September, Gilbert reached *hurricane* strength with maximum sustained winds of 118 kph while it continued to get stronger. On 12 September, Gilbert interacted heavily with the island of Hispaniola (Haiti and the Dominican Republic) without making landfall. Gilbert was already a major hurricane, category 3, when it crossed directly over Jamaica that same day with maximum sustained winds of 202 kph gusting to 260 kph, its central pressure down to 960 millibars (Figure 8.2).

Incredibly, Hurricane Gilbert maintained its intensity as it dissected Jamaica despite its interaction with the island's mountainous terrain. When Gilbert emerged over the warm waters of the Caribbean off the western coast of Jamaica, it gained intensity so rapidly that over a period of less than 24 h, its central barometric pressure dropped from 960 to 888 millibars during the afternoon of 13 September. At the time, that was the fastest drop and the lowest barometric pressure ever recorded at sea level. That same day, Gilbert rushed very near the Grand Cayman islands, where wind gusts of 250 kph were recorded over land, and continued to get even stronger as it aimed for the Yucatan peninsula of Mexico.

Hurricane Gilbert made landfall on the island of Cozumel the morning of September 14, 1988 and emerged over water to make another landfall in Cancun as a category 5 hurricane causing significant widespread damage. It then traversed the Yucatan to emerge over the Gulf of Mexico in the early morning hours of 15 September, where it regained intensity as it continued on its NNW course at 28 kph toward yet another landfall, north of La Pesca in the east coast of Mexico the night of 16 September, the Day of National Independence (Figure 8.3).

Under a favorable atmospheric environment, a decaying Hurricane Gilbert moved inland and tracking south of Monterey in the northern industrialized region of Mexico, where the intense rains it generated caused deadly and damaging flash floods even as the cyclone degraded to a tropical storm and was in the process of becoming a tropical depression. The storm finally turned to the north and moved

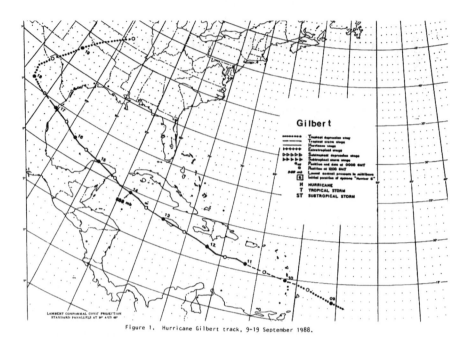

FIGURE 8.1 Track of Hurricane Gilbert as of September 8, 1988, when it was classified as a tropical depression. (Adapted from NOAA—Technical Memorandum NWS NHC #42.)

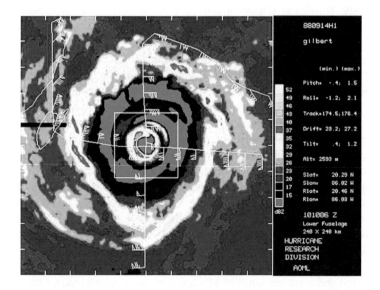

FIGURE 8.2 Graphic showing data collected from a hurricane-hunter plane at 2593 m on September 14, 1988 at 5:10 a.m., when Hurricane Gilbert's eye was 90 km east of Cozumel. Note the closed system of circulation with a well-defined eye. (Adapted from NOAA—Hurricane Research Division.)

Hurricane Gilbert—1988

FIGURE 8.3 Satellite view of September 14, 1988 showing Hurricane Gilbert, already a category 5 and with 1000 km of diameter, approaching landfall in Cancun. Without meteorological information from Mexico, the minimum atmospheric pressure of 900 millibars and the sustained maximum wind speed of 290 kph and landfall were estimated based on measurements from the hurricane-hunter plane flying at 3000 m. (Adapted from NOAA.)

over Texas, Oklahoma, and Missouri where it was absorbed by another storm system traversing the United States from west to east.

BALANCE OF HURRICANE GILBERT

The final balance from the crossing of Hurricane Gilbert over Mexico was 202 deaths, mainly from flash floods in the northern regions of the country; thousands of injured; and more than 60,000 homes destroyed or otherwise rendered uninhabitable. Storm surge of 5–6 m in Cancun and environs caused catastrophic erosion and damage to the famed beaches, scouring and undermining of foundations of numerous hotels, as well as heavy damage to most of the external infrastructure and landscaping throughout the hotel zones along the coast. Extreme rain generated by the hurricane affected not only Cozumel, Cancun, and the coastal region but also the interior of the country and especially the mountainous regions where flash floods near Monterey lead to several deaths and heavy damage.

Estimates of direct damage caused by Gilbert range from $2.5 to more than $3.0 billion dollars, but these numbers do not include loss or degradation of the tourism and commercial function, business interruption, or the heavy loss of foreign income from tourism while the lengthy process of recovery, reconstruction, and repairs to the heavily damaged hotels, tourism infrastructure, and beaches was underway. More importantly, these dollar figures do not account for the value of lost lives or human suffering.

High winds generated by Gilbert destroyed or damaged the canopy of forests throughout vast regions in Quintana Roo and the rest of the Yucatan peninsula. As a consequence of this, vast areas of forests were covered by broken branches,

116 Hurricane Mitigation for the Built Environment

uprooted trees, and dead foliage, which became fuel for wild fires the following year, in 1989. In Quintana Roo alone, forest fires lasted more than three months and totally destroyed 1400 square kilometers of forest.

Gilbert was the first category 5 hurricane to make landfall in North America since Hurricane Camille hit the coast of Mississippi in 1969. Given its intense winds and record-breaking central pressure of 888 millibars, Gilbert was considered the strongest hurricane of all times, one for the record books, until 2005 when Hurricane Wilma, also a category 5 tropical cyclone, recorded a central low pressure of 882 millibars as it moved in the Caribbean toward, you have guessed it, the coasts of Quintana Roo and the region of Cancun.

FROM THE LESSON BOOK OF HURRICANE GILBERT

Hurricane Gilbert, just like many other disaster-causing natural hazards, left us with a number of critically important lessons we need to learn. There were lessons for each and all of those who survived the direct attack of that tropical cyclone, for emergency management and civil defense authorities, for the teams of scientists who tracked every minute of this tropical cyclone from its genesis over the Atlantic to its final decay, for those to whom Gilbert was only an item in the evening news on television or the morning newspaper, but also for those who, like I do, have a personal interest in learning as much as possible from nature so that we may find ways to mitigate its impacts.

At the same time, there were also lessons for all of those who then or at some other time were considering the feasibility of various business projects, be it of a commercial nature, in tourism, or in some other type of activity, in Cancun proper or in some nearby resort or anywhere else in the state of Quintana Roo.

How many of us have learned a lesson from Hurricane Gilbert? Even more importantly, how many of us believe that Hurricane Gilbert did leave some lessons for us to study? What lessons did we actually learn? Which of these lessons would we consider to be useful and practical? How many of us can state, with any certainty, that we have in fact applied some lesson taught by Gilbert?

It would be of interest to learn who or how many of those that were considering the feasibility of developing or investing in projects in the region affected by Gilbert either continued with their project or changed their minds? How many of the architects or engineers working on design projects, to be built in Quintana Roo, revised or changed their design criteria after having witnessed the performance of buildings under the impact of Hurricane Gilbert? How many of the public and private financial institutions engaged in the financing of projects in the affected region walked away from a given project, or modified their financial terms and conditions?

It is also relevant and important to ask: What new codes or standards have been adopted in Cancun, Quintana Roo, or throughout the larger Caribbean or Gulf region to improve design and strengthen the construction of new buildings and houses to reduce the potential for damage from the impact of future hurricanes? What enhancements, revisions, or changes have been incorporated into emergency plans by those responsible for civil defense to correct or improve that which did not meet its intended objectives, or that which did not work well during emergency management actions taken before, during, and after the impact of Hurricane Gilbert?

Hurricane Gilbert—1988

Beyond all of the questions we may ask relative to the impact of Gilbert, I believe the most important interrogative for all of us is if we, on an individual basis, truly see the impact of a hurricane and a resulting disaster as an opportunity for learning and improving?

It is in the spirit of contributing to such a learning process and to the intention of improving that I write these lines. If after having read this book, the only thing a reader has learned is to ask how to mitigate the impact of a hurricane, and the process of asking if this is helpful in the decision-making process, then we could conclude that the main objective of this book has been accomplished.

TYPIFYING DAMAGE CAUSED BY HURRICANE GILBERT

In November 1988, just three and a half weeks after the passage of Gilbert, I visited Cancun on a research and learning trip, to take as much advantage as possible from the lesson book being offered to all.

In Chapter 11 of this book, a detailed description of various types of damage to buildings and infrastructure, together with recommendations on how to mitigate each case, is offered.

I want to share with you, however, what at the time was my first diagnosis, my *first impression* if you will, based on what I had seen after conducting a visual assessment of the hotel zone in Cancun and other areas of the region hit by Hurricane Gilbert.

Relative to this, I come back to the topic of lessons and the opportunity for learning that is offered in the aftermath of a disaster, to emphasize just how important it is to visit the affected area, *ground zero* as it is often called, as soon after the impact as it becomes possible to do, keeping prudence and safety in mind. It is during the immediate aftermath that we can identify the direct causes of damage with the greatest clarity. This is the best time to carry out empirical research and forensic investigations on *causality*, meaning the sequence of events that have culminated in the type and specific amount of damage that we observe. To all those who may be interested, regardless of the reasons, I strongly recommend trying to visit the impacted area as soon as possible once the emergency phase has been declared over. There are invaluable lessons that can only be learned at that time.

So I visited Cancun just a few weeks after the impact of Hurricane Gilbert and as soon as I could arrange for lodging and access to the areas of heaviest damage. My main objective during this visit was to acquire as much data as possible about the causes and magnitude of damages, so that I could then complete a preliminary assessment of the disaster. My methodology in the field included the following:

1. A fast automobile sweep of as many damaged areas as possible to gather a general vision of the impact and its consequences
2. A follow-up inspection on foot, as much as it was possible to do so safely, and by phases of key damaged areas
3. Documenting examples of damage by way of photography and recorded notes
4. Interviewing of several individuals who had witnessed the impact, or who may have been responsible for preparedness measures ahead of the impact,

or who were in positions of authority or management in both the public and private sectors and were able to offer important commentary, ideas, or recommendations regarding the damage that had taken place

Upon returning from my trip, my methodology included the following tasks: classification and ordering of all photographs by type and location of documented damage, transcribing, and cataloguing my field notes, and exhaustive research of available sources of meteorological and scientific data about the tropical cyclone itself.

On the basis of the saying a picture is worth a thousand words, in the following, I share several photos and comments that illustrate the types of damage caused by Hurricane Gilbert observed during my postdisaster visit to Cancun.

DAMAGE TO THE BEACH

Together with a wonderful tropical climate, sunshine, and a warm hospitality, the white sand beaches are the prime attractions Cancun offers tourists from all over the world. Storm surge generated by Gilbert eroded and obliterated most of the beaches, and also caused heavy damage to retaining walls used by the hotels to protect and anchor their outdoor recreational infrastructure (Figures 8.4 and 8.5).

DAMAGE TO OUTDOOR INFRASTRUCTURE

In order to make their sites as attractive as possible for their guests, most hotels include terraces, swimming pools, bars, gardens, and other recreational facilities as

FIGURE 8.4 The 5–6-m storm surge generated by Hurricane Gilbert eroded the beach, undermining retention walls used by many of the hotels. As a result of the damage to the retention walls, the external infrastructure in many of the hotels was damaged (swimming pools, terraces, and gardens). In some cases, storm surge undermined the foundations of several buildings, causing severe damage, including total structural failure in some. It is important to recognize that the use of retention walls has contributed to weakening of the beach since the sand is constantly attacked by wave energy reflecting off these walls.

FIGURE 8.5 Beach destruction caused by Hurricane Gilbert was mainly due to three factors: (i) The common practice of building hotels as close to the beach and the ocean as possible, without considering the risk that comes with this. (ii) The use of retaining walls to allow building of external recreational infrastructure by the beach. These retaining walls reflect wave energy, considerably weakening the sand's cohesiveness. (iii) The hydrodynamic pressure of a storm surge of up to 6 m above mean sea level, without counting the waves that continued forming above that level. The figure shows a ship weighing thousands of tons propelled by storm surge against a building, causing serious damage.

close as possible to the beach. The construction and maintenance of such outdoor infrastructure is usually made possible by the construction of retention walls to hold compacted and leveled grounds fronting on the beach (Figure 8.6).

The picture shows major damage to outdoor infrastructure caused by storm surge and beach erosion during a hurricane.

FIGURE 8.6 After the retaining wall failed, a swimming pool and a terrace, built near the water, were totally destroyed by Hurricane Gilbert's storm surge.

Damage to Foundations

During my post-Gilbert visit to Cancun and surrounding areas, I documented numerous cases where storm surge had caused damage to the beach, resulting in severe damage to retention walls and the outdoor infrastructure beyond. I also documented several cases where the energy of storm surge was such that its impact continued beyond the beach and areas of outdoor infrastructure, causing erosion and scouring of the grounds, and even undermining of foundations to a degree that resulted in structural damage to the building itself (Figure 8.7). In at least one case, the extent of this type of damage was such that it led to the demolition of a multistory wing of a hotel. In several other cases, partial demolition was also necessary (Figure 8.8).

Damage to Building Envelope

The *building envelope* is that "box" consisting of all exterior walls and the roof, which protects building occupants, the building interior, finishes, and contents from the elements. The building envelope is one of the main lines of defense to mitigate or avoid potential damage during a hurricane. The building envelope, which also includes all exterior openings, such as doors, windows, skylights, ventilation devices, and other components, must be considered as strong as its weakest component. The reason for this being that breaching of the building envelope during a hurricane usually starts with failure of one such weak link. Once such failure occurs, it does not matter how strong the rest of the building envelope is; at this point, its integrity has

FIGURE 8.7 Damage due to undermining of foundation. The picture shows a foundation system consisting of a concrete slab and running foundation, and compacted soil behind an unreinforced retaining wall. The system is inadequate for beachfront construction, since the building literally floats on the ground, without actually being anchored to it.

Hurricane Gilbert—1988

FIGURE 8.8 Total structural failure of a building due to lack of adequate foundation and the undermining of its footings after hurricane storm surge eroded the beach.

already been compromised and damaging elements from the hurricane are already inside the building, causing damage.

During the post-Gilbert assessment, I documented numerous cases of breaching of the building envelope and extensive damage caused by forces generated by *wind pressure* and impacts of *flying debris*. Figures 8.9 and 8.10 show damage to the building envelope.

FIGURE 8.9 Damage to the building envelope includes window breakage and destruction of architectural metal work. Once the building envelope is breached, wind, rain, and flying debris attack the interior of the building.

FIGURE 8.10 Damage to the roof of a building, a component of the building envelope. This corrugated aluminum roof was probably detached by uplift created by wind pressure and breaching of the building envelope, allowing hurricane winds inside the building, leading to the collapse of the steel structure that supported the roof. This is an example of structural damage resulting from damage to the building envelope.

DAMAGE TO BUILDING INTERIOR

The main, and the most important, function of a building is to shelter and protect its occupants, their property, contents, equipment, the building interior, and the activities, provision of services, and other functions taking place inside. Documented damage to the interior of many buildings, which in some cases may have involved injuries or the death of some occupants, is testimony to the failure of each of those buildings in fulfilling existing expectations of protection (Figure 8.11).

FIGURE 8.11 Interior damage due to failure in the building envelope, which allowed the wind to penetrate and cause damage. The ceiling was completely detached and its support structure also shows damage.

9 Ten Years Later— Higher Vulnerability

A decade after the catastrophic impact of Hurricane Gilbert, I again visited Cancun to take another look and assess the relative vulnerability of the place to the impact of future hurricanes, taking into account the 10 years of growth in terms of population, urban development, and commercial activity, as well as the implementation, or lack thereof, of practical lessons left by Hurricane Gilbert.

Three principal aspects caught my attention during this visit in 1998:

1. The explosive growth in population, urban development, and human activity experienced by Cancun and the surrounding regions, since my visit in 1988, which meant there were considerably more population and property at risk and a more vulnerable region in 1998 than ten years earlier. Also, the clearly obvious total recovery of the region from all the devastation and destruction that I had observed in the aftermath of Hurricane Gilbert.
2. A marked difference and improvement regarding civil defense organization and capabilities both at the state and municipal levels. Enhancements in this area were evident not only in the organizational structure and assigned human resources of the municipal civil defense in Cancun and in the support provided by the State Office of Civil Protection, but also in the newly added scientific and technological tools to assist in decision making, such as meteorological information provided by a weather station and radar operating near Cancun International Airport. In this regard, I still remember the total lack of meteorological data regarding Hurricane Gilbert in 1988, which is why I was so positively surprised to see that 10 years later, there was now an interactive process of communication between civil defense authorities and the local meteorological service, as well as with NOAA in the United States. All of this resulted in a much improved emergency management structure, especially relative to hurricane warnings and alerts, evacuation orders, and the activation of shelters.
3. On the negative side, I found an almost total lack of evidence that practical lessons learned from damage caused by Hurricane Gilbert had been applied in the design of new buildings or the retrofitting of existing facilities, or to management and maintenance of the beach. I found it worrisome to see the same weaknesses in design and construction, which had contributed to the level of damages caused by Hurricane Gilbert, were still evident in most if not all of the new buildings and urban development that had taken place over the course of those 10 years.

During this visit in 1998, I basically used the same methodology for my field assessment and research than I had used back in 1988. The main difference this time around was the absence of actual damage and debris, and this time I had an official host who provided invaluable support in facilitating visits and on-site inspections at numerous hotels. Just as I had done before, I documented my observations with photography, digital in this case, and written and recorded field notes. A great advantage during this visit was the opportunities to interview civil protection authorities and personnel as well as several managers and staff members at several hotels to discuss their emergency plans and the safety of their buildings in case of future hurricane impacts.

PRELIMINARY ASSESSMENT

On the basis of my observations and the interviews and discussions with hotel personnel, and civil defense authorities at the municipal and state levels, my initial assessment in 1998 included the following key findings:

1. The vulnerability of the place, and consequently the risk, had grown considerably since the impact of Hurricane Gilbert mainly for the following reasons:
    a. From 1988 to 1998, the population of Cancun had grown by more than 50% and it already hovered around the half a million mark. Similar or even greater rates of population growth had also taken place in many other communities in the region, including Cozumel, Isla Mujeres, Puerto Morelos, and Playa del Carmen.
    b. The total number of hotel rooms had more than doubled to around 25,000 units.
    c. The number of annual tourist visitors, both international and domestic, had also grown significantly.
    d. Hurricane activity in the Atlantic basin had entered, as of 1995, a new multidecadal period of increased annual cyclogenesis, which, based on historical records and the opinion of scientists, could last for the next 25–30 years. This increase in the possible number of tropical cyclones generated in the Atlantic basin also increases the annual probability of hurricane impact in Cancun and many other places along the coastal region of Quintana Roo.
    e. Based on all of the above, I concluded that the added population, urban development and infrastructure, and larger number of visitors, meant there was much more that was at risk in 1998 than in 1988. If to this we add the higher probability of impact resulting from the projected higher annual probability of tropical cyclones in the Atlantic basin that is expected to last from 20 to 30 years, the logical conclusion is that not only is the value-at-risk much higher, but the risk of damage is also higher. In summary, the vulnerability of the place was much higher in 1998 than it was in 1988.

Ten Years Later—Higher Vulnerability

2. Save rare exceptions, the impact of Hurricane Gilbert had not been taken advantage of as the unequaled opportunity that it was, to learn lessons and implement enhancements and solutions, especially in the design, construction of new buildings, or the repair and renovation of existing ones.
3. There were still no codes or standards for building design and construction establishing minimum requirements for addressing external loads generated by hurricanes.
4. In contrast with these deficiencies and increased vulnerability and risk, I found considerable improvement in the field of emergency management as a result of the following initiatives and actions:
   a. A more capable emergency management structure was now in place at the state and municipal levels.
   b. A statewide education and outreach campaign was in progress to raise awareness to the hurricane vulnerability of Quintana Roo among the general population. This outreach effort emphasized the need for all state residents to remain alert during hurricane season and cooperate with local authorities with respect to evacuation orders and warnings to be prepared and take measures for the protection of life and property.
   c. A comprehensive training and continuing education effort was launched for emergency management personnel, involving a series of lectures and workshops.
   d. The addition of hurricane-related data and information acquired by the local meteorological and radar station was affording emergency management authorities improved decision making for the protection of the general population and visitors.
   e. Perhaps the most promising new development was a collaborative effort between emergency management authorities and the University of Quintana Roo, which among other objectives planned to develop advanced training and educational initiatives that would include seminars and workshops offering new management tools for civil defense, including the Red Cross and branches of the military.

POTENTIAL FOR DAMAGE

When comparing all that I had seen and evaluated during three different visits to Cancun and the surrounding region in 1979, 1988, and 1998, I was confronted by the following questions: What is the risk of recurrent hurricane damage for Cancun, and the region, going forward? What is the potential for damage to Cancun the next time a major hurricane makes landfall?

My answers, after the 1998 visit, are summarized below:

1. I anticipate a much more organized and effective implementation of emergency plans to protect the local resident population and those tourists who may elect to remain in the area when the next hurricane approaches. In my opinion, these actions by emergency management authorities in Cancun

FIGURE 9.1 View of the southern beach in Cancun, to the west of "Punta Nizuc," which in 1998 was the least developed sector of the Cancun hotel district. What is evident in this picture, however, given that I took it during low tide, is how the use of retention walls has resulted in the disappearance of the sandy beach.

and neighboring municipalities, supported by state civil protection authorities, will contribute to protecting lives and property, while also reducing risk from future recurring hurricane impacts.
2. In my opinion, most of the built environment, including hotels and other buildings along the coastal zone, continues to be unprepared for an effective performance under the impact of a major hurricane. I believe that, save some exceptions, the existing inventory of hotels and residential buildings in the coastal region as of 1998 has a high potential for damage from the impact of future major hurricanes.
3. As long as no code or standard incorporating hurricane-resistant criteria exists for the design and construction of buildings in this vulnerable region, future hotels and other buildings will share the same high risk of damage from hurricane impacts, as those already built prior to 1998.
4. The beach has a high probability of once again being destroyed by storm surge generated by a future major hurricane, because the same practices that contributed to so much damage during the impact of Hurricane Gilbert continue to be part of the "business-as-usual" approach that prevails in the region (Figure 9.1).
5. The prevalent use of reinforced concrete or masonry for the construction of housing, both single family or multifamily units, gives this sector of the built environment a clear capability for performing well under the impact of future hurricanes. Some weaknesses remain however. For example, I have noticed the almost total absence of hurricane shutters to protect windows and doors from the impact of flying debris during hurricanes (Figure 9.2). This will undoubtedly result in instances of breaching of the building

Ten Years Later—Higher Vulnerability

FIGURE 9.2 The design detail of these balconies in a Cancun hotel is attractive and also offers privacy for hotel guests. However, it also represents a high potential for damage from expected forces generated by wind-velocity pressures during a hurricane.

envelope leading to damage to the interior and contents, and possible injury to occupants, not to mention possible structural damage as well. Also, I noticed the same inadequate methods continue to be used for the installation of roofing tiles, which as we saw during Gilbert contributed to the generation of flying debris missiles that caused so much damage.

10 Hurricane Wilma—2005

Being a researcher and student of hurricanes, what took place in October 2005 is fresh in my mind. If the Atlantic hurricane season of 2005 broke many records, the month of October in particular was in its own right one for the record books.

In addition to a tropical depression that was generated in late September and was still active early in October, six tropical cyclones were generated in the Atlantic basin during October 2005, of which four became hurricanes and two reached tropical storm intensity. To these cyclones, we must add a subtropical depression that also formed during this record-setting month of October. At the end of October, the 2005 Atlantic hurricane season had already counted a total of 23 named tropical cyclones, including 13 hurricanes, of which seven were major hurricanes (sustained winds of 177 kph as a minimum) based on the Saffir–Simpson hurricane intensity scale.

It all started toward the middle of the second week in October 2005 when atmospheric conditions in the Caribbean and the Gulf of Mexico became rather complicated. Unstable atmospheric conditions, including tropical waves, rain, thunderstorms, and low pressure prevailed over most of the Caribbean, while a dome of high pressure dominated over the Gulf of Mexico, and an anticyclone developed over the Atlantic to the east-northeast of the Caribbean.

In the afternoon of 15 October, a tropical depression formed near the southwestern coast of Jamaica. Because of the conjunction of atmospheric factors described above and the resulting complex environment, the new system moved rather slowly and erratically for the first couple of days, until steering currents began to move it along a variable track toward the south and southwest, while it intensified slowly until it reached tropical storm strength during the early morning hours of 17 October.

The storm named Wilma encountered favorable steering winds over the central Caribbean that pushed it on a west-northwest course starting on 18 October, while a favorable ocean-atmospheric environment caused it to get much better organized and to strengthen rapidly until it became a hurricane later on the same day.

Right after sunset on 18 October, Wilma initiated a phase of explosive growth rarely seen before any tropical cyclone, such that during the late night on 18 October and the early morning hours of 19 October, it had already reached category 5 strength in the Saffir–Simpson scale. In only 24 h, Wilma had gone from being a tropical storm with 110 kph sustained winds to a category 5 hurricane with sustained winds of 276 kph; quite an unprecedented and unheard of event in the history of cyclonic activity in the Atlantic basin.

As surprising as the explosively rapid intensification of Wilma was, the cyclone continued, surprising the scientists, the meteorologists, and all of us who were following its progress with great interest, when later on 19 October as its maximum sustained winds were peaking at 295 kph, its eye began to contract until it measured a reported 3.7 km in diameter, the smallest hurricane eye ever measured by scientists in the history of the National Hurricane Center in the United States.

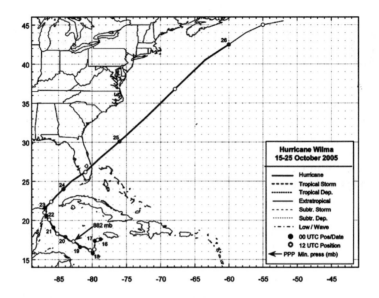

FIGURE 10.1 Map illustrating the "best track" of Hurricane Wilma on the basis of satellite observations. Data acquired by hurricane-hunter flights and other data captured via a variety of means and instruments. (Adapted from NOAA—NHC.)

Wilma gave us one more record-breaking surprise when also on 19 October a hurricane-hunter aircraft penetrated the cyclone and measured a minimum barometric pressure of only 882 millibars at sea level. This is the lowest minimum pressure ever recorded in a hurricane generated in the Atlantic basin. What is even more interesting about this is that data acquired via satellite-mounted remote-sensing instruments showed the central minimum pressure got even lower shortly after the hurricane-hunter aircraft had traversed the eye of Wilma. Based on such additional readings, the scientific consensus is a best estimate of 880 millibars. Quite a record indeed! (Figure 10.1).

While I witnessed, awestruck and increasingly worried, the incredible display put up by Wilma, I remember asking myself just as others who were also tracking the storm may have also done: How far will this hurricane go? How long will this system continue to generate such incredible energy?

My preoccupation had to do with the growing possibility that Wilma could hit Cancun or Cozumel, or the nearby Mayan Riviera, a region where I had done so much of my work. In this regard, I want to share that on 17 October, shortly after this system became a tropical storm named Wilma, I sent an electronic mail message to my good friend former President of the University of Quintana Roo and now member of the State Legislature, Efrain Villanueva Arcos in Chetumal, Quintana Roo, which I translate and transcribe partially below:

....*Monday, 17 October 2005 15:34:29-0400 (EDT)*
Dear Efrain:
Tropical storm Wilma is growing stronger over the Caribbean and it is now located between Jamaica and Nicaragua. All indications are that it may become a hurricane

in the next 24–48 hours. The cyclone is aiming toward Cancun and Cozumel by the end of this week. I will keep you informed. Attached is one of the latest satellite images. ...

Ricardo A. Alvarez

As if to answer my questions, just as furiously as it had intensified into a monster hurricane, Wilma started to lose some intensity on 20 October when its maximum sustained winds went down to 240 kph, turning it into a still strong category 4 hurricane. At the same time, the miniscule record-breaking central eye disappeared to be replaced by a much larger one 70–72 km in diameter. Wilma would keep its new large eye, fluctuating between 70 and 95 km in diameter for the next few days (Figure 10.2).

Wilma touched land on the island of Cozumel on 21 October, causing severe damage, and on the same day crossed the strait, making a new landfall just south of Cancun where the brunt of its right-front (relative to its track of forward motion) quadrant destroyed most of the beach causing vast amounts of damage in the coastal hotel zone and farther inland. Coinciding with landfall, complex and disturbed atmospheric conditions over the Gulf of Mexico and mainland United States deprived Wilma of steering winds, which caused it to meander aimlessly over the northeastern region of the Yucatan for a period of 48 h. Hurricane Wilma was virtually "stalled" over the region for 2 days. During this period of time, it dumped a veritable deluge of rain over most of the region; a total of 1574 mm of rain were measured over Isla Mujeres during a 24-h period.[*] Similar amounts were recorded in Cancun and most of the northeastern Yucatan peninsula.

FIGURE 10.2 Water-vapor satellite image of October 21, 2005 showing the central eye of Hurricane Wilma over Cozumel Island as it was moving toward Cancun. The overall diameter of the tropical cyclone system was 1000 km at that time. It was certainly a monstrous powerful storm. (Adapted from NOAA.)

---

[*] National Meteorological Service of Mexico.

132 Hurricane Mitigation for the Built Environment

Finally, and not a moment too soon for the residents of the affected region, in the early morning of Sunday, 23 October, Wilma emerged over the Gulf of Mexico as a strong category 1 hurricane and aimed for the Florida peninsula. A favorable environment of quite warm waters in the southern Gulf of Mexico and strong steering wind currents caused Wilma to intensify again to a category 3 hurricane with maximum sustained winds of 195 kph, while being pushed toward Florida at 35 kph.

Wilma made landfall near Cape Romano on the west coast of Florida before dawn on 24 October as a category 3 hurricane. Strong wind currents propelled the storm at speeds in excess of 45 kph as it traversed the peninsula while its maximum winds decayed to 175 kph, still a strong category 2 storm. Just over 4 h after its landfall in Florida, Hurricane Wilma reached the Atlantic Ocean where it regained strength as it moved parallel to the U.S. coast at speeds that may have exceeded 90 kph until 27 October when an extra-tropical cyclone absorbed it near Halifax, Canada 10 days after having seen its genesis over the central Caribbean Sea.

Given its multirecord-breaking history, although it lasted only 10 days, it appeared to many that Hurricane Wilma would never go away.

BALANCE OF HURRICANE WILMA

Without a doubt, Hurricane Wilma was one for the record books. For starters, the month of October 2005 equaled a record that had been set back in 1950 when six named tropical cyclones also generated in a single month.

Wilma set new records and broke numerous records. Not only did Wilma set a new record for the lowest minimum central pressure when it reached below 822 millibars on 19 October, but it also went through periods of 6, 12, and 24 h during which it registered the fastest drops in central pressure ever recorded in the annals of the National Weather Service; for example, the central pressure dropped 54 millibars in just 6 h on 19 October, breaking the previous mark of 38 millibars set by Hurricane Beulah in 1967. The previous day, on 18 October, the central pressure had dropped by 83 millibars in 12 h, breaking the previous record of 48 millibars in 12 h by Hurricane Allen in August 1980. Hurricane Gilbert had set a record when its central pressure went down by 72 millibars in 24 h back in September 1988, but Wilma went beyond that with a drop to 97 millibars in 24 h just 2 days before impacting Cozumel and mainland Mexico in October 2005.

While the previous narrative on the topic of central minimum pressure and record-breaking pressure drops may appear repetitive, it is nevertheless quite important as it contributes to our understanding of the kind of storm that Wilma was. The key factor here is that the minimum central pressure is a much more accurate gauge of hurricane intensity than wind velocity.

Unfortunately, other than remotely sensed data, from satellite-mounted instruments or from hurricane-hunter airplanes, there was very little specific data on surface winds and storm surge relative to Wilma's passage over Mexican territory, probably because of a lack of appropriate instrumentation to acquire such important data for the study of hurricanes. Regarding this, I discussed this matter with civil protection officials during my visit to Cancun in November 2005, encouraging them to develop the local capability for data acquisition, using specialized instrumentation,

Hurricane Wilma—2005

including portable units to measure surface wind fields that are capable of performing under hurricane conditions.

In my opinion regarding this need for instrumentation to acquire critically important data, Wilma left positive lessons, in the sense that it helped us identify an important gap that must be closed. However, the balance will only be considered a positive one to the degree that pertinent authorities take actions to fulfill the existing need.

In the meantime, it is important to understand that we do have data on maximum sustained wind, on wind gusts, and on the depth and velocity of flow of storm surge from Hurricane Wilma at several coastal locations, based on measurements and observations from hurricane-hunter aircrafts and satellite-mounted instrumentation. This means that we are working with the best *possible estimates* and not actual hard data; this is neither the best we can do nor what we should aim for going forward.

Other data and numbers that can help us quantify differences and similarities in damage, performance in preparedness, response, and in recovery in Hurricane Wilma when compared with Hurricane Gilbert include the following:

- During my post-Wilma visit, I received reports of deaths caused by Hurricane Wilma; the actual number of victims varied according to the source of the information. Even though one single death if one too many, the reality regarding Hurricane Wilma is that the number of deaths was quite low, especially when one considers the intensity of the cyclone. This outcome is a reflection of the professionalism, planning, and the dedication of local and state civil protection authorities.
- Usually, it takes quite some time before reliable and certifiable data on the cost of damage become available. I did however gather several estimates from a variety of sources during my visit in November 2005, and subsequently through correspondence over the course of several months with colleagues and contacts in Quintana Roo. Estimates of insured damage ranged from $5.0 to $8.0 billion. There were estimates of $15.0–$20.0 million in daily loses to the tourism industry in Cancun alone. In contrast with this, a source from within the insurance industry reported that close to a year after the disaster, insurance claims for damage to buildings and infrastructure from property owners in Cancun only totaled $2.5 billion. It is clear that some unexplained differences and discrepancies in the numbers remain to be resolved over time.
- Having visited Cancun and environs after the impact of Hurricane Gilbert in 1988 and after Hurricane Wilma in 2005, in my opinion, the total amount of damage to tourism installations was much higher in 2005 than in 1988. However, the severity of damage to individual buildings was clearly higher in 1988 than with Wilma in 2005. I believe this is mainly the result of the tremendous growth in urban development in general, and in the tourism infrastructure in particular, between 1988 and 2005, which resulted in a much larger inventory of buildings and facilities that were at risk when Wilma hit than there were at the time of Hurricane Gilbert.
- Damage to the beach was truly catastrophic. I estimated, on the basis of my visual inspections, that 95% of the sandy beach was obliterated by

the impact of storm surge generated by Hurricane Wilma and the erosion and scouring that it caused. I believe damage to the beach from Wilma was much higher than that caused by Hurricane Gilbert. The main reason for this increased damage was the multifold increase in the lineal meters of retaining walls constructed along the beach, for the "protection" of so many new hotels and other construction fronting on the beach that had been added over the last 17 years. These walls reflected the energy of the rushing waters and breaking waves with dire negative consequences for the beach.

- The destruction and damage to the tourism infrastructure has resulted, as it would be expected, in heavy economic losses and loss of jobs in the region. Increases in jobs in the construction and public works sectors during the recovery and rebuilding period that followed the disaster were not enough to offset losses in the tourism sector. However, despite the fact that the impact of these negative factors was still evident during the first quarter in 2007, informal queries revealed that close to 90% of all hotels in Cancun were back in operation some 15 months after the disaster event caused by Hurricane Wilma in 2005. This is truly a remarkable recovery by anyone's standards, but especially when compared with similar cases in other countries.

- In tallying the positives and negatives, a definite positive in my opinion was the immediate, effective, and decisive effort mounted by the public sector in the aftermath of the impact. From the initial response, operations of search and rescue, to restoration of communication and basic public services, debris removal, to the demolition of unsafe structures, and the start of actual repairs, this major effort benefitted from the collaboration of municipal and state agencies and the full support of the federal government. This was truly outstanding. I personally witnessed the initial phases of this during my visit a few weeks after the passing of Hurricane Wilma in 2005. This was definitely a positive balance.

WILMA LESSON BOOK

More important than characterizing or quantifying the balance from the impact of Hurricane Wilma is to identify and review the many lessons left to us by the visit of this natural hazard. Our study of these lessons must include all that we have learned and that which remains to be learned from this event.

Following are the lessons that I consider most important for those of us who might have some interest, whatever that may be, in Cancun or the Maya Riviera specifically or Quintana Roo in general, or in hurricanes and in all we can do to mitigate their impacts.

1. The first and perhaps most important lesson to heed is *impacts will repeat!* It is quite clear, based on the historical record, that Quintana Roo and more specifically the area impacted by hurricanes Gilbert and Wilma and several other tropical cyclones over the years is the region that is most vulnerable

to hurricanes in all of Mexico. If we learn this lesson and reside in or are interested in this region, then we should be prepared for future hurricane impacts.

2. Those lessons that are learned from past impacts will be applicable to new impacts. A clear example of this is how effective the emergency management effort mounted by civil protection authorities in Cancun and neighboring communities truly was, which is in part a reflection of lessons learned from Hurricane Gilbert and other impacts, as much as it is of a sustained effort of learning, education, training, planning, and public outreach mounted by the authorities at the municipal and state levels in Quintana Roo.

3. *Damage will be repeated!* We clearly saw this with Wilma, when damage to the beach, the buildings, and infrastructure were to a large degree a repetition of the same type of damage caused by Hurricane Gilbert in 1988, keeping in mind of course the differences in scale due to the tremendous urban development in the region over the intervening 17 years. Such repetition of damages, meaning of the same type and in some cases to the same building, means there are *some lessons that we have not learned yet.* To provide evidence of these lessons that remain to be learned, I offer the following:

    a. Save some rare exceptions, hotels and other buildings along the coastal zone in Cancun and other communities continue to be built using criteria that clearly failed or performed inadequately under previous impacts. Why, if not because the lessons have not been learned?

    b. The impacts continue to be wasted as opportunities for incorporating mitigation measures, during the process of repairs and reconstruction, that can reduce the potential for damage the next time there is an impact; and there will be a next time, and almost certainly several next times!

    c. New buildings continue to be sited as close as possible to the sand of the beach and the water, utilizing retention walls to hold the ground and allow outdoor recreational infrastructure to be built, being woefully oblivious to how this approach has so clearly contributed to the vulnerability and past damage of the beach.

4. *Codes and standards for the design and construction of hurricane-resistant buildings are clearly needed.* I am personally a witness that this topic was discussed in the aftermath of Hurricane Gilbert in 1988, as it has also been discussed over the past 10 years in several conferences, workshops, and other venues throughout Quintana Roo in which I was a contributor or participant. This topic was again on the table, this time perhaps with an added sense of urgency in the aftermath of Hurricane Wilma, but as I write these lines, it remains a pending item.

5. *Storm surge can destroy the beach.* It is true that the surge generated by Wilma and by Gilbert destroyed the beach in Cancun. Equally true is the fact that the remedy used both after Gilbert and after Wilma was exactly the same, to pump sand from some offshore source to rebuild the beach up to a

given height and width. After Hurricane Wilma, the government of Mexico paid a reported $25–$30 million to a Belgian company to renourish the beach in Cancun by pumping sand from some 30 km offshore. In an effort to make the beach stronger, its width was increased from a before-Wilma average of 25 m to approximately 42 m after the hurricane. As I have stated before, this method of repairing the beach does nothing to mitigate potential damages next time, because it does not address the root causes of the damage, which is building so close to the water and the extensive use of retaining walls. The true lesson here is that pumping sand to rebuild the beach is at best a temporary measure that does not reduce the potential for damage from recurring future impacts.

6. *Some hotels and buildings in the coastal region suffered only minor damage.* Each one of those buildings that did survive virtually unscathed must be considered as a lesson from which we can all learn. What specific characteristics, such as location, elevation above ground, total height, type of component of the building envelope, structure, foundations, shape of the building, etc., might have contributed to such good performance under the impact of the hurricane? Each one of these buildings, which emerged basically intact, in a manner of speaking, from the impact of Hurricane Wilma merits being studied and analyzed as an important lesson. I am referring especially to those buildings that despite having sustained exterior damage had no breaching of their envelopes, and reported no significant damage to their interior and contents; or buildings whose structure and foundations maintained their integrity despite severe erosion and scouring near or around the building caused by storm surge. Although the opportunity for in-depth analysis of instances of these cases has passed because most repairs have been completed, it will never be too late to identify the few such unscathed buildings in order to evaluate what common characteristics of their design and construction may have contributed to their successful performance under the impact of Hurricane Wilma?

7. The best time to assess causes of damage and for identifying effective mitigation measures for future hurricane impacts is as soon as it is safely possible after the event, before repairs and reconstruction work has begun. In the case of Hurricane Wilma, in my opinion, this will have to be filed with the wasted lessons, because most hotel property owners when confronted with the dilemma of losing business for failing to repair and get the property ready for the fast approaching peak of the season, opted for repairing and rebuilding as fast as possible, wasting the opportunity for integrating mitigation measures to strengthen their facilities against future impacts. In other words, the buildings were repaired or rebuilt and brought back to their exact condition just prior to the hurricane event.

8. *A culture of hurricanes saves lives.* One of the most important lessons learned is that all of the efforts by local and state civil protection authorities over the course of several years dedicated to training, planning, education efforts and public outreach, and the timely implementation and execution of emergency plans, resulted in an orderly and timely evacuation of the

vast majority of tourists, the timely and efficient activation of shelters for visitors and the general population, and above all in having accomplished this with a minimal or no loss of life and few injuries caused directly by the hurricane.

TYPIFYING DAMAGES CAUSED BY HURRICANE WILMA

A few days after the passage of Hurricane Wilma over Cancun and surrounding areas and its impact over my own home-base in South Florida, I received a phone call from Efrain Villanueva Arcos, a member of the state legislature in Quintana Roo, Mexico, requesting my services to help assess damage and offer recommendations for the recovery and rebuilding process, and basically just asking me, "How soon can you get here?"

I asked for a couple of days to get organized and assemble a team for field work before determining specific dates to be there in "ground zero." I then proceeded to call my good friend and hurricane research collaborator for several years going back to 1997, Dr. Timothy "Tim" Reinhold, PhD, a structural engineer and Senior VP for Engineering and Research at the insurance industry funded Institute for Business & Home Safety (IBHS), to invite him to join me for a visit to ground zero in Cancun. Tim immediately accepted this unique opportunity to go and record the lessons left by Hurricane Wilma. I also contacted Dr. Hugh Gladwin, an anthropologist and Director of the Institute for Public Opinion Research (IPOR) at Florida International University (FIU), affectionately called "Huq" by me and others after his name was printed in that manner while we both gave a major workshop on hurricane vulnerability and mitigation at the University of Quintana Roo, in Chetumal back in 1998, and who was a previous collaborator of mine in applied hurricane mitigation research for various years while I served as Deputy Director of the International Hurricane Research Center (IHRC) at FIU and as PI for a major research grant under the Residential Construction Mitigation Program funded by the State of Florida and coordinated by the Division of Emergency Management of the Department of Community Affairs (DCA). Huq also accepted my invitation without hesitation.

And so it was that just a few days after the disaster caused by Hurricane Wilma, here we all were, the team of Alvarez, Gladwin, and Reinhold, in Cancun, accommodated in rooms in one of only four hotels that were operational in the area at the time.

During our visit, we briefed State Legislator Arcos and received extensive logistical support from Roberto Vargas Arzate, Director of Civil Protection (Emergency Management) for the Municipality of Benito Juarez where Cancun is located; from Mario Stoute, PhD, the Chief Scientist in the Office of Civil Protection; and also from Jesus de la Torre, an engineer with General de Seguros, one of the largest casualty insurers in Mexico. Support from these individuals proved invaluable in allowing us access to practically any site or damaged building in the area so that we could inspect it in detail and at close range, and in facilitating numerous interviews with owners, managers, and engineering staff at several hotels as well as with public officials and first responders throughout the region.

Just as I had done 17 years before after Hurricane Gilbert in 1988 here I was, this time with my colleagues Reinhold and Gladwin visiting Cancun and its surrounding areas in the aftermath of Hurricane Wilma, at the request of the office of the Governor of the State of Quintana Roo, with two principal objectives: (a) to assess on-site and catalog patterns and types of damage to hotel buildings, public infrastructure, housing, and the beaches and (b) to interview civil protection officers, hotel administrators and managers, and project engineers in order to evaluate the effectiveness of preparedness measures as well as the initial response during the Wilma event. The results of the field work were summarized in a written report titled *The Impact of Hurricane Wilma on Cancun: Preliminary Report of Field Visit from 30 November through 6 December 2005*, which was submitted to the state government in January 2006.

DESTRUCTION OF THE BEACH

I was not able to obtain official data on the magnitude of storm surge generated by Wilma, but estimates based on data from the National Hurricane Center in the United States and my own field observations indicated that the maximum storm surge elevation along the beach of the main hotel zone ranged from 4.6 to 5.0 m, which is below the 6.1 m surge estimated to have been caused by Hurricane Gilbert (1988). In any case, the energy and extent of the surge was enough to cause catastrophic damage to the majority of the beach, as shown in the pictures that follow (Figures 10.3 and 10.4).

Related to storm surge, but not to the damages to the beach, I observed several cases of floating debris that had been propelled by the water and were capable of causing considerable damage. Figure 10.5 documents an example of large floating debris moved by storm surge during Wilma.

FIGURE 10.3 Destruction of the Cancun beach caused by storm surge during Hurricane Wilma. The original water line was some 30 m beyond the current line shown here.

Hurricane Wilma—2005

FIGURE 10.4 Heavily damaged retention wall at a beachfront hotel in Cancun. Many of these retention walls performed well in preventing damage to the hotel buildings they protected, but these structures have contributed extensively to beach damage, especially as the rushing waters of storm surge have reflected off these walls, eroding the sandy beach in front of them. Note in this picture how some retention walls in the distance are built much closer to the water than the one nearer the front of the picture.

FIGURE 10.5 Mid-size boat carried inland more than 100 m by storm surge. In this picture, one can appreciate the vast amount of sand left behind as the surge retreated back to the sea, which is a common occurrence in a coastal region affected by a hurricane.

Damage to External Infrastructure

Virtually all of the hotels fronting on the beach have a vast gamut of outdoor infrastructure for the relaxation and enjoyment of their guests, often built as close as possible to the water. Just as happened during Hurricane Gilbert (1988), storm surge generated by Hurricane Wilma (2005) destroyed or damaged a good portion of such outdoor infrastructure. Public utility installations for power distribution, communications, and public illumination are among the rather important components of external infrastructure (Figure 10.6).

Just in case we were in need of having confirmation of something we already knew, Hurricane Wilma reminded us that wind and water are the main *damaging components* of a hurricane together with *flying* and *floating debris* propelled by these elements.

Outdoor infrastructure presents a rather particular problem, because in most if not all cases, their design characteristics are dependent on the function, which requires most components and elements of outdoor infrastructure to be totally exposed to the elements. Examples of this exposure and vulnerability are the cables and posts used for transmission and distribution of electric power to individual hotels, buildings, and houses, or similar installations for telephone communications or cable television, or for public lighting, streets, and road signs, and even commercial billboards often mounted on posts or atop buildings. Equally exposed are a number of elements of a recreational nature that are highly vulnerable because of their exposure to the elements (Figures 10.7 and 10.8).

Damage to Building Foundations

Buildings constructed near the beach or the water or on the beach itself have a high potential for damage to their foundations. The amount of such damages becomes much

FIGURE 10.6 Recreational area of terraces and swimming pool at a beachfront hotel on the island of Cozumel built right on the beach at the edge of the water. This exterior infrastructure was heavily damaged by storm surge and wave action despite being elevated 4 m above mean sea level and being protected by retention walls.

Hurricane Wilma—2005　　　　　　　　　　　　　　　　　　　　　　　　　　　　　　**141**

FIGURE 10.7 Photo showing a typical "palapa," a decorative building covered by a thatched palm frond roof that is commonly used around the grounds of many hotels to provide shelter from the sun for guest recreational activities. What is interesting in this case is that the typical rough timber structure, using trunks and branches of trees, was replaced by galvanized steel tubes. An analysis of damage revealed the assembly was top-heavy and presented a large surface to the wind, which resulted in an overturning moment that exceeded the structural loading capacity of the central post.

FIGURE 10.8 Metal structure used to support commercial billboards overturned by the wind. This is a typical example of a "sail" catching wind and being damaged by it. Close inspection revealed inadequate anchoring supports plus corrosion at the base of the structure rendering the whole assembly incapable to resist external forces that were not unexpected.

FIGURE 10.9 Example of a building built on the beach lacking adequate foundation. Close inspection of this particular building revealed a total absence of deep columns anchoring the structure to adequate load-bearing levels of the ground to resist the weight of the building and the combination of live loads and external environmental loads applied by a hurricane.

larger when such foundations are poorly designed or just plain inadequate for their expected performance. In the course of field observations, both after Hurricane Gilbert (1988) and Hurricane Wilma (2005), I found numerous cases of totally inadequate foundations as a result of their design, location, and the expected external loads from the impact of natural hazards such as hurricanes and storm surge. The probability of severe structural damage to a building increases exponentially as a result of storm surge causing erosion and scouring that undermine its inadequate foundations (Figure 10.9).

Damage to the Building Envelope

While I inspected the zones most affected by Hurricane Wilma, the most obvious damages to me, those that were clearly visible, were those to the external infrastructure and the building envelopes. I am referring to damage to external walls, windows, exterior doors, and to the roofs of buildings. I was not surprised by the amount and extent of damage throughout the main hotel zone along the beach of what used to be Cancun Island. But I was indeed surprised by the incidence of cases of breaching of the building envelope with considerable or severe damage to the interior and contents of so many buildings that clearly had lacked hurricane shutters or other means of protecting their most vulnerable components of the building envelopes, such as glass curtain walls, windows, and doors, against the impact of flying debris. After having seen so much of the same type of damage from Hurricane Gilbert in 1988, I had expected to see widespread use of hurricane shutters or impact-resistant doors and windows (Figures 10.10 through 10.13).

Hurricane Wilma—2005 143

FIGURE 10.10 Picture showing an industrial-type building with extensive and severe damage to its building envelope constructed of unreinforced masonry units that were incapable of resisting positive and negative pressure forces during the hurricane. Note how the pattern of failure changes where interior walls provided lateral support for the taller exterior wall.

FIGURE 10.11 Example of a building with a strong main structure capable of resisting hurricane forces, and a weak building envelope lacking protective devices against the impact of flying debris and external loads generated by wind pressure. Note how every single window is broken.

FIGURE 10.12 Photo showing damage to a glazed portion of the building envelope of a multistory hotel in Cancun. This specific area is a lobby on one of the lower levels of the hotel. All of the glass in the envelope sustained severe and extensive damage leaving the interior exposed to hurricane condition and extensive damage also.

FIGURE 10.13 Photo showing damage to the roof of a shopping mall in the hotel strip area of Cancun. The semicylindrical roof consisted of a light steel structure covered by a translucent fabric membrane that was damaged by hurricane winds and flying debris. Also shown here is damage to the windows. This is an example of an interesting architectural design concept unfortunately executed with materials that were inadequate for the expected impacts of hurricane winds.

Damage to the Interior of Buildings

When considering the potential for damage to the building envelope, it is of utmost importance to consider that the main reason for protecting its integrity is to protect the occupants, ensure the continuity of function sheltered by the building, and prevent damage to the interior and contents. Stated differently, the most important thing is not to protect the physical building for its own sake, but to do so as the shelter that it is for human life and human activity.

It is impossible to prevent all exterior damage to a building during a hurricane, but if we prevent the breaching of the building envelope and major structural damage, the building will be capable of continuing to function as a shelter of life and human activity inside it.

In this regard, it is important to highlight that often the higher cost is not the damage to contents, equipment, finishes, or the interior of a building, but rather the cost of interrupting or considerably degrading the function of the building or business and the related human activity taking place inside it, not to mention the safety and well-being of the lives of the occupants of the building. Over the years, I have witnessed firsthand how numerous businesses have had to close permanently, not as a result of the cost of repairing damages, but for the cost represented by having had to shut down their commercial activities for unacceptably long periods of time as a consequence of damage caused by a hurricane (Figures 10.14 and 10.15).

FIGURE 10.14 Photo shows damage to the interior and contents of a hotel caused by wind and water penetrating the building during Hurricane Wilma (2005). Note the damaged windows and imagine the wind, wind-driven rain, and flying debris penetrating this space and causing the damage seen here. Also note that this photo shows two adjacent guest rooms where the dividing wall between the rooms was partially demolished by the wind.

FIGURE 10.15 Another example of the implacable and destructive combination of hydrodynamic pressure, floating debris propelled by storm surge, positive and negative forces generated by wind-velocity pressure and the impacts of flying debris, and its capacity for causing catastrophic damage to unprotected structures. In the building shown in this particular picture, a major contributing factor was the use of totally inadequate materials in the construction of the building envelope. In the face of such catastrophic destruction in a place of such well-known vulnerability, it is important to ask: What design criteria did the design team use for the construction of this building? Why was a wholly inadequate material used for the building envelope? Why did this building not have protective measures to mitigate the expected impacts of storm surge and floating debris?

FIGURE 10.16 Photo shows an architectural feature often used in hotels and buildings with large central atriums, which allow natural light into the building while making an often dramatic architectural statement. During my visit to the Cancun region in 1998 to assess vulnerability 10 years after Hurricane Gilbert (1988), I had called attention to these specific features and the potential for damage resulting from inadequate performance under hurricane forces. This picture speaks for itself; this particular skylight and many others in the area did not perform well under the effects of hurricane winds, confirming the fears I had expressed 7 years before Hurricane Wilma caused this damage.

Hurricane Wilma—2005

FIGURE 10.17 Photo showing damaged roof-mounted equipment, which mainly resulted from inadequate anchoring to resist the force of hurricane winds. This type of damage was widespread throughout the region.

OTHER DAMAGES

As one may imagine, in addition to the types of damage mentioned and illustrated here, the range of types of damage is such that it would be impossible to document them all without unreasonably extending the number of pages in this book. In this regard, it is important we recognize Hurricane Wilma in 2005 as being quite similar to other major hurricanes that have hit coastal tourism resorts in Mexico and other countries. However, I would like to end this section by illustrating, via Figure 10.16 (opposite page) and Figure 10.17 (above), a couple of examples of other types of damage that were quite prevalent throughout the whole region hit by Hurricane Wilma.

11 Classification and Mitigation of Damages

Gilbert (1988) and Wilma (2005), two powerful tropical cyclones, over a period of just 17 years, caused two major disasters in Quintana Roo. They destroyed beaches and caused severe to catastrophic damage everywhere. Damages repeated and some lessons never learned. Such are the consequences of these natural hazards to which this paradise consisting of Cancun, the Maya Riviera, Isla Mujeres, and Cozumel is so vulnerable.

I intend to group and classify observed damages documented on site, and offer comments relative to those mitigation measures that could be implemented to reduce the potential for damage from the impact of future hurricanes. In this regard, we can all be sure that there will be future hurricane impacts in this paradise.

This classification of damage and comments about mitigation is offered as a helpful checklist for those critical aspects that must be considered by all of those who want to come to develop and build new projects in paradise, as well as for those who are already here and have built or invested in working hotels and other projects, because it is never too late to take a careful look and to assess the vulnerability of an existing building or site in order to characterize potential impacts and to identify and implement effective mitigation measures through renovation or retrofitting initiatives.

These comments are mainly based on the damages observed and documented by our research team during a field visit in November of 2005 some 4 weeks after the disaster caused by Wilma.

BEACH DAMAGE

The damage to the beach caused by Wilma in 2005 was a repetition of what I had seen after Gilbert in 1988, but the overall extent, if not the severity, of damage was much more widespread this time around. This was mainly due to the increased vulnerability resulting from the fourfold increment in the number of buildings that had been sited on the beach itself or very near to it over the intervening 17 years. In other words, there were many more people and buildings at risk, and much more that could be damaged 17 years later. In this regard, it is important to mention that despite all of the work done after Gilbert to restore damaged beaches and 17 years of natural accretion, these had not fully recovered by the time Wilma hit.

During this process of assessment, I was able to compare photos taken just a day or two after the passage of Wilma with my own field observation just 4 weeks later and, to my surprise, verify that some natural partial beach restoration was already underway through a process driven by alongshore currents and tides. Encouraging as this sign of *natural beach reconstruction* was, which I had already observed in some

Florida beaches after Hurricane Andrew (1992), it clearly is a very long-term process and not enough by itself to help Cancun and neighboring resort communities restore beach-dependent tourism in the shortest possible time.

Most of the damage to the beach was a direct result of buildings being sited so close to the water and the extensive use of retention walls to make this possible. Retention walls on the beach reflect the energy of tides and waves, weakening the beach and continuously contributing to loss of sand and erosion, which in turn makes it increasingly more vulnerable to the impact of storm surge and waves generated by future approaching hurricanes (Figures 11.1 and 11.2).

On the basis of information provided by local and state sources during my initial post-Wilma visit to the region, I understood the government's decision was to use the traditional beach renourishment approach of pumping sand from offshore sources as the most expeditious method for restoring the beach. It is hard to argue with the logic of using this approach given the impending onset of high tourist season as the recovery and rebuilding efforts got under way; in this regard, however, although this may have been the fastest way to restoring one of the main assets attracting tourists to these parts, I would like to make clear that beach nourishment is not a long-term solution to the problem.

What could or should be done to avoid a repetition of beach damage the next time there is an impact from a major hurricane? To restore the beach to its prestorm condition by pumping sand and grading the terrain will neither mitigate nor resolve the combination of factors that contribute to its vulnerability.

FIGURE 11.1 Damage to the beach. The rocks seen in this picture are 2 m below what was the original level of the sand before the impact of storm surge generated by Hurricane Wilma (2005). This damage is typical of what we saw throughout the entire area, but mainly on the eastern side, and it is quite similar to the damage caused by Hurricane Gilbert (1988).

Classification and Mitigation of Damages

FIGURE 11.2 Another example of typical damage to the sandy beach and to external infrastructure at a beachfront hotel. The extended white area seen in the water beyond is due to the millions of cubic meters of sand that were eroded by storm surge. Consider that the level of the sand reached to the top of the retention wall shown in the photo. The use of retention walls is widespread and typical of what is done to be able to build as close to the water as possible while protecting the building foundation and grounds. Unfortunately, this method of construction is a major contributor to erosion of the sandy beach and damage from storm surge.

MITIGATION

When considering alternatives to mitigate damage to the beach from the impact of hurricanes, it is paramount to use a holistic approach treating the beach in its entirety as a natural system, meaning as a unit, rather than as a collection of individual local beaches. A key objective of this approach is to implement comprehensive solutions avoiding unintended consequences. It may be prudent to explore the feasibility of implementing a range of possible solutions, including assisting nature by adopting measures to help create a new dune, or constructing offshore structures to break the waves or dampen the energy of onrushing surge, which will at the same time preserve the viability of marine fauna and flora, and also consider complementing these defensive measures by hardening strategic points along the sandy beach or by reintroducing effective natural defenses such as mangrove forests and wetlands.

In this regard, it is clear that no single measure is capable of solving the complex combination of factors that contribute to this repetitive damage; consequently, we must search for a mix of complementary partial solutions if we are to have a good probability of reducing the potential for damage to the beach from recurring major hurricanes in this region.

Careful planning, based on a comprehensive assessment of area-specific vulnerability and the characterization of expected impacts over time, will be required to design and implement an effective mitigation plan tailored for the parameters that exist in Cancun, in Playa del Carmen, in Cozumel, or whatever the particular location happens to be. This planning effort must, for example, balance the optimal location of any offshore surge-dampening structure so that it preserves the attractive character of the beach for the pleasure of visitors, protects existing marine ecosystems in the area, while also being effective in defending the sandy beach from the worst impacts of storm surge and breaking waves.

The cost of doing this will be considerable, especially when taking into account that some of the components involve major engineering works, but on the flip side, the benefits to be derived from ensuring the continued viability of tourism as the economic engine of the region could surpass implementation costs by a wide margin.

Finally, I would like to emphasize that what has been addressed in the preceding paragraphs is only part of the total mitigation solution for the beaches in paradise; to be truly effective, the combination of physical and structural measures mentioned above must be complemented by other equally important components. These other parts of the solution include coastal management, land-use planning, and comprehensive development policies, as well as codes and regulations for any new projects to be developed near the beach, which will prescribe appropriate setbacks to respect the dune and other natural environmental features, as well as design criteria that will be effective in anchoring the structure in solid ground and a minimum elevation for the ground floor slab above a specific level of expected coastal inundation and storm surge during the projected service life of any new building. Such regulatory provisions must also limit and regulate the construction of retention walls along the coastal zone. I submit all of these provisions from a conceptual perspective only, as it will be undoubtedly necessary to conduct pertinent studies and assessments before adopting standards and regulations to simultaneously foster the enjoyment of the beach and its protection against erosion and storm surge.

BUILDING DAMAGE

Based on direct observation, without the use of instrumentation or testing, I categorize damage to buildings in the following sequential manner.

FOUNDATIONS

I observed and documented several instances where the foundations of buildings had been undermined by storm surge. In some of these cases, I also observed other structural damage, including to main load-carrying members, floor slabs, and walls, but without a detailed forensic analysis in each case, it was impossible to determine the causality of damage. In my opinion, however, I believe foundation damage clearly was a direct contributor to the major structural and interior damage in many of the buildings.

Another prevalent problem, which I observed repeated in several cases, was the use of structural systems where load-bearing columns continued through all levels of a multistory building, which upon reaching the foundation and the ground below lacked spread footings, piles, or another clear mechanism to anchor them to deep load-bearing soil strata. While this lack of adequate anchoring for major structural members was clearly on display in buildings where erosion and scouring caused by storm surge had laid bare the foundations and the ground below, I saw nothing to make me think that the rest of the structure and foundation of most other buildings

Classification and Mitigation of Damages

FIGURE 11.3 Typical example of lack of adequate foundation and damage caused by erosion and undermining from the impact of storm surge.

had been treated any differently. In this regard, I want to emphasize that an examination of the structural plans for a given building would be the only sensible method for determining how the main structure was actually anchored to load-bearing ground.

I must mention that I had already observed such a lack of spread footings and anchoring piles in many of the damaged buildings in the aftermath of Hurricane Gilbert back in 1988 (Figure 11.3).

From these field observations, it is clear that the lack of proper foundations, footings, and anchoring piles is a major contributing factor to structural damage when storm surge and its erosion and scouring effects affected the underside of numerous buildings located on or near the beach.

Mitigation

All of those buildings that lacked deep and properly anchored foundations are basically "floating" on top of the ground, resting on concrete slabs and shallow foundations, kept in place by friction with the ground below and their enormous mass. Because of their construction based on reinforced concrete structures and main walls, these buildings can be categorized as very strong "reinforced concrete boxes" that are capable of remaining in one piece even after having suffered some damage when the ground below has been eroded and scoured by storm surge. However, despite such strength in their construction, as it had already been observed during Hurricane Gilbert in 1988, there is always a high probability of major structural damage under the circumstances described here.

To mitigate the potential for damage stemming from inadequate foundations, the first step is to conduct comprehensive soil analyses and tests and acquire geological data in order to determine at what depth there is enough load-bearing capacity to support and anchor the mass of the building and also resist the highest combination of loads that could result.

Beyond this initial step, it must be given that buildings sited in the coastal zone must incorporate deep foundations, including columns with spread footings in deep soil, or deep piles with caps to anchor the footings and the main structure of the building.

STRUCTURE

The short duration of my field visit after Wilma, in November 2005, and emphasis of visual assessment as the main method for documenting damage did not really allow for any detailed forensic work to verify the extent and type of structural damage to buildings otherwise impacted by wind, water, and debris during Hurricane Wilma. If we take into account that most of these buildings have reinforced concrete structures, it might appear unlikely, but certainly not impossible, for some of those buildings to have sustained some serious structural damage beyond the damage to foundations that I have already described. Related to such possibility of structural damage to reinforced concrete buildings, I did, however, document several instances of serious structural damage to reinforced concrete components of the outdoor infrastructure common to many of the hotels in the area, which confirms that given the right combination of damaging forces and design deficiencies, even reinforced concrete can suffer considerable structural damage during hurricanes (Figure 11.4).

An important conclusion to be drawn from these observations is that, in order to assess the extent of structural damage to a building and the causality of such damage, a detailed analysis is needed and in some cases, instrumentation and testing are also required. Having the original as-built structural drawings for the specific building is of great help in most cases.

FIGURE 11.4 Structural damage to external infrastructure at this beachfront hotel.

Classification and Mitigation of Damages

Mitigation

The measures listed below, among others, can be effective in mitigating the potential for structural damage under the impact of a hurricane:

1. For new buildings, those in the design phase, the most important consideration to mitigate potential structural damage is to use design criteria that reflect the specific vulnerability of the site and expected impacts where the building is to be built. What this means is that, regardless of whether there is an officially adopted building code or not, design criteria for resisting wind forces must be based on a basic wind speed that is congruent with expected hurricane wind velocities in the region. Said differently, the basic wind speed must at the very least reflect maximum sustained wind speed or wind gusts experienced during historical hurricanes in the region. Taking Cancun as an example, since there have been previous hurricane impacts in the area with wind gusts measured in the range of 240–280 kph per hour, it would make sense to use design criteria for wind forces based on the probability of such historical measurements being repeated in the future. The same line of thought applies to design criteria relative to hydrodynamic pressure from hurricane-generated storm surge in the specific area, as well as wave impact and impacts from flying and floating debris.
2. Design the main structures of buildings by creating a direct and effective load path from the roof and external periphery of a building to the foundation and the ground below. To accomplish this, it becomes mandatory to use deep foundations, or foundations anchored to deep soil layers by way of piles and pile caps, for all buildings located near the beach or in site on the coastal zone where the upper layers of the ground may not have adequate load-bearing capacity.
3. Ensure that the design of the building incorporates, as much as possible, the concepts of symmetry, centricity, redundancy, and margin of safety, discussed previously, but with special emphasis in assessing the center of mass, center of stiffness, and the aerodynamic center as they relate to the wind silhouette of the building, to design for resulting eccentricities so that it will be capable of resisting the resulting loads, torsion, overturning moments, and other effects. To support the design effort, wind tunnel studies should be conducted for major projects or any project that deviates from typical "boxy-shape" buildings.

ROOFS

Although the majority of roofs are definitely part of the building envelope, I have decided to discuss them separately, in terms of observed damage and possible mitigation of the same, to help in typifying damage patterns.

Toward this objective, I will discuss damage by type of roof, as follows.

Main Tile Roofs

A "main" roof is that which covers a fully enclosed building or part thereof and, as such, it is considered to be an integral component of the building envelope. All of the cases that I documented during my visit were roofs covered by straight barrel, also known as mission style, clay tile installed on a bed of mortar over a concrete slab or wood sheathing.

In most cases, the damage observed led me to conclude that it had occurred when negative wind pressure acting on the roof generated uplift (suction) that exceeded the resistance provided by adhesion to the mortar bed under the tile. This resulted in tiles being dislodged and flying off, leaving most of the mortar adhered to the roof itself. These tiles became windborne debris generating missiles that may have caused damage to neighboring buildings.

There were some common patterns of damage, which were repeated in many, if not most, of the buildings with damage to this type of roof. For example, while damage in terms of missing tiles ranged from 20% to 60% of the total roof area, nearly all (90%–100%) of the tiles on the ridges were missing. In the case of gable roofs, damage on one slope approached 80%–100% in terms of missing or damaged tiles, while on the opposite slope damage rarely exceeded 10% of the total area. I attributed this to the prevalent angle of attack by the wind (Figure 11.5).

FIGURE 11.5 Example of roof tiles damaged by hurricane winds that became flying debris. While most hotels and other high-rise buildings in the area do not use tiles for a roof covering, there is wide use of this type of roofing material for secondary roofs and external infrastructure and in housing or other low-rise residential buildings. Most of these tile coverings have a strictly decorative role and are installed atop a waterproofed reinforced concrete roof. The risk from the damage shown in this picture is the generation of flying debris, which can inflict damage to surrounding buildings and property.

Classification and Mitigation of Damages

In some cases, the pattern and quantity of lumps of mortar that were left still adhered to the roof itself indicated that poor quality of installation may have been a contributor to the damage I saw. From the appearance of the damaged roof, it was clear that the mortar used to install each tile was not, in numerous cases, enough to cover the complete underside of the tile leaving voids and a lower level of resistance to wind uplift forces.

Visual inspection of tile roofs provided important empirical evidence relative to the causality of damage. It became clear for example that in many cases damage appeared to have started near a corner to propagate along the roof edges and throughout most of the roof field in the direction of the mean winds, which was discernible from the overall pattern of damage in the vicinity of the specific building being inspected. It was easy to trace the "domino effect" that had started when one or two tiles near the corner had been damaged and dislodged allowing the wind to penetrate below neighboring tiles, which, in turn, became dislodged and damaged, repeating the cycle of one damage resulting in additional damage as vortices had propagated from the corner up. There was also plenty of evidence of broken roof tiles transformed into windborne debris causing damage to the envelope, especially windows, of neighboring buildings.

Other damage that was visually evident could be categorized as the indirect result of the original direct damage sustained by the roof, things such as roof fissures causing water penetration that damaged the interior and contents and also mold developing over time on ceilings, interior walls, and finishes.

On the basis of what I saw in terms of damage to these types of roofs, I recommend priority be given to the careful analysis of methods for installing roof tiles as well as ensuring a quality installation. It is of the utmost importance to minimize the kind of damage described here in order to strengthen and ensure the integrity of a critical component of the building envelope.

SECONDARY TILE ROOFS

Secondary roofs are those installed over balconies, terraces, and other semiopen spaces, or over secondary structures that are part of the external infrastructure, which consist mainly of tiles installed over a wooden structure, which is made of dimensional lumber with minimal finish, but it could also consist of rough lumber or even tree branches. In most cases, roof tiles had been installed by mechanical means consisting of light gauge copper or galvanized steel wire to tie each one to the wooden structure. This type of installation proved quite incapable of resisting the pressures exerted by hurricane winds resulting in 90%–100% damage to the roof covering. Given the extent of this damage, one can identify these kinds of roofs as major contributors to flying debris during the hurricane and damage to windows, exterior walls, and roofs in neighboring buildings. In some rare cases, I also observed secondary roofs where tiles had been installed with mortar over wood sheathing attached to the wood structure, which also suffered extensive damage under the impact of the hurricane (Figure 11.6).

Special attention needs to be paid to the construction of these secondary roofs, which mainly have a decorative rather than utilitarian purpose, because their damage led to considerable damage elsewhere due to the generation of windborne debris.

FIGURE 11.6 Debris from a clay tile roof where individual tiles were tied to the substrate using thin gauge galvanized steel wire ties as can be seen in this photo. Practically all roofs using this mode of installation sustained catastrophic damage.

Mitigation

In general, every tile roof, be it the main roof or a secondary one, and for that matter every tile installed on a house or building even if only for decorative purposes, must be considered susceptible to damage under the effects of wind pressure, wind gusts, and the impact of windborne debris. A common consequence of damage to tile roofs during hurricanes is that they themselves become sources of windborne debris when broken or dislodged tiles become airborne, propelled by the wind turning the tiles into veritable missiles capable of inflicting damage to neighboring houses and buildings.

On this basis, we may conclude that the methods of installation used to install roofing tiles can contribute to mitigating the potential for damage to the roofs themselves.

Relative to methods of installation for roofing tiles, some possible mitigation alternatives to consider are the following:

1. Combine methods of installation in order to achieve redundancy, stronger anchoring, and enhanced performance of roofs under hurricane impacts. For example, use a foam adhesive instead of mortar to install roofing tile, and combine this with the nailing of each tile to nailing strips. The adhesive foam provides a chemical method of installation that is highly effective because it provides much better surface coverage and stronger adhesion than mortar. The nailing of tiles provides a mechanical anchoring method.

Classification and Mitigation of Damages

The combined use of both methods results in roofs that are stronger and perform better under hurricane loads thereby reducing the potential for damage during future hurricanes.

2. Pay special attention to methods of installation of tiles on the ridges and peak of a roof because field observations consistently show that such roof elements are generally more susceptible to damage from wind pressures than the rest of the roof, except perhaps for roof corners. The method of installation of ridge tiles may contribute to considerably reducing the potential for damage. A method that has proven effective in this regard is the use of adhesive foam and nails to anchor individual tiles, rather than the traditional mortar bed method, plus the addition of a ridge board such as it is prescribed in the Florida Building Code, which has proven helpful in enhancing both mechanical and adhesive anchorage of roof tiles.

3. The slope of a tile roof may contribute to increasing the potential for damage under wind loads. For example, a low-sloping tile roof approaches the characteristics of a flat roof and becomes much more susceptible to damage from wind uplift, negative pressure, than more inclined roofs. Consequently, paying attention to the slope of the roof will reduce the potential for damage from uplift forces.

4. Empirical knowledge, confirmed by wind tunnel tests, shows that the shape of the roof itself is an important factor in its performance under the influence of hurricane forces. Generally, a hip roof, one that slopes in four directions, performs far better than a gable roof. Consequently, it is recommendable to build hip roofs whenever the design concept allows it.

5. Finally, it is important to note that the shape of the individual tiles used on the roof will also contribute to its performance under hurricane conditions.

FLAT ROOFS

Save for rare exceptions, most of the hotels and other buildings I observed in the area affected by Hurricane Wilma had flat built-up roofs consisting of waterproofing coatings or membranes applied to the surface of a concrete slab, or asphaltic or elastomeric membranes over other substrates.

In assessing flat-roof damage, I documented numerous cases where the adhesive strength of the asphaltic or elastomeric covering was not enough to resist the uplift pressures generated by hurricane winds. As a result, large pieces of the roof covering were ripped off, leaving the underlayment or the concrete slab itself exposed. In some other cases where there was no concrete slab, but the covering was attached to another type of material or to the structure itself, the damage I observed showed large areas of the roof where the covering had been peeled off by wind uplift, leaving gaping holes in the roof and the supporting structure exposed to the elements. These kinds of flat-roof damage generally lead to water penetration and vast amounts of damage to the interior and contents of the building.

In typifying flat-roof damage, I recommend basing it on the complete roof system in each case, including the covering, underlayment, base, supporting structure, and other components (Figure 11.7).

FIGURE 11.7 Severely damaged flat roof under uplift forces generated by hurricane winds. Failure of the roof left the interior of the building exposed to the elements leading to significant damage to the interior and contents.

Mitigation

Mitigation measures to reduce the potential for these types of damage to flat roofs include the following:

1. Use covering materials and roofing systems that meet the expected pressures that will be generated by hurricane winds at the height of the roof above ground; I am referring to actual expected pressures, not those based on the minimum code requirements for basic wind speed. The first step involves the project engineer calculating negative pressures that could be generated at roof height by hurricane category 3, 4, and 5, and then deciding which performance level is most appropriate for your building. In using this approach, there might be a tendency to think you are increasing costs by going beyond the minimum requirements of the building code, but the reality is that technology and manufacturing methods have made considerable progress in recent years, as a result of which the range of available roofing systems is quite wide in addition to meeting much higher performance standards with very little or no increase in unit cost. Most currently available roofing systems have been subjected to testing protocols to determine their capacity for sustaining negative and positive pressures and have, as a result, some type of certificate of product approval issued by the testing authority. In the absence of this type of certificate of product approval, there are field or laboratory tests to determine such capacities.
2. Build as much redundancy as possible in the design and construction of your flat roof. Such redundancy may be achieved, for example, by installing a secondary moisture barrier, when the roof covering consists of several layers of coatings and membranes. This secondary moisture

Classification and Mitigation of Damages

barrier will act as a second line of defense in cases where the upper layers and first moisture barrier may have failed during a hurricane due to an impact by dislodged roof-mounted equipment, windborne debris, or extreme uplift forces acting on the roof. Another example of redundancy in flat-roof construction is the use of drains to reduce the accumulation or ponding of water during or after an extreme rain event. By all means, go beyond the minimum requirements of applicable building codes and establish design criteria based on expected future, not historical, extreme rain events, and then add drainage capacity to allow the system to perform effectively even when some of it may stop working because of damage or blockage by debris during a hurricane. Whenever possible, combine internal drains with downspouts and gutters and scupper drains.

3. You may also reduce the potential for damage to a flat roof by paying special attention to the method of anchoring the roof covering to its base in the case of mechanically attached coverings and the whole roof assembly to the structure. Both the specific type of anchor used and the fastening schedule, the distance between individual anchors, are important components of this mitigation approach. Relative to this, two criteria are key in reducing potential damages: One is the capacity of an individual anchor to resist or counteract wind-uplift forces, and the other is its capacity for preventing covering pull-through (the covering membrane is pulled off the roof while the fasteners remain in place) caused by negative wind pressure. You mitigate the first effect by ensuring total uplift force acting on any individual fastener is well below its capacity, usually by specifying a fastening schedule that reduces the tributary area supported by one single fastener. Membrane pull-through is mitigated by specifying a larger head diameter for the fastener and also by using metal washers under the anchor head. In this regard, it is recommended to conduct roof-covering uplift tests in the field once the roof construction has been completed.

SKYLIGHTS

In the course of post-Wilma field work in Cancun and environs, I inspected numerous hotels and other high-rise buildings that had large pyramidal skylights crowning their roofs. In most cases, these components of the building covered full building-height interior spaces allowing natural light into its interior while making spectacular architectural statements.

Most of these skylights consist of translucent or transparent pieces of polycarbonates or similar materials anchored to a supporting steel structure. In at least two cases, I observed a steel cable running through the individual pieces providing an additional means of anchoring.

Many of these skylights suffered 90%–100% damage or loss of their cover under the impact of Hurricane Wilma. Careful observation revealed such damage resulted from a combination of strong negative pressure above the structure caused by hurricane winds flowing over it and strong positive pressure applied to the underside by wind penetrating the building as a result of a breach in the envelope most probably

FIGURE 11.8 Example of a large pyramidal skylight crowning a central building-height space in this 12-story hotel. Breaching on the building envelope generated a combination of positive pressure from below and uplift (suction) from above with catastrophic results for the skylight and the interior of the building when wind and rain penetrated.

caused by windborne debris. The two forces (external negative and internal positive) combined into a much larger load that exceeded the capability of the skylight cover, resulting in the documented damages.

A consequence of this damage was the penetration of wind, rain, and debris into the building causing vast damage to the interior, finishes, contents, and furnishings.

While these skylights are used as architectural elements that add a dramatic and quite spectacular touch to interior spaces, they are nevertheless weaknesses in the building envelope contributing to an increased risk for the building, its contents, and occupants. There are, however, design criteria, and methods and materials that allow for the safe construction of these architectural features and preservation of the integrity of the building envelope. It behooves the architect and engineer of record to research these aspects or to consult with mitigation experts regarding effective measures to protect the roof from the impact of hurricanes (Figure 11.8).

Mitigation

To mitigate potential damages to skylights from hurricane impacts, the best approach is to tackle the three main causes of observed damage, which in my opinion were the following:

- The use of weak and ineffective anchoring method to attach light, flexible, and otherwise strong skylight covering to the supporting structure.

Classification and Mitigation of Damages

- The use of glass or other heftier skylight covering anchored to rather flexible structures that lacked the capacity for maintaining integrity under hurricane forces.
- Some skylights were strong enough to have capacity to withstand negative pressures, but failed anyway as a result of breaching of the building envelope at some lower level, which generated a combination of positive pressure on the underside of the skylight with the negative pressure above it. The net result was a combination of loads that exceeded by far the design capabilities of the skylight.

Mitigation is achievable through the use of covering materials, supporting structures, and anchoring methods that are capable of withstanding expected negative pressures, while the rest of the building envelope is hardened or protected by deployable hurricane mitigation devices to prevent breaching of the envelope at levels below the skylight.

A rather important element for achieving adequate strength is for the engineer of record to define design criteria for the skylight that are based on maximum expected net pressures based on negative external pressures and realistic estimates of positive internal pressures at the location of the unit, and its elevation above ground.

METAL ROOFS

During the course of our field work, our team also inspected several buildings and other structures, such as gasoline filling stations, covered by metal roofs. Most of the roof covering was aluminum, but there were some corrugated zinc-coated steel roofs as well. In practically all the cases observed, there was extensive damage to these metal roofs. In some cases, the metal sheets had been ripped off from the structure, and in others, there was partial delaminating of the metal, but in all cases, we saw abundant evidence of damage from the impact of windborne debris.

The main causes of damage were the following:

- The gauge of the sheet metal used for the covering was inadequate to support uplift forces applied by hurricane winds.
- The type of fastener used or the fastening schedule were inadequate to perform effectively.
- Mismatched covering gauge and size of fasteners allowed covering pull-through.
- Poor maintenance, or lack of it, allowed corrosion to spread, weakening structural components, fasteners, and the roof covering itself.
- Impacts of windborne debris (Figure 11.9).

Mitigation

Most of what has been said before regarding mitigation measures for various types of roofs also applies to reducing the potential for damage to metal roofs. The starting point should always be the proper analysis and definition of expected uplift forces to establish design criteria, followed by the selection of metal roof covering material of

FIGURE 11.9 Damage to a roof with a covering of corrugated galvanized steel resulting from the combination of uplift forces and internal pressure caused by a breach of the building envelope most probably by flying debris. Note the damaged windows.

a gauge that is capable of performing under the expected loads, and specification of a fastening system and schedule that is capable of sustaining the design forces without failure and of preventing pull-through uplift of the metal sheets. Clearly, all of this is possible, but only to the extent that the supporting structure performs effectively in maintaining the roof covering in place while also being effectively connected to the main structure of the building. Beyond this, it is equally important to consider the role of proper and timely maintenance as a contributor to mitigation, because sites near the ocean coastal environment are prone to corrosion problems unless proper preventive maintenance is carried out on a regular basis as the corrosion will eventually undermine the structural capability of metal roofing systems.

DECORATIVE ARTISAN ROOFS

Several of the buildings visited had some areas covered by nontraditional roofs or by what would best be characterized as artisan roofs. These were roofs built with thatch, palm fronds, canvas, vinyl, or other covering materials and structures ranging from wooden poles to lightweight metal frames, which invariably suffered considerable damage under the effects of Hurricane Wilma. In most cases, these lightweight nontraditional coverings were badly torn apart or totally ripped off from their supporting structures (Figure 11.10).

Mitigation

Careful assessment of causes of damage to these artisan and nontraditional roofs showed that the main problem was that these types of roofs were not treated with the

Classification and Mitigation of Damages

FIGURE 11.10 Example of decorative artisan tile roof on the balcony of a guest room at one hotel in Cancun. While the rough lumber structure survived mostly undamaged, poorly attached clay tile became flying debris.

same level of attention used for main roofs. It was apparent that these artisan roofs were considered more as decorative elements with emphasis on aesthetics rather than on their structural integrity and capacity to perform effectively under hazard conditions.

Based on this, in terms of mitigating potential damage, the first recommendation is to treat these artisan and nontraditional roofs exactly as one would a main roof. What this means is that one needs to start by characterizing expected impacts in terms of external wind loads at the height of the roof above ground and then specify the materials, fasteners, and fastening schedules that will give the complete system the required structural capacity to perform effectively and maintain its integrity under hurricane conditions. As an alternative, the designer needs to focus on the larger structural elements and their connections to ensure they will remain in place, and not become windborne debris, while allowing the lightweight thatch or other light roof covering materials to be blown away.

BUILDING ENVELOPE

By definition, all exterior walls with its cladding and components, including windows, exterior doors, ventilation grilles, and other elements, together with the roof are considered to be the building envelope.

For purposes of this discussion, to simplify the process of categorizing typical damage and identifying mitigation alternatives in each case, we have already addressed issues related to the roof and we will now address those related to the walls and exterior openings.

To simplify this process, observed damage is classified on the basis of the materials used in the construction of the exterior walls.

REINFORCED CONCRETE OR MASONRY WALLS

In general, based on extensive visual inspection of numerous buildings in the Cancun and Maya Riviera region, reinforced concrete and reinforced masonry exterior walls, which are prevalent throughout the region, sustained minor to moderate damage during Hurricane Wilma. Most of the damage observed consisted of loss or deterioration of paint or stucco, nicks, and chipping, and some minor superficial hairline cracks, due to forces applied by wind pressure and extreme rain or the impact of windborne debris. In those cases where buildings were subjected to the impact of storm surge, breaking waves or floating debris, damage to these types of exterior walls ranged from moderate to extensive and, in some cases, even catastrophic.

Unreinforced masonry exterior walls fared much worse with several instances of major or catastrophic damage caused by wind pressure and/or the impact of windborne debris. This type of wall invariably sustained total collapse or significant damage when impacted by storm surge and breaking waves.

Mitigation

Empirical data from field observations and analysis of causality make it clear that damage sustained by these types of walls were caused by the following:

1. Inadequate, or total lack of, reinforcing steel, rendering the walls incapable of performing effectively under external loads generated by wind and water during hurricanes
2. Inadequate, or total lack of, protective devices to prevent or reduce the impact of storm surge and breaking waves on these walls

Given these contributors to the observed damage to the walls, the following approaches may prove effective in mitigating future impacts:

1. Avoid using unreinforced masonry in or near the coast in hurricane vulnerable regions, or establish dimensional limits (width and height) on unreinforced masonry filler walls between structural members.
2. Establish design criteria, such as strength of concrete and minimum reinforcing steel, for reinforced concrete walls on the basis of expected loads from future major hurricanes and effective performance levels relative to the occupancy and life-safety parameters of each building.
3. Design and build hazard mitigation structures and devices, based on site-specific vulnerability studies and characterization of expected impacts, to modify or protect from expected hazards in order to reduce the potential for damage to these walls.

Classification and Mitigation of Damages

GLASS AND ARCHITECTURAL METALS

In most cases, observed damage to glazing components of the building envelope ranged from severe to extreme, regardless of building height or type of glazing system, installation method or glass type used. A recurring contributing factor to such damage was the almost total absence of hurricane shutters or other impact-resistant protective devices designed to protect glazed surfaces from the impact of windborne debris, in the buildings inspected. Another widespread cause for the observed damage was the lack of adequate reinforcement, bracing, or support in glazing installation, which is reflective of lack of knowledge or concern relative to the increase in wind loads as a function of building height, or the specific location of glazing components with respect to corners of the buildings or changes in direction of the plane of the building envelope. It is clear that the absence of a local building code (at the time of and prior to the impact of Wilma) establishing requirements for design criteria and performance based on expected wind loads has translated into a generalized lack of measures to ensure the integrity of the building envelope, especially its glazing components, under hurricane conditions.

The main causes of damage by type of glass and installation were as follows:

1. *Heat-strengthened glass curtain wall*: A common component of the building envelope consists of glass curtain walls using heat-strengthened glass sheets installed directly in grooves cut in the concrete slabs or supported by metal angles and by adhesives. This method of installation, especially the one using grooves cut into the slab, proved ineffective in resisting the cycling between positive and negative wind-velocity pressures, allowing the glass to come off the groove, breaking and falling to the ground, or being pulled off the envelope, becoming the most dangerous kind of flying debris. Impacts from wind-driven debris were also contributors to breakage of these large sheets of glass. This type of glass breaks into large pieces and shards, generating tremendous risk to people and property in the vicinity.

2. *Tempered-glass curtain wall*: More prevalent than heat-strengthened glass is the use of tempered-glass sheets in building envelope curtain walls, which in the totality of the buildings inspected used the groove-in-the-slab method of installation, and in some cases also used vertical tempered-glass sections, ribs if you will, installed perpendicularly to the face of the curtain wall to buttress and provide additional support. The main causes of damage were the already identified combination of cyclic loading between positive and negative pressures and the impact of flying debris. Risk associated with this type of system in case of breakage is much less than with the previous system because tempered glass will break into small sized, basically square or rounded, pieces and there is no chance of large pieces becoming flying debris (Figure 11.11).

3. *Sliding glass doors, windows, and other glass and aluminum curtain walls*: These types of installations of glazing systems are quite common for hotel room balconies or terraces and the rooms themselves. These systems use annealed or regular untreated glass and anodized aluminum

FIGURE 11.11 Picture illustrating what is described in this section. Glass installed directly in a groove in the concrete slab with a bead of caulking. Additional support was provided by glass vertical fins at the joints of two sheets of glass. A combination of wind pressure and flying debris may have contributed to extensive breakage in this type of installation.

profiles. Damage to these types of components, which was extensive and widespread, was caused by the combination of windborne debris impacts and cyclic wind-pressure loading plus the addition of mostly inadequate installation methods. In most cases, the fasteners and fastening schedule used to anchor the aluminum frames to the building lacked the capability for sustaining the loads generated by wind pressure. For example, a typical installation in every room of one particular hotel in Cancun had an aluminum and glass curtain wall between the room and the balcony. The curtain wall was 4 m wide by 2.5 m high and consisted of two 1.2-m-wide fixed panels on each side and a two-panel sliding glass door in the center. Basically, all of these curtain walls, in all of the rooms, suffered the same kind of damage. The aluminum frame was deflected and pushed in by the wind until it became disconnected from the concrete wall, and the glass broke. Close inspection revealed that the aluminum frame was attached to the concrete wall by three #10 × 2″ masonry screws on each side and by only one screw at the top at the center of the opening. Every single one of the screws connecting the top frame to the wall had been sheared off (Figure 11.12).

Mitigation

In summary, damage sustained by these glass and glass–aluminum curtain walls can be attributed to the following causes:

Classification and Mitigation of Damages

FIGURE 11.12 The glass exterior wall and sliding door in the balcony of a guest room in a Cancun hotel was so poorly anchored to the building itself that it failed under the force exerted by wind pressure during Hurricane Wilma. This glazed assembly spanned 4.0 m horizontally by 2.5 m vertically and was anchored by three fasteners at each jamb and only one fastener at the head. This type of assembly was rather typical in several of the hotels we inspected.

- Lack of protection against the impact of flying debris
- Usage of large glass sheets installed in grooves in the concrete without a metal frame or other additional means of support
- Selected fasteners and fastening schedule attaching aluminum frames to the building incapable of resisting wind loads during the hurricane

To mitigate these damages, the following measures are recommended:

1. Install protection against the impact of flying debris. There are a wide range of available products for this purpose, from removable hurricane shutters to various types of fixed devices, which have been tested and passed impact protocols.
2. As an alternative to external impact protection, install impact-resistant glass, making sure the product has been tested using recognized and widely accepted testing protocols and has a certificate of product approval from a certified and recognized agency, such as those issued by Miami-Dade County in Florida.
3. Reduce the size of glass sheets and make sure they are supported by properly sized metal frames and, in cases where the span of glass between supports exceeds specific dimensions, especially in height, use additional structural members to brace the glass curtain and limit its deflection so that it will be capable of resisting expected cyclic loading generated by the wind.

4. Increase the gauge of all aluminum members, increase the size of fasteners, and enhance the fastening schedule by reducing the distance between individual fasteners to effectively reduce the tributary area and the loads supported by each anchor.

OTHER EXTERIOR WALLS

Some of the most severe damage observed in the Cancun area, in the aftermath of Hurricane Wilma, can be directly attributed to the type of materials used in the construction of the building envelope. I would like to share three examples to illustrate the role of specific materials or components used in the building envelope and the resulting damage:

1. A particular reinforced concrete building was clad in a curtain wall consisting of square aluminum panels attached by metal screws to two aluminum angles on each side, which in turn were attached to a supporting frame fabricated with steel angles anchored to the reinforced concrete structure. Close inspection of this cladding system revealed the connection between the square aluminum panels and the supporting steel frame was rather weak and not capable of resisting the negative pressures that developed over the building. Consequently, many of the aluminum panels were ripped off the building, becoming windborne debris, especially in the higher floors where wind pressures were higher. The main deficiency here was in the connection between the individual panels and the supporting substructure (Figure 11.13).

FIGURE 11.13 This building has a reinforced concrete structure and a building envelope consisting of lightweight aluminum panels supported by a lightweight steel structure. The fasteners and fastening schedule used to anchor individual panels to the supporting structure did not resist negative pressure during Hurricane Wilma. Numerous panels were sucked off, becoming flying debris.

Classification and Mitigation of Damages

2. Also documented were several cases where standard 1/2″ drywall panels attached to a supporting substructure made of steel angles were used to clad the exterior of a building. It appears this particular cladding material was selected because of its light weight and ease of fabrication to achieve specific architectural effects and shapes, which would have been much more difficult to build and more costly using more traditional materials and methods. Unfortunately, the very same characteristics that made this material attractive for the specific architectural purpose were also the main contributors to its poor performance under hurricane winds or the impact of windborne debris, which caused many of these panels to be damaged or ripped off the building, becoming flying missiles themselves (Figure 11.14).

3. The third example is the case of a building where both the roof and exterior walls, the whole building envelope, were built using a material commonly known as "exterior insulation finishing system" or by the resulting acronym "EIFS." This material is lightweight and easy to use in terms of cutting, installing, and finishing with stucco and paint, for example, and in addition, it has good insulating qualities that make it ideal to reduce cooling loads and energy demand for the building. Usually, EIFS is attached to a structure of metal studs anchored to the main structure of the building, which in this specific case was reinforced concrete. The main problem with this material is its total lack of structural capacity to resist the impact of windborne or floating debris, or wind loads, or the impact of storm surge. In this case, it was clear that major breaching of the building envelope led to water and wind penetration, resulting in catastrophic damage to the building interior and contents in addition to the building envelope damage (Figure 11.15).

FIGURE 11.14 Example of inadequate material used on the building envelope of this church in Cancun. Drywall and steel studs were used in this case, proving incapable of sustaining external forces generated by wind pressure during Hurricane Wilma.

FIGURE 11.15 The EIFS used for this Cancun building envelope proved totally inadequate to sustain wind forces and the impact of flying debris during Hurricane Wilma.

Mitigation

When considering how to reduce the potential for damage to the building envelope, more specifically the exterior walls as components of the building envelope, it is critical to keep in mind the synergistic interdependency that must exist between the various components of a building (see Chapter 5). Within this context, the most effective mitigation for exterior walls starts with the use of building materials capable of performing under the impact of expected external loads during hurricanes, which means maintaining integrity under the impacts of wind pressure, hydrodynamic pressure from storm surge, breaking waves, windborne debris, and floating debris, and being capable of transferring such loads to the main building structure. This also means all connections between exterior walls and the main structure must be designed to ensure the integrity of the entire system and an effective loads path from the building envelope to the main structure and the building foundation. In essence, effective mitigation is achieved to the degree that design criteria for the building are established on the basis of expected impacts and level of performance during the projected service life of the facility and not only on the minimum requirements of applicable building codes.

Consequently, it is critical to avoid using materials such as drywall, poorly anchored panels, or EIFS as the main components of exterior walls in regions vulnerable to hurricanes.

EXTERNAL INFRASTRUCTURE

As is typical of most coastal tourism centers, not only in Cancun and the Maya Riviera, but also in Florida, the Caribbean, and most everywhere else, the infrastructure is

Classification and Mitigation of Damages

built to support the main building functions and also activities for the comfort, recreation, and enjoyment of guests.

Much may be learned from reviewing how such external infrastructure performed and sustained damaged during the impact of Hurricane Wilma.

RETAINING WALLS

In an effort to build as close to the beach and the water as possible, design professionals often use retaining walls to create an elevated site to "protect" the main building and external infrastructure from the tides and waves. In the course of field work in the aftermath of Wilma, I came across numerous instances of such retaining walls severely or catastrophically damaged by the hydrodynamic pressure of storm surge, which in the case of Hurricane Wilma was estimated to have reached 5 m above mean sea level, plus wind waves riding above it. Considering that one cubic meter of sea water weighs approximately one metric ton, it is rather simple to conclude that very large dynamic loads impacted those structures.

In assessing the causality of the observed damage, other contributing factors were identified. For example, the initial impact of incoming storm surge eroded the beach, removing vast quantities of sand. As the surge got higher and traveled farther inland, it started interacting with the retaining wall, and the resulting reflected waves contributed to further beach erosion that at some point started to also contribute to undermining of the retaining wall foundations. As this process continued, waves breaking against the retaining wall, and storm surge itself got over the wall, causing damage to the grounds and infrastructure "protected" by the wall itself. Eventually, as the surge returned to the sea, it caused erosion and undermining behind the wall from the land side, leading to further weakening of the structure. The end result of the described process was structural failure, partial or even total collapse of the retaining wall, and considerable damage to the protected infrastructure, including swimming pools, terraces, landscaped areas, and other appurtenances located landward of the wall (Figure 11.16).

FIGURE 11.16 Retaining wall and outdoor infrastructure at this beachfront hotel in Cancun demolished by the impact of storm surge.

FIGURE 11.17 External recreational area in a beachfront hotel in Cancun totally demolished by the storm surge generated by Hurricane Wilma.

TERRACES AND SWIMMING POOLS

Numerous swimming pools and terraces along the main "hotel strip" in Cancun and elsewhere were directly impacted by Wilma's storm surge and waves, which beyond causing direct damage from the impact itself also transported and deposited large amounts of sand, rocks, and debris both during the incoming and outgoing phases of the storm surge. All of this caused extensive damage to these facilities (Figure 11.17).

BALCONIES AND RAILINGS

Although technically and physically part of the building, I have grouped balconies and terraces that protrude beyond the main plane of the building envelope together with other external infrastructure. Many balconies and terraces, especially at higher elevation and upper floors of the building, sustained extensive damage. Balcony railings, commonly made of aluminum, were often ripped off their anchors (Figure 11.18).

EXTERIOR CEILINGS

The architecture of some buildings includes overhangs and roof eaves, cantilevered floors, or large open spaces underneath higher portions of the building and other shapes, leaving many external ceiling areas exposed to the elements. Save for rare exceptions, most of the buildings observed, where these conditions were present, had used materials normally intended for interiors or more sheltered spaces to build these exterior ceilings. I am referring to drop ceilings consisting of acoustical panels, or lath and plaster ceilings, attached to a supporting framework of angles hanging from wires attached to the underside of the structural slab above or to structural members, or perforated or semiopen lightweight aluminum panels similarly installed. None

FIGURE 11.18 The railing in this upper-floor balcony was ripped off its supports.

of these ceiling systems are intended for exterior installation where they will be exposed to environmental forces not encountered inside a building, and it was clear no special reinforcement or adaptive modification had been made to account for expected conditions in the external environment. These installations suffered extensive damage from wind pressure, wind-driven rain, and the impact of flying debris.

In a few of the buildings inspected, repairs were already underway or had been completed, even though it had been only three and a half weeks since the hurricane event, using exactly the same materials and installation system as before. In other words, they were returning these buildings to their exact prestorm condition, entirely missing the opportunity for incorporating mitigation measures to reduce the potential for damage from future hurricanes. In fact, this approach basically guarantees that the observed damage will be repeated with the next impact of a hurricane (Figure 11.19).

ROOF-MOUNTED EQUIPMENT

Most of the hotels and other buildings had several pieces of electromechanical equipment, chimneys, communication towers, solar panels, water tanks, and so on mounted on the roof, which sustained and/or caused considerable damage during Hurricane Wilma. Careful assessment of damage revealed that the main cause was failure of the main anchoring system, allowing a given piece of equipment to be displaced and in some cases to be totally ripped off its supports, causing damage to the roof. In other cases, the main anchoring system performed well, but secondary means of anchoring failed. Such was the case of an array of solar heating panels installed on raised steel frames attached to the flat roof of a high-rise hotel. Each of the solar panels measuring 1.80 m × 0.90 m was attached to the supporting steel frame by two small (50 mm × 25 mm) steel tabs spaced 1.0 m apart at the top and bottom, which were not enough to maintain the panels in place under the strong

FIGURE 11.19 The exterior ceiling covering the underside of the structure was totally ripped off by the winds of Hurricane Wilma.

wind-uplift pressures generated over the roof of this high-rise hotel. Worth noting in this case is that while most of the solar panels were dislodged and some became windborne debris, the supporting steel frames remained in place attached to the roof. This was possible because loads acting on those structures actually decreased as the solar panels were dislodged.

There were also cases of extensive damage to roof-mounted equipment such as AC units resting on a metal base and radio and cellular phone communication towers and antennas being kept in place by guy cables (Figures 11.20 and 11.21).

FIGURE 11.20 Typical example of roof-mounted equipment. These AC units were attached to their bases by one screw and tab at each corner, clearly inadequate to keep them in place under hurricane wind loads.

Classification and Mitigation of Damages

FIGURE 11.21 Guy-wire communication tower damaged by wind.

OTHER EXTERIOR-MOUNTED EQUIPMENT

In addition to roof-mounted heating, ventilation and air conditioning (HVAC) equipment, I also visited several hotels and buildings that had these kinds of equipment installed outdoors at ground level, in some cases out in the open and in others behind mostly decorative barriers, not so much to protect them but to hide them from view. In most of the cases, these installations showed a range of common deficiencies such as

- Widespread, and in some cases severe, corrosion in their anchoring systems and the pieces of equipment themselves.
- Lack of protection against the hazards of wind and water during hurricanes.
- No protection against the impact of windborne and/or floating debris during hurricanes (Figure 11.22).

PARKING LOTS

Parking areas adjacent to many hotels, condominiums, and other commercial facilities such as restaurants, shopping centers, and others sustained extensive damage caused by storm surge or inundation resulting from the extreme precipitation event that poured more than 1500 mm of rain over the region in a span of 48 h. Observed damage included erosion of pavement, undermining of base material in parking areas and roadways, and differential settling of various areas. Other contributing factors to this widespread damage included poor construction in terms of base materials, inadequate compaction, and poor quality of surfacing materials, as well as lack of proper drainage in most of the lots visited (Figure 11.23).

FIGURE 11.22 Outdoor infrastructure at ground level.

Exterior Lighting, Masts, and Traffic Lights

Large numbers of electrical and street lighting posts, towers supporting high-voltage transmission lines, posts and cables for traffic lights, flag poles, masts of various kinds, street signage, and similar kinds of infrastructure sustained extensive damage from wind, the impact of flying debris, and also from falling tree limbs or uprooted trees.

FIGURE 11.23 Parking lot in the Cancun hotel strip flooded by storm surge and extreme rain.

Classification and Mitigation of Damages

In assessing causes of damage to this class of infrastructure, several contributing factors were identified. First, most of these are tall slender structures that cantilever from the ground up and are anchored in various manners, usually having a light fixture or other appurtenance attached at or near the top of the structure. The net result, in simple terms, is a long cantilevered structure fixed at one end with a concentrated load at the opposite end that will tend to bend and overturn under pressure from hurricane winds, sometimes to the point of failure when external loads exceed the design criteria for the structure.

Another contributor to the observed damage was lack of preventive maintenance resulting in deteriorated and weakened structures—often a result of corrosion that is a prevalent problem in the marine environment of the coastal region—with reduced capacity for sustaining external loads during hurricanes.

In many cases, it was evident that eroded or waterlogged ground had lost much of its capacity for supporting the post, mast, or other such structure, becoming a major contributing factor to the damage observed.

In the specific case of traffic lights, most of the observed damage fell into one of the following three modes: the traffic light crashed to the ground after being ripped off its supporting cables by the force of the wind, the cables from which the traffic light was hung snapped and the traffic light and cables crashed to the ground, or in some extreme cases, one or both of the poles supporting the cable and the traffic light broke or overturned and the whole assembly crashed to the ground.

It is important to note that at the time of this visit, less than 4 weeks after the landfall of Hurricane Wilma, a vast effort to replace or repair damaged electrical transmission and distribution infrastructure as well as street lighting and traffic devices was already underway. In fact, many of these structures had already been repaired or replaced in an effort toward restoring important public services to the area. Laudable as these efforts were, I should mention that all of this damaged infrastructure had been, and was being, restored to prestorm conditions without taking advantage of the opportunity to incorporate mitigation measures to reduce a repetition of the observed damage during the impact of recurring hurricanes (Figure 11.24).

FIGURE 11.24 Street lighting and electrical infrastructure damaged by wind.

Piers, Tiki Huts, and Others

Post-Wilma field inspections from Isla Mujeres and Cancun to Cozumel and Playa del Carmen, and points in between revealed several piers that had been severely damaged during the hurricane. Save perhaps one exception, all of these piers were built with pairs of reinforced concrete piles connected by a reinforced concrete beam, a superstructure of dimensional lumber topped by wood planks and wood railing. All of the piers seen had been totally or partially demolished. All or most of the wood components had been ripped off or otherwise damaged by storm surge, breaking waves, and floating debris, leaving only the reinforced concrete pilings in place. Close inspection of these pilings revealed widespread corrosion of the reinforcement and anchoring devices and spalling of the concrete, possibly the result of the observed corrosion and also salt penetration, which most probably played a major role in contributing to damage in these structures (Figure 11.25).

A rather common element of outdoor infrastructure in many hotels and other facilities is the tiki hut, or *palapa* to use the local term, which consists of a wood or, in rare cases, a metal structure covered by a thatched roof constructed of palm fronds. Many of these structures, but not all, also had a protective rope net on top of the thatched covering to reinforce it and help keep it in place against wind forces. These *palapas* are typically built in two ways: One consists of a central column, usually a heavy timber either round or square, but in some cases, it could also be a metal pole, topped by a structure of the same material and the thatched palm frond covering with or without the reinforcing rope netting. The other common method of construction involves a rectangular or square structure supported by four corner timber or metal columns and a thatched hip roof covering.

Contrary to what some may think, given the artisan nature of these structures, by and large, they performed quite well under the impact of hurricane winds. In fact, all

FIGURE 11.25 Pier damaged by storm surge.

Classification and Mitigation of Damages

of the many *palapas* that I inspected had little to mostly partial damage consisting of partial loss of covering and isolated cases of structural damage. The only structure of this type that I saw demolished, toppled over, had a central steel column and structure that was corroded at its base, which became the main point of failure under hurricane wind pressures.

Close observation of these *palapas* and subsequent analysis revealed their generally outstanding performance under hurricane conditions results from the porosity of the roof covering and the semiopen construction, which allowed for wind pressures to basically equalize above and under the roof. In addition, the roof covering sheds part of the upper layers, increasing the porosity and allowing more wind to pass through, reducing external loads on the structure. It is quite an effective design, and perhaps one that merits more study and research to determine how much of these beneficial qualities may be replicated or adapted in some fashion to other types of roof coverings. In any case, this is food for thought.

LANDSCAPING AND GARDENS

Landscaping in general sustained extensive damage. From loss of fronds, foliage, and partial loss of canopy to uprooting of trees, and widespread damage to shrubbery, most of the vegetation along the coastal region and well inland showed the brunt of the impact. Despite massive loss of foliage and some cases of uprooted units, palm trees appeared to have performed the best under the impact of hurricane winds and extreme rain. Other kinds of trees sustained far worse damage, including numerous instances of uprooting, which is mainly due to the fact that these trees are shallow-rooted because of the proximity of the water table and water logging of the mostly sandy soil.

Damage to trees resulted in considerable indirect and consequential damage. When trees were uprooted and toppled over under wind pressure, sidewalks and curbs were also damaged, as well as electrical and communication lines. Broken tree limbs became flying debris inflicting damage to neighboring buildings and structures. As a consequence of these damages, communications and electrical power supply were also interrupted (Figures 11.26 and 11.27).

SIGNS AND BILLBOARDS

Many outdoor signs from stand-alone billboards, to banners, and illuminated neon signs attached to buildings or structures suffered damage. Damage to commercial neon signs ranged from molded plastic pieces or individual letters being perforated or torn apart by flying debris or ripped off by wind pressure. Damage to billboards fell into two categories: (i) the aluminum or wood panel on which the sign itself was painted or pasted was totally or partially torn off the supporting structure, or (ii) the entire stand-alone structure toppled over after performing as a large sail catching wind and being overturned by the force of the wind acting on the surface of the panel above. These are examples of the *sail effect* when large exposed surfaces come under extreme pressures from hurricane winds and the loads that develop exceed the capabilities of the supporting structures (Figure 11.28).

FIGURE 11.26 Damaged landscaping near the beach in Cancun hotel strip.

Mitigation

Mitigating potential damage to external infrastructure presents a rather interesting challenge. First, the function of these components requires that they be located outdoors, fully exposed to the elements and hazards generated by a hurricane. Despite such exposure, it is entirely feasible, in most cases, to mitigate impacts by implementing a range of practical and effective measures.

Toward that end, our approach should simplify and focus on the basics that have already been identified, such as sails, wind-catchers, proper anchoring, damaging

FIGURE 11.27 A large tree uprooted by the winds of Hurricane Wilma in the streets of Cancun.

Classification and Mitigation of Damages 183

FIGURE 11.28 The total force sustained by the large sail that was this roof-mounted outdoor sign exceeded the loading capacity of the supporting structure, particularly the connections between the top and lower portions.

components, external loads, characterization of impacts, impact modifiers, and other factors.

We can identify specific mitigation measures by revisiting each of the components of outdoor infrastructure listed here, and taking a look at the damage each sustained:

Retaining walls: I would like to start by recommending abandoning the use of retaining walls, most of all because they are a significant contributing factor to the destruction of sandy beaches, and also because of their intrinsic vulnerability as a function of their location. In those cases, where it may be absolutely necessary to build a retaining wall or keep an existing one, I would suggest using design criteria and construction methods that are different than those observed in the area. What is critically important is to anchor these walls deep down into the ground, using pilings that reach deep into load-bearing layers in the ground to prevent undermining of the wall due to erosion. Coupling retaining walls with structures or devices that can dampen the energy of breaking waves and onrushing surge will reduce loads generated by hydrodynamic pressure and wave impact, and hence the potential damage. Combining retaining walls with dunes and vegetation on the seaward side adds a natural protective barrier to help absorb the impact of surge and waves. In this regard, the use of vegetation is critical to anchoring the soil in place to maintain an effective natural barrier. And there are other effective engineering approaches that could be used that should be well known to practicing engineers.

Terraces and swimming pools: One of the most effective methods to reduce or avoid much of the damage observed is to build these infrastructure components at a safer distance from the beach and at higher elevations to minimize possible impacts by storm surge. The use of surge deflectors, which are devices designed to absorb most of the energy of the onrushing water thereby reducing hydrodynamic pressure and the resulting external loads acting on the infrastructure, is also recommended. Such surge deflectors may be designed as decorative elements as long as they also have the required structural capacity.

Balconies and railings: Most of the damage seen in these building components resulted from failure of anchoring devices under the impact of wind loads. Consequently, the most effective mitigation measure is to use higher capacity anchors and a denser anchoring schedule to increase the overall capacity of a railing to resist external forces generated by hurricane winds.

Exterior ceilings: Damage to these components occurred mainly because they were generally treated as mere decorative elements to cover pipes, conduits, or other utilities or to provide a finished surface to the underside of a slab or structure. To reduce such potential for damage, the first step is to treat these elements as integral component of the building envelope. As such, these components must be designed to perform under specific design criteria determined by the project engineer, taking into account elevation above ground, exposure, and other factors. Considering all of the above, the next step is to choose adequate materials, supporting systems, anchors, and anchoring schedules.

Roof-mounted equipment: There are two proven and effective approaches to mitigation when it comes to roof-mounted equipment. The first is to avoid installing equipment on the roof altogether, if at all possible. The second, and equally effective approach, and one which I tried on several projects in Florida with excellent results, relies on the installation of anchoring devices attached directly to the main structure of the building, and in the use of galvanized steel straps or stainless-steel cables with turnbuckles or other tensioning devices placed over the piece of equipment itself and attached at an angle to said anchoring points to tie it down.

In the case of communication towers or antennas to be installed on the roof of a building, the design itself can make an important contribution to mitigate potential damage. For example, using tubular members rather than angles and preferably a tripod design in the construction of the tower has proven quite effective in improving performance under hurricane conditions. In the case of guy-wire-supported towers, it is recommended to run sets of guy-wires all the way to the top of the tower without leaving that top portion of the tower to cantilever beyond the last set of wires, as is the common practice.

Other exterior-mounted equipment: Often, mechanical equipment is installed outdoors but at ground level. In these cases, recommended mitigation measures include a slab or foundation to elevate the equipment and also a protective barrier around the perimeter, to protect against flooding and the impact of flying or floating debris. Equally important and recommended is the use of anchoring devices with the capacity to keep the equipment in place under the impact of hurricane winds. A periodic maintenance program to

Classification and Mitigation of Damages

combat corrosion in this marine environment, preventing it from becoming a contributor to future damage, is recommended as an effective mitigation measure.

Parking lots: Elevation above adjacent roadways and streets, high quality of construction with well-compacted and deep base materials, and a sturdy surface, preferably a porous one to contribute to drainage and reduce ponding of water, in addition to properly sloped surfaces and an effective and redundant drainage system are all good contributors to mitigating the type of damage observed. Collaterally, it is advised to provide deep footings for light poles, masts, and posts for signage to reduce or prevent overtopping under wind pressure as the ground becomes waterlogged. Shade trees used through parking areas should be braced by timbers or by cables to prevent uprooting and damage to the pavement.

Regarding trees, all trees and not only those around parking areas need to be subjected to an annual maintenance program of preventive pruning in anticipation of the hurricane season, reducing canopy volume and increasing porosity to allow easier flow of wind-reducing forces acting on the tree during hurricanes. Younger trees must be buttressed with timber tripods and/or supporting cables until they become mature enough to strengthen their capacity for resisting wind pressure during hurricanes. All of these measures will reduce or prevent the uprooting and overturning of trees as well as resulting indirect damages to the parking area itself.

Exterior lighting, masts, and traffic lights: Numerous galvanized steel posts used for public lighting on the streets or on the grounds around hotels or other buildings were bent and damaged by the force of the wind. There were also painted steel posts that in most cases were snapped off at the base because of corrosion. Recommended mitigation measures include the following: One used rather effectively by electric utilities in Florida is to replace galvanized steel posts with spun-reinforced concrete or prestressed reinforced concrete posts designed to withstand extreme winds and wind gusts expected for the region. Another alternative is to keep using galvanized steel posts, but upgrade to a heavier gauge and increased cross section to have a stronger unit with enhanced capacity for resisting expected wind loads. With respect to plain steel painted post, the best mitigation is to avoid using them and replace those that were damaged with one of the two alternatives described above.

In the case of cable-suspended traffic lights, I would recommend switching to the "mast-arm" supported design, which was developed in the aftermath of Hurricane Andrew (1992) in Florida and has been used there since that time and in several other hurricane-vulnerable regions with excellent results. The mast-arm design provides a much lower wind profile than the post and cable system and consists of a hefty gauge galvanized-steel post with an attached cantilevered arm at the top, to which the traffic lights themselves are attached often in a horizontal rather than a vertical position, which reduces the wind profile further. In this design, additional reinforcement is used at the connecting points between the post and the arm, and between the post and the foundation.

Equally effective as a mitigation measure for this type of infrastructure is to pay special attention to the design of the foundation and method of connecting the post or mast to the same. Depth of foundation is paramount to counteract the overturning moment induced by wind loads, as well as the reduced holding capacity of waterlogged soils.

Another method for mitigating potential damage is to move the electrical distribution cables underground in order to avoid damage from wind loads, or falling trees or tree limbs, during a hurricane. When considering this specific mitigation alternative, it is important to note that the cost of maintenance for subterranean installations is higher than for aerial cables, and also that special precautions will need to be taken to prevent damage from flooding and uprooted trees. Also, subterranean electrical distribution line installation may not be cost effective once all risk factors and corresponding protective measures are taken into account.

Piers, tiki huts, and others: At a risk of becoming repetitive, mitigating these structures and facilities is all about quality of materials, the integrity and capability of connections and anchorage, the depth and adequacy of design of foundations, and design criteria in term of expected impacts. Mitigation is also about avoiding, or designing for, the "sails" and "wind-catchers" that have been mentioned herein and their role as damage-contributing factors.

Piers require special attention because by function they must be in contact with the water, where they will receive the brunt of the impact of storm surge and breaking waves, as well as possible impacts of floating debris and/or boats moored there or anchored nearby during a hurricane event.

The understructure and foundation, consisting of wood or reinforced concrete pilings, must be embedded deep enough into the ground to reach soil layers with the bearing capacity to sustain loads from hydrodynamic pressure, the impact of breaking waves, and impacts from floating debris. Structural cross bracing between vertical supporting members is strongly recommended. Connectors and anchoring devices must be of stainless steel, galvanized steel, structural aluminum, bronze, or other noncorrosive material to ensure that structural capacity is maintained during the useful life of the structure.

Additional mitigation is achieved by leaving narrow spaces between boards that make up the horizontal traffic surface of the pier, diffusing the energy of water and waves impacting the structure. The same measure also works for secondary piers, or finger piers, where the traffic surface is often made of heavy gauge aluminum or stainless-steel members that are perforated and also spaced, leaving small narrow voids between them in order to dissipate the energy of impact from waves or surging water.

Building piers high enough to be above the waves helps mitigate damaging impacts, but when this alternative is not possible, floating piers are also used to mitigate potential damage. These piers are connected to vertical pilings by devices outfitted with rollers allowing them to roll up and down as the level of the water changes.

Classification and Mitigation of Damages

In summary, mitigation for these exposed structures is achieved through measures to strengthen and harden the structure as much as possible to resist expected impacts and to modify such expected impacts in a way that external forces are reduced as much as possible.

Landscaping and gardens: The main criteria for mitigating potential damage to landscaping and vegetation were covered when discussing trees in and around parking areas and may be summarized as follows: Use well-developed mature native trees, maintained through an annual pruning program, to reduce canopy and promote more effective interaction with hurricane wind fields. Use wooden timbers to buttress the trees against wind loads, or use cables and collars to provide additional support to sustain environmental forces, especially when dealing with juvenile or recently planted trees.

But above all of these measures, I believe the most effective one is to use native species, which are already acclimated to the place and the hazards that affect it, including hurricanes, and which have in some fashion adapted to conditions in the coastal region, including salt content in marine breezes and in the soils.

Signs and billboards: In assessing damage sustained by billboards and outdoor signs under the impact of Hurricane Wilma, several contributing factors were identified, including the following:

- Most billboards and signs are top-heavy structures, where the sign itself is a large sail that catches a lot of wind and therefore transfers large external loads to its supporting structure.
- The entire system, consisting of the sign itself, its supporting structure, and its foundation, works as an inverted pendulum while resisting wind forces during a hurricane, which makes the structure prone to torsion and overturning.
- Following the load path from top to bottom, there are two points of critical connections where failure typically occurs. One is the connection between the sign itself, the big sail, and its supporting structure; the other is the connection between the supporting structure and its base and foundation, which is where the external forces are finally transferred to the ground, and the pivot of rotation for the complete assembly sustains the overturning moment generated by the push of the wind on the sign above.
- Corrosion and lack of proper preventive maintenance to combat it, especially in the marine environment prevailing in the coastal region, were major contributors to failure of these structures and resulting damage.
- The overall design of the complete billboard/outdoor-sign assembly itself was a major contributor to damage in many of the cases observed.

Knowing the most common weaknesses that contribute to damage allows concerned parties to identify mitigation measures that will be effective in reducing the potential for damage from future hurricane impacts, counteracting them through enhanced, stronger design methods and criteria. In this respect, focusing on the connections and points of anchorage identified above is recommended. The top-to-bottom load path will be most effective in direct relation to the capability of such connections and anchoring points to maintain their integrity and resist external forces during a hurricane. Effective mitigation can be achieved by enhancing the performance of the system by strengthening the connection between the structure and base and by ensuring that the foundation itself is deep enough to work in conjunction with the ground to resist external forces, especially the overturning moment and torsional loads.

Taking a careful look at the design of these structures and making, what in reality amounts to minor changes, will enhance performance while interacting with hurricane winds. Using a combination of tubular steel components and spoilers (to reduce vortex shedding) rather than angles to build the supporting structure makes a significant difference on how it interacts with wind, and in the loads generated by wind pressure on such structural elements. Using galvanized, or stainless steel, or structural aluminum, for the supporting structure will virtually eliminate corrosion as a damage-contributing factor and also simplify preventive maintenance.

When using corrosion-resistant materials may not be possible, painting the entire structure with a rust-resistant base and several coats of rust-resistant paint together with a strict preventive repainting program will also mitigate the potential for damage from hurricane impacts. As an alternative, prepainted powder-coated heat-cured components could be used to build the billboard supporting structure, offering a superior resistant surface.

Regarding the large panel on top of the structure, where the billboard itself or sign is pasted on, or painted, or otherwise installed, the main recommendation is to do everything possible to reduce external loads generated by the wind. One possibility is to use perforated materials, such as aluminum sheets, and to also perforate the sign itself to take advantage of porosity to allow some wind to bleed through the structure thereby reducing the total load applied to the sail.

No hazard mitigation approach will be as effective as it could possibly be without a collateral preventive maintenance program involving periodic inspections of the entire assembly, looking for signs of corrosion, loosened connectors, deterioration of the ground around the base, ponding water, moisture damage, and other potentially weakening conditions that must be remedied immediately to preserve the integrity and structural capabilities of the structure.

BUILDING INTERIOR

Breaching of the building envelope during a hurricane, whether caused by wind, storm surge, or the impact of debris, allows wind and water inside the building, often causing extensive damage.

Interior walls: In inspecting damage to the interior of buildings affected by Hurricane Wilma in Cancun and surrounding areas, it was clear that interior masonry walls in older buildings suffered considerably less damage than drywall or plaster walls used with increased frequency in newer buildings. There was extensive damage to these drywall interior walls and partitions throughout the entire hotel strip in Cancun and neighboring areas in the path of Hurricane Wilma (2005). Unsurprisingly, there was a clear transitional demarcation of types of wind damage between interior walls in the higher floors and those in lower levels of multi-story buildings that had sustained breaching of the building envelope. The extent

Classification and Mitigation of Damages 189

of damage was much more severe in higher floors where some drywall partitions were totally ripped off by the pressure of winds penetrating the building combined with external pressures. Wind damage to these types of interior walls was not as severe in the lower floors. An assessment of causality to determine the causes of these damages pointed to a breach in the envelope, perhaps a broken window or balcony door, allowing hurricane winds to penetrate inside, causing rapid pressurization in the entire space or floor where it occurred, placing extreme loads on these walls, to the point where entire segments were ripped off their points of attachments to the building structure. In other cases, numerous individual drywall panels were damaged or ripped off, but most of their interior skeleton remained in place. It is also clear to me that in addition to wind, wind-driven rain as well as rain pouring in through damaged roofs also penetrated the interior causing additional damage. Drywall loses whatever little structural integrity it possesses when wet to the point where it is easily damaged by the impacts of wind and water. The observed damage was also partially due to the impact of pieces of furniture, decorative objects, and other content being propelled by the wind and hitting these interior walls. Extensive as these damages were in the higher floor, they pale in comparison to those caused by storm surge, waves, wind, and debris in the ground floor and other lower floor levels in the building. It is clear that drywall interior walls are no match for the forces of the most damaging components of hurricanes. While damage to interior walls, especially those made of drywall or similar materials, was extensive due to wind in the higher floors, damage in the ground floor was often catastrophic due to storm surge and wave impact.

The materials and methods of construction used in these interior walls were quite inadequate for a number of reasons. Metal studs, in most cases galvanized steel, used to build the supporting structure were gauge 30 or 28 in most cases, below the minimum 25 gauge typically used in the United States. Typical spacing between vertical studs was 0.60 m, far beyond the 0.40 m to 0.30 m typically used in the United States, plus the fact that in most cases there was no horizontal member bracing the assembly. The net result of this was that individual studs that were 11%–25% thinner than the minimum gauge commonly used in the United States had a tributary load-carrying area 50%–100% larger than what is acceptable in common practice, resulting in 50%–60% higher loads, clearly a formula for failure. Additionally, drywall panels used for these walls were 9.5 mm thick rather than the 12.7 mm commonly used in the United States for these types of applications. In summary, the materials and methods of construction for these interior walls used in many of the buildings we inspected in Cancun and neighboring areas resulted in a final product that was well below normally acceptable standards in the United States (Figure 11.29).

Ceilings: Drop ceilings constructed of drywall or insulating materials supported by a light metal structure suspended from wires attached to the underside of the roof slab, also sustained considerable damage once there was a breach in the envelope and wind and water penetrated the inside of the building. It is clear that in constructing these ceilings, little to no consideration was given to the possible effects of dynamic loads. Rather, these installations were designed to carry their own weight with aesthetic effects being the major consideration. Consequently, the observed damage should not have been surprising or unexpected, and it can be expected to repeat with each future

FIGURE 11.29 View of the interior wall in a hotel guest room. This example is typical of damage observed throughout the building. The wall structure consists of thin 12-mm-thick studs at 600 mm on center without horizontal cross bracing. It is clear that this system had no capacity to perform well under the impact of strong winds.

impact by a hurricane. In summary, inadequacy of materials and methods of construction coupled with totally inadequate design criteria will always result in extensive damage when the building envelope is breached during a hurricane (Figure 11.30).

Floors: Generally, finished floors made of ceramic, porcelain, Saltillo, or similar kinds of tiles, as well as granite, marble, or stone suffered minor damage under the impact of wind and water during the hurricane. Most of the damage came from accumulated debris, sand, or ponding water, which required extensive clean-up and perhaps refinishing these floors. Beyond this, there were some instances of nicked or broken tiles or sections of the floor caused by the impact of debris and other objects pushed by the wind or water inside the building.

There were totally different outcomes when the floor was finished in wood or carpeting. Damage to these type of finishes were extensive and caused mainly by water that penetrated the building either as rain or storm surge. Wet or waterlogged carpeting that could not be immediately dried up always resulted in a total loss. Even in cases where the level of interior flooding was minimal, only a few centimeters deep, and drying techniques were applied with the utmost expediency, the development and spread of mold could not be avoided. Mold infestations in the interior of a building frequently led to seriously adverse consequences for the health of occupants, as many individuals are allergic to mold and its spores. Often, the only solution to this problem is to use aggressive and intensive remediation measures, which carry a high price tag given the level of expertise and equipment that are required.

Although not widely used in Quintana Roo, wood floors sustained considerable damage. Most of these floors were finished with parquet or tongue-and-groove planks, glued directly to the floor slab. Observed damage ranged from warped or cracked wood, to dislodged or loosened pieces due to failure of the adhesive. It was

FIGURE 11.30 View of drywall-suspended ceiling damaged by hurricane winds after a breach of the building envelope. The ceiling assembly is rather weak and has no capacity to sustain even minimal external loads due to minimal thickness of material and spacing of supporting metal channels.

clear that the kinds of wood and methods of installation used for these floors were inadequate for the impacts of water, wind, and debris sustained during the hurricane.

Electromechanical equipment, infrastructure, and others: Breaching of the building envelope to one extent or another had actually occurred in most of the buildings we inspected in the aftermath of Wilma (2005) in Cancun and surrounding coastal areas. Breaching of the building envelope exposed the interior of the building to wind pressure and extreme loads generated inside. Air conditioning, ventilation, and electrical and lighting installations were especially susceptible to damage from the resulting dynamic-loading regime. In the course of inspections, several instances of flexible air-conditioning ducts that had been shredded to unrecognizable pieces by the force of the winds inside the buildings were documented (Figure 11.31). Similarly, numerous cases of ventilation ceiling fans, lighting fixtures, and other components of a building air conditioning and ventilation (ACV) and electrical installations totally destroyed or seriously damaged by the forces of hurricane winds flowing throughout interior spaces were also documented. There was at least one documented case in which direct damage caused by wind triggered indirect damage by water when the fire-sprinkler system suffered damage from wind forces, resulting in broken pipes and a deluge of water flooding several floors of a high-rise hotel in the Cancun strip.

Electrical installations, except perhaps for exposed lighting fixtures, cables, and poorly anchored conduits, are generally better protected than other infrastructure components against the impact of wind. The outcome however is quite different in terms of damage when it comes to the impact of water, particularly salt water, on

FIGURE 11.31 What remains of a cylindrical flexible AC duct after being hit by winds of Hurricane Wilma (2005) after a breach of the building envelope.

electrical installations. Salt water flooding caused by storm surge is capable of causing extensive damage to electrical infrastructure, especially in the lower levels of a building. This flooding can penetrate conduit lines through wall outlets, causing considerable damage to critical switchgear, transformers, bus lines, and other electrical controls. Because salt water is highly corrosive, some of the damage may not be apparent at first, but rather starts to show over time as small pinhole-sized rust spots on the cowlings and exterior of pieces of electrical equipment, usually a sign of larger damage inside.

Contents

External forces generated by wind pressure, the hydrodynamic pressure of storm surge, or the impacts of flying or floating debris or of breaking waves are capable of breaching the building envelope, allowing all damaging components of a hurricane inside. Often, the result of this chain of events is considerable damage and destruction of the contents of the building, especially those pieces of furniture or décor that are not attached to the building itself (Figures 11.32 and 11.33).

Furniture: Although the clean-up and recovery process was already underway by the time my colleagues and I arrived on ground zero, we were still able to inspect several hotels and observe large numbers of pieces of furniture destroyed or severely damaged both in common areas and in the guest rooms themselves. It was surprising that in most cases, no protective precautionary measures had been taken to protect furniture ahead of the hurricane impact for which ample warning had been received. In this regard, it is worth mentioning that in a major hotel we visited, desks, chairs, night stands, minibar, television set, telephone and lamps, linens, drapes, paintings,

Classification and Mitigation of Damages

FIGURE 11.32 Lobby furniture in a hotel breached by storm surge generated by Hurricane Wilma still crusted with sand, shells, and other materials. In many cases, furniture covered by the storm surge remained in one piece, but they were completely saturated by moisture, salt, and sand, which caused permanent and irreparable damage.

and other works of art in each guest room were all placed inside the bathroom. The bathroom door was closed and locked for the duration of the expected impact. The purpose of taking these measures during the execution of the hotel's preparedness plan was to protect most of the furniture, décor, and objects of greater value, leaving outside, in the guest room space, the largest piece of furniture, the bed, but also the one of lesser relative value. As a result of these precautionary measures, this particular hotel preserved most of its guestroom furniture and contents without damage, which allowed it to resume operations much faster than competitors that did not take similar preparedness actions ahead of Hurricane Wilma's landfall. This is a

FIGURE 11.33 Interior finishes, décor, and furniture damaged by wind and water after a breach of the building envelope during Hurricane Wilma (2005).

good example of how preparedness and the execution of an emergency plan made an important contribution to mitigating the impact of the hurricane.

Decorative elements: Our field observations and inspection of several hotels in the region affected by Hurricane Wilma in Cancun and environs confirmed that décor, furniture, and other decorative objects or elements in common areas of hotels, such as lobbies, bars, restaurants, and other similarly large open spaces, regardless of level at or above ground, have a much larger probability of being damaged as a result of a breach in the building envelope than those inside the guest rooms in the hotel. In this regard, the lack of protective devices to shield the building envelope from some or most of the expected impacts and/or the lack of protective preparedness measures taken ahead of the approaching hurricane were indeed major contributing factors to the extensive damage observed.

Mitigation

Regarding potential damage to the interior and contents of a building, especially one located in the coastal region near the beach and ocean, undoubtedly the best mitigation is to design and build the building envelope using materials and components capable of resisting the impacts of flying or floating debris, and possessing the hardness and integrity to sustain expected wind pressures, as well as external forces and impacts generated by windborne or floating debris, by breaking waves and storm surge. In this respect, it is critically important to keep in mind that the building envelope is as strong as its weakest component. Consequently, such weak components need to be constructed with impact-resistant materials or protected by permanently installed or deployable devices that are impact resistant and which must be installed using design criteria and anchoring systems capable of resisting the expected loads.

As long as we are able to maintain the integrity of the building envelope, the interior and contents of the building will be protected. But in anticipation of an eventual breach of the building envelope, it is essential to consider which mitigation measures may prove effective in reducing the potential for damage to the interior and contents of the building.

Assuming an otherwise hurricane-resistant building, one incorporating mitigation in its design criteria and built with materials, components, and construction methods to ensure effective performance under the impact of a hurricane, including preservation of the integrity of the building envelope, here are some recommendations to mitigate potential damages to the interior and contents in the remote eventuality of a breach in the envelope allowing the penetration of wind and water in the interior space:

1. Nonstructural interior walls must be reinforced and built to sustain some level of wind pressures. For example, interior walls constructed of steel studs and drywall can be strengthened considerably by implementing the following changes:
   a. Use gauge 20 (1.01 mm nominal thickness) "C" shape galvanized 100-mm-wide steel studs rather than the lighter gauge channel-shape steel studs commonly used in the buildings in Cancun and surroundings areas.

Classification and Mitigation of Damages

    b. Install studs at 400 mm on center, rather than at the 600 mm spacing commonly used in those buildings.

    c. Install a transversal stud at mid-height between vertical studs to provide lateral bracing.

    d. Anchor both the bottom and upper channels to the slab using fasteners and a fastening schedule (center to center distance between fasteners) specified by a structural engineer.

    e. At a minimum, use 16 mm nominal thickness drywall panels on both faces of the wall or partition rather than the 12 mm thick panels used in several of the inspected buildings.

2. Drop ceilings also need to be strengthened to be given the capacity for resisting some level of dynamic wind loading. Regardless of what type of material is used, be it drywall, acoustical panels, lightweight metal panels, or something else, it is critically important to pay particular and careful attention to the design and construction of the supporting structure for the ceiling, making sure it is designed to sustain expected external loads and that it has the strength and rigidity and is attached to the building structure in such a way as to limit deflection and movement of the ceiling under wind loads. A general recommendation is to use at a minimum 1.219-mm-thick (18 gauge) or better yet 1.626-mm-thick (16 gauge) galvanized steel members to construct the ceiling supporting structure.

3. Use galvanized steel-sheet AC ducts firmly anchored directly to the main structure of the building by way of steel straps or steel hangers and frames, rather than the flexible round ducts commonly used in many of the hotels and buildings in the Cancun area, which invariably suffered total failure and damage once they were subjected to wind loads.

4. Regarding interior finishes, such as wall veneers of wood or other materials, ceiling treatment for light fixtures, fine carpentry, built-in furniture, wood and glass decorative elements, ceiling lamps and wall sconces, ceiling fans, and similar items, it is important to consider that at some point they may all come under the effects of external loads during a hurricane. Consequently, every decorative element must be built and installed in the strongest manner possible and must be treated as an integral component of the building itself, capable of supporting its own weight and of sustaining additional forces without failing.

In closing, we should reflect on the following:

All the damage described, which our team cataloged on the ground during our field visit to the Cancun region, is the result of past events and there is nothing anyone can do about them. What we can do in reading these lines is to consider these examples as lessons about causes and causality of damage, which we must learn and apply to avoid seeing a repetition of these damages next time there is a hurricane passing over the same region.

It is rather important to keep in mind that hurricane mitigation applies equally to projected buildings not yet built as it does to existing buildings. Also, that it is a relatively simple process to incorporate mitigation concepts—hurricane mitigation measures—during the design phase of a new building, allowing us to get intended results at the lowest possible cost. However, it is never too late and indeed possible, and necessary, to consider incorporating mitigation measures in buildings that already exist by way of retrofitting or remodeling projects.

Implementing hurricane mitigation measures in an already-existing building must always start with the site-specific assessment of relative vulnerability of the building and its external supporting infrastructure. This assessment allows us to generate an inventory of weaknesses and that which is susceptible to being damaged during a hurricane and also to identify alternatives to mitigate future recurring hurricane impacts in each case.

Investing in hurricane mitigation today may be the difference between suffering some damage and being able to continue to function as a viable commercial enterprise and suffering catastrophic damage leading to long-term interruption on function while repairs or reconstruction are under way, or perhaps even the total and permanent shutdown of a business.

Investing in hurricane mitigation may be, without a doubt, one of the best business decisions one can make based on a return on investment perspective. I state this opinion based on studies by the Institute of Business and Home Safety (IBHS) in the United States that project a return of 5–7 times for each unit of currency invested in mitigation. We are talking of a rate of return on investment from 500% to 700%. In the same manner that all it takes is one hurricane impact to badly damage a building or a business, it only takes that one impact to recuperate an investment in mitigation in terms of avoided damage and the ability to continue to function.

Food for thought, indeed!

12 Future Impacts

Now it is time to pause and mentally take stock of all the information, knowledge, and ideas we have shared up to this point, and to think about what will happen in the future when new hurricanes—and it is a certainty that there will be future hurricanes—hit our coastal paradise?

What factors will be at play in the future that could influence the potential for damage generated by recurring hurricanes in Miami Beach, or along the Gulf Coast, or in Jamaica or Haiti, Quintana Roo, or in Cancun, or any other paradise of interest? What influence will we have, if any at all, over such contributing factors and if so, which specific factors are there that we may be able to influence?

What measures can we implement to reduce the potential for damage from future hurricanes, knowing fully well that there will be future hurricanes? When do we need to start taking mitigating actions?

In this respect, we need to consider two types of contributing factors capable of affecting the characteristics of future hurricane impacts on a given community, region, or site:

- Natural factors
- Anthropogenic factors

NATURAL FACTORS

In considering natural contributors, it is important to understand that the behavior of cyclonic activity that may directly impact a region of interest, say in Quintana Roo, in South Florida, or any other place, will always depend on the complex interaction between ocean and atmosphere at the time. Recognizing this fact, let us now put aside those factors that drive annual variability in cyclogenesis in a given region, and concentrate rather on the longer-term tendencies, such as may occur over decades.

To clarify this idea, let us accept that there may be considerable variability in cyclonic activity from one year to the next in a given region for a number of reasons. What is important however is to keep in mind that regardless of the kind of cyclonic activity experienced during a single season, it only takes one impact to cause catastrophic damage; consequently, it behooves all of us to anticipate what may confront us in terms of expected hurricane impacts in a future that may be quite different from what we have experienced in the past. In this regard, we must by all possible means avoid surprises regarding such future impacts.

Regarding such long-term tendencies affecting future hurricane impacts in our region of interest, let us consider the following.

CLIMATE CHANGE

If there is one certainty, it is that nature is in a constant state of change. Just like gravity, change is a constant in nature. Some changes take place quite rapidly, while others may take years, decades, centuries, millennia, or even millions of years. Some of these natural changes occur in fairly regular cycles or in oscillations.

With respect to climate change, putting aside all of the polarizing ideology-driven noise clouding the evidence science offers us with ever-increasing clarity, there are two specific components capable of directly affecting the characteristics of future hurricane impacts: (i) global warming and (ii) sea level rise.

Global Warming

There is irrefutable scientific evidence that planet Earth has cycled between periods of intense coldness, the glacial ages, and periods of rather warm temperatures, the interglacial ages. These cycles last approximately 100,000 years and are driven by a range of factors, including the orbital mechanics of Earth around the sun, changes in the inclination of Earth's axis relative to the plane of the solar system, changes in the levels of concentration of various atmospheric gases, and the increasingly more noticeable influence of human activity that has contributed to an accelerating rate of warming over the past 180 years.

Global warming is evident in the melting and retreat of glaciers worldwide, in the clear and progressive reduction of sea ice in the Arctic Ocean during the northern hemisphere summer, as well as in the melting of the ice sheet in Greenland and Antarctica and the calving of icebergs and very large ice platforms the size of some small states. Global warming is evident in the many visual and physical signals nature gives us and also in the data acquired by scientific instrumentation deployed throughout our planet on land, over water, and in the atmosphere.

Beyond its capacity for driving sea level rise, a factor that will influence hurricane impacts, global warming also increases the capacity of the atmosphere for holding moisture as water vapor. In summary, because of global warming, the air is loaded with increasingly more water.

A more humid atmosphere may be raising the threshold for precipitation to occur, but when it does actually take place, the same higher moisture content in the air results in more intense and even extreme rain events.

Considering hurricanes are cyclonic systems that draw water from the ocean and the troposphere from hundreds of thousands of square kilometers around their centers of circulation, it is simple to conclude that the incidence of "wet" hurricanes, those generating large amounts of rain, may continue to increase in the future as a consequence of global warming.

Hurricane Wilma already gave a sample of things to come in 2005 when it dumped more than 1500 mm of rain over Cancun, Isla Mujeres, and northeastern extreme of the Yucatan peninsula in less than 48 h.

With the prospect of an increase in extreme rain events associated with future hurricanes, we can only conclude that flooding and flood-generated damage to the built environment, housing, and infrastructure will also continue to increase with each passing year.

Future Impacts 199

Relative to such potential for damage, it is important to highlight that extreme rain leads to waterlogged soils that lose much of their capacity to support trees, light poles, traffic and street signs, masts, and other types of infrastructure, which then under the impact of hurricane winds may be toppled, overturned, uprooted, and damaged.

Extreme hurricane-generated rain may also contribute to health problems and environmental contamination and should be considered as a cause of consequential postevent damage. Run-off from torrential rain becomes a mode of transport for a wide range of contaminants that had been stored in damaged houses and buildings, fecal matter from damaged sanitary infrastructure, including septic tanks, which become focuses of disease, infection, and contamination for humans and also for animals and plants, which may eventually also be consumed by humans.

When rainfall amounts are such that they exceed, indeed overwhelm, the capacity of local storm drain infrastructure and the absorption capacity of the ground, flooding will ensue. In some cases, factors will combine to produce prolonged flooding events, where ponding water may remain for several days or even weeks in a particular area, creating a propitious environment for mosquitoes and infestations by other pests that carry the risk of disease for the local population.

Returning to the topic of damage to buildings and houses, let us keep in mind that extreme rain will most probably coincide with the impact of hurricane force winds and flying debris and, depending on location, also the impacts of storm surge, waves, and floating debris. Under such a scenario, it is not difficult to visualize how the combination of these external forces may breach the envelope of the building or house, allowing wind-driven rain to penetrate the interior. A direct consequence of this will be damage to the interior, contents, furniture, finishes, and the interior infrastructure of the affected building. In the longer term, another consequence of these damages will be the development of mold and fungi inside the house or building, which at best could be cured through a process of aggressive and prompt cleaning, but at worst, could turn into a serious health issue especially when mold propagates into difficult-to-access areas such as HVAC ductwork, above ceilings, or behind drywall. Numerous pulmonary, respiratory, or skin diseases and allergies are caused by the conditions I have just described.

Extreme rain events generating high rates of precipitation over short periods of time, say, for example, 120–150 mm/h, can easily exceed the drainage capacity of some roofs. This could represent serious problems for large flat roofs, especially those supported by structures having large spans between main members that are commonly found in gymnasiums, theaters, warehouses, and some industrial use buildings. When the drainage capacity of a given roof is insufficient to evacuate the amount of rain falling on it, water will pond, generating additional loads, which in some cases may exceed the design criteria for the roof, causing structural failure.

From the previous discussion, it is clear that to the extent it will lead to increased instances of extreme precipitation during hurricane events, global warming will become a significant contributor to potential damage from recurring hurricanes over the service life of a house or building located in hurricane-vulnerable places such as Cancun, Miami, Florida, the Caribbean and so many more in Central America, Mexico's Pacific coast, the U.S. Gulf Coast, and other innumerable hurricane-vulnerable places throughout the world.

200 Hurricane Mitigation for the Built Environment

This prognosis for potentially more damaging wet hurricanes in the future must be viewed as our call to action. This is a time for building design professionals to establish and practice a new design paradigm, one in which design criteria are based on expected future impacts over the projected service life of a building and not on past trends or the historical record. This is a time for closing the gaps between science and implementation relative to characterizing expected impacts that may affect a house or building 30, 50, or 75 years after it was built. This requires design professionals and industry to develop and implement materials, systems, and methods of construction that will effectively sustain and mitigate the expected impacts from future wet hurricanes that were described above.

Sea Level Rise

The other component of climate change that will have a direct effect of future potential damage during hurricanes is sea level rise or, as some science purists will call it, sea level change. While the term *sea level change* correctly describes the fact that owing to a combination of factors, the mean level of the sea relative to the land is rising in some cases and receding in others, I will purposely only address sea level rise because it is the component that has and will continue to have a direct effect in the potential for damage from future hurricane impacts in the coastal regions that are of interest here in Florida, the Gulf Coast, the Carolinas and other states along the Atlantic seaboard, as well as Cancun, the Maya Riviera in Quintana Roo, and many other places in the Caribbean and elsewhere.

I had read and knew about sea level rise for quite some time, but only had concrete and direct evidence of this phenomenon some 18 years ago while conducting an assessment of vulnerability for a major hospital facility located on a barrier island in Florida.

When assessing the vulnerability of a facility located in the coastal region, one must consider the possibility of damage caused by storm surge or wave impact and any consequential coastal flooding. For this purpose, flood maps, surge atlases, and hydrographic studies are important sources of data and information to use while conducting a vulnerability assessment such as the one I have mentioned.

I remember the flood maps and other studies available to me at the time projected surge levels for each of the five categories of hurricanes (based on the Saffir–Simpson scale) and coastal flood depths on the basis of a reference datum known as the National Geodetic Vertical Datum or NGVD for short. While the concept of a geodesic vertical datum is quite clear and simple, in this specific case, NGVD referred to a datum measured back in 1929. All the site plans and other drawings for the facility I was studying indicated building elevations based on NGVD.

My main concern at the time was whether the water level I needed to use to assess potential storm surge and wave levels the same in 1996, which is when I was conducting my assessment, as it had been in 1929 when NGVD had been established. From my basic knowledge of sea level rise, I believed the level of the water at the specific location would certainly be higher in 1996 than what it had been in 1929; consequently, all the available sources of information specific to the facility and the site were providing me with data that were no longer accurate.

After researching several sources of information, including tide gauge data, I was able to determine that mean sea level at the project site in 1996 was approximately

Future Impacts

0.2 m higher than in 1929. It was proof that sea level had risen driven by global climate change. Since that particular time in 1996, I have had numerous opportunities to research the topic of climate change, sea level rise, and what it means for vulnerable coastal communities in Florida, in Quintana Roo, and in other places.

On the topic of future tropical cyclone impacts, which is central to this chapter, it is clear that sea level rise will affect such impacts in at least two ways:

- The height of storm surge at a given location, everything else being equal, for a specific intensity of hurricane will be higher with each passing year. As a consequence of this, storm surge will penetrate farther inland with each new impact.
- Progressively deeper waters at a specific location will result in faster flow of storm surge and higher waves. In turn, this will result in progressively stronger hydrodynamic pressure and breaking wave impact and consequentially higher external forces exerted on buildings and infrastructure in the coastal region that are impacted by the hazard. This means the potential for damage from such impacts will grow higher in the future as a result of sea level rise.

MULTIDECADAL CYCLES OF TROPICAL CYCLONE ACTIVITY

Cyclogenesis in the north Atlantic basin, which is of interest because this is where tropical cyclones affecting the region where I have conducted the research used as a foundation for this book are generated, oscillates between cycles of high annual activity and cycles of low activity.

Cycles of annual cyclonic activity in the Atlantic basin are driven by a combination of factors including the system of deep and surface currents, which mix and circulate ocean waters, as well as cyclical atmospheric changes over the North Atlantic that affect atmospheric pressure and also the salinity of the water.

It is beyond the scope of this book to provide a scientific discussion of how these various contributing factors drive changes in cyclonic activity in the Atlantic. Suffice it to say that the historical record gives clear evidence of the oscillation between cycles of high annual cyclonic activity lasting from 20 to 30 years and cycles of low annual cyclonic activity lasting from 15 to 20 years.

NOAA's Hurricane Research Division maintains records indicating the Atlantic basin entered a cycle of high annual cyclonic activity around 1995, which continues today. Most every year since 1994, with the exception of 1997, 2006, 2009, and 2014 when El Niño events deterred cyclogenesis, saw annual hurricane seasons above the historical average. Of special notice were the 2005 season that generated 28 named storms, including 15 hurricanes, 7 of them major, and also 1995, 2010, 2011, and 2012 with seasons that generated 19 tropical cyclones each.

So here we are more than 20 years into the current cycle of high annual cyclonic activity in the Atlantic, which appears to be taking yet another pause in 2015 while a strong and strengthening El Niño persits off the Pacific coast of Peru. How much longer will it last? No one knows at this time, but what is important is to consider this North Atlantic oscillation as a recurring natural occurrence and a by-product of

202 Hurricane Mitigation for the Built Environment

natural processes that will contribute to future cyclonic impacts in Florida, the Gulf, the U.S. Atlantic seaboard, the Caribbean and obviously Cancun, the Maya Riviera, and the many other coastal communities in the state of Quintana Roo, Mexico that I have referred to here.

ANTHROPOGENIC FACTORS

Anthropogenic is a fancy term used to refer to that which derives from or relates to human activity. What this means is that we are talking about things and measures that we humans can control, which could in one way or another contribute to, affect, or modify future hurricane impacts in Quintana Roo, Florida, or any other hurricane-vulnerable region that may be of interest.

In thinking about human factors that have the capacity for influencing to one degree or another how the impact of a natural hazard, say a hurricane, may affect a region, a community, a site, or one specific building or structure, it is important to keep in mind that characteristic of vulnerability already discussed here: the *interactive* nature of vulnerability.

Relative to this, let us consider that the vulnerability of a place, be it a whole region, a community, or just one given building, requires two components: a *source* of potential damage, meaning the hazard, and a *receptor* of such potential damage meaning the place or structure impacted by the hazard.

Potential damage results from the interaction between said source and receptor, in other words, from the impact of the hazard. How much damage actually takes place depends as much on the damaging components particular to the hazard as it does on the capacity of the community or building to resist the impact itself.

When considering the impact of a hurricane, we already know that wind and water and flying and floating debris are the main damaging components. We also know the methods and equations for calculating the external forces, the loads, and the said damaging components can apply to a building under specific circumstances. In summary, we have the knowledge and capability for characterizing the impacts and quantifying the external loads generated by the hurricane on the building itself. The types and amount of damage that results depend in large measure on the capacity of the impacted building for sustaining such loads.

A building with a strong well-designed structure, a building envelope protected against debris impacts and capable of sustaining expected pressures, will incur far less damage than another building whose envelope is breached because it lacks adequate protection, resulting in extensive damage to the interior and contents and potentially, even structural failure.

The same statement applies relative to the performance under hurricane conditions of a high-rise hotel built with shallow foundations near the beach and the ocean, when compared to a similar type of hotel built with deep foundations, elevated above the expected levels of storm surge, and sited farther from the water most probably landward of the existing dune. I am confident that, based on the concepts and information of preceding chapters, we are capable of predicting which of these two buildings will perform most effectively while interacting with a hurricane.

Future Impacts

The above comparisons help us identify several factors that are capable of modifying the impact of a hurricane on a site-specific basis. I am referring to the anthropogenic factors mentioned before, including the following:

- Urban planning and land use
- Zoning regulations
- Building location and siting
- Elevation of ground floor slab
- Building design criteria
- Methods and materials of constructions
- Building codes and standards
- Mitigation measures applied to the building and/or the site
- Research and development of building materials and components
- Impact tests
- Emergency plans
- Assessment of vulnerability prior to building design and construction
- Relevant education of building design and construction professionals
- Education of the public
- Hazard alert and warning system

These and other aspects are part of a family of anthropogenic factors that can help us define what kinds of hurricane impacts we will see in the future, during the projected service life of our new building, relative to potential damage.

The challenge in front of us is quite clear. We already know that Cancun, the Maya Riviera, and other coastal locations in Quintana Roo, Mexico, and for that matter in Florida, or the Gulf, are among the most hurricane-vulnerable anywhere. We know quite well what the damaging components, causes of direct damage, of a hurricane are. We have seen with our own eyes the damages, often repeated damage from previous impacts, which a hurricane can generate in any one of these vulnerable communities. Through a dedicated process of assessment and field work, we have identified the main causes of damage and, in many cases, the causality that led to specific results. We are also quite certain that there will be future hurricane impacts in any one of these places we like to call paradise. It has already been said that it is not a question but really a matter of when future impacts will occur.

In the specific case of Cancun, Maya Riviera, Cozumel, and others in the state of Quintana Roo, Mexico hit by Hurricane Wilma, I will venture to say that damage from any future hurricane impact will most probably be an amplified repetition of what we saw in 2005, just as those were in turn an amplified repetition of what took place in 1988 when Hurricane Gilbert devastated the same region, but only if we continue the *business-as-usual* approach without changing anything, and we continue designing and constructing buildings in the same manner we have done up until now, locating our buildings as close to the water and beach as possible. The same exact statement can be made about Florida, North Carolina, Texas, Mississippi, New Jersey, and many other vulnerable coastal regions around the world.

Reducing the potential for damage from future hurricane impacts rests entirely in our hands. We must assess vulnerability on a site-specific basis and incorporate effective mitigation measures during the design phase of every new project we start in one of these vulnerable locations. By the same token, we must practice vulnerability assessment and mitigation as we retrofit or remodel existing buildings, or as we prepare to repair and rebuild those that were damaged by the last hurricane impact.

We must close existing gaps in defenses resulting from anthropogenic factors.

Paradise awaits us, be it Cancun, the Maya Riviera, or Miami Beach, Hollywood Beach, or any one of so many other wonderful and beautiful places—it is there waiting for us. We have the knowledge at hand; it is up to us to take needed actions to make it a *paradise protected!*

13 Hurricane-Resistant Buildings

It is time to ask: what can we conclude from all that has been presented and discussed in all the previous chapters here?

Within the context of the specific region where field studies and research were conducted to validate my theories and methodology for the practice of hurricane mitigation applied to the built environment, and keeping in mind that this is applicable to most other hurricane-vulnerable places in Florida, the Gulf coast, the Caribbean, or elsewhere in the United States and the world, I submit that for me the most important takeaway knowledge includes the following:

- The Mexican Gate to the Caribbean, that is, the state of Quintana Roo, with Cancun, Cozumel, Playa del Carmen, Tulum, Xcaret, Xel-Ha, and so many other wonderful resorts along the Maya Riviera, is also a major economic engine and the main generator of tourism revenue for the country. It is truly a paradise. It is a *vulnerable paradise.*
- Quintana Roo is, and will continue to be, the most hurricane-vulnerable region in Mexico.
- Past hurricane impacts, such as those of Gilbert (1988) and Wilma (2005), in addition to causing extensive damage also left important lessons about how the location of buildings, the materials and methods of construction used, their structural design, and their architecture, have all been determining factors in their performance while interacting with a hurricane, and also in the type and amount of damage sustained during the event. There is much that we can learn from these lessons.
- Concerning the specific region of Cancun and environs, in general, it is clear the emphasis from the start has been the development of new projects and the construction of new buildings and infrastructure to foster and take advantage of the tourism industry. These objectives have been met with great success, but unfortunately without paying much needed and warranted attention to the vulnerability of the place and without taking advantage of opportunities to mitigate the potential for damage from future hurricane impacts.
- An example of this approach is what I witnessed in the aftermath of the disaster caused by Hurricane Wilma when, in general, the priority was how quickly a hotel building could be repaired and put back in operation in order to take advantage of dates and schedules that were pertinent within the international tourism industry. In most cases that I saw, save rare exceptions, this objective was met at the cost of not taking advantage of opportunities to incorporate effective hurricane mitigation measures during the process of

repairs and reconstruction. As a result, most of the hotels and other buildings are as, or even more, vulnerable today, because of unattended hidden damage, than before the impact of Hurricane Wilma. Consequently, the probability is high that repeated or amplified damages to these buildings will occur next time a hurricane pays a visit to the area.

- Despite the destructive impact of Hurricane Gilbert (1988) on pretty much the same region hit by Wilma (2005), the experience of other impacts throughout Quintana Roo in the intervening years, and the damage to the built environment and infrastructure witnessed by all and extensively documented by many, all of the construction and extensive urban development in Cancun and neighboring communities took place without the benefit of an adequate building code. It was not until April 2007 that the municipality of Benito Juarez, where Cancun sits, adopted a new building code that for the first time included wind loads as a basis for establishing design criteria for buildings and infrastructure in the area. In other words, it was this building code of 2007, abrogating the code of 1991, which for the first time recognized hurricanes and the need to address potential impacts by establishing minimum wind design criteria to regulate building construction in this vulnerable place.

- In my opinion, while the Municipality of Benito Juarez Building Code of April 25, 2007 is a welcome step in the right direction, there is an urgent need to support this building code with a program of plan review, permitting, research, testing, and product approval protocols and procedures, as well as project inspection to ensure field implementation of the letter of the law really results in stronger, safer, better-performing buildings and structures under the impact of future hurricanes. Without this suite of collateral, complementary procedures, this building code will lack teeth, remaining a collection of printed pages. Also needed is a well-defined protocol and procedure for proposing and adopting changes to the building code, preferably a process that includes proper examination and debate of the technical merits of a specific proposed change before it may be recommended for approval and subsequent adoption by resolution of the legislative authorities of the municipality. Relative to this, in my opinion, the testing protocols and product approval regulations established for the High Velocity Hurricane Zone (HVHZ) of the Florida Building Code (FBC), and the procedures for proposing, reviewing, recommending, and adopting changes to the FBC are quite effective and would constitute an excellent model to emulate not only in the Municipality of Benito Juarez but elsewhere in Quintana Roo and other hurricane-vulnerable regions.

- Beyond these efforts in Benito Juarez, I am not aware of similar codes or norms being adopted in other coastal jurisdictions in Quintana Roo, even though I have information from various professional collegiate associations of engineers and architects discussing this issue and addressing it in some fashion by way of workshops and conferences. But as of 2014, there is no statewide building code in Quintana Roo, and most municipalities outside of Benito Juarez have not adopted a building code requiring hurricane wind loads as a basis for establishing design criteria. It is clear however that much remains to be done in Quintana Roo and other hurricane-vulnerable area in Mexico, both in the Gulf and the Pacific in terms of reducing the potential for damage to buildings from recurring hurricane impacts.

- In regard to this specific building code, speaking of the Municipality of Benito Juarez, it is my opinion that most of those who participated in the drafting of it or who were involved in its adoption by resolution of the Municipal Council view it as a stand-alone end-product in itself, as a solution, and not as the absolute minimum requirements for the design and construction of buildings established by law in this jurisdiction that it really is. In my opinion, much remains to be done in terms of educating building design and construction professionals to recognize that having a building code is just the initial step, that it is really up to each involved professional whether individually or as a team to assess in each case what the site-specific vulnerability is for a new project, and what design criteria relative to the structure and form of a building beyond the minimum requirements of the code may be necessary to mitigate the expected impacts of wind and water from future hurricanes, during the projected service life of the new building.
- There are natural processes and hazards that are beyond our control, such as a hurricane that is generated and hits our community. On the other hand, there are also actions and factors that we can control, such as the design criteria we use for the construction of a new building. What is critically important is for us to recognize that we must learn from what is beyond our control, and that we act upon what we can control, all with the objective of reducing and managing our risks.
- Perhaps the most important takeaway is how those in other hurricane-vulnerable communities, say in Florida, Texas, Mississippi, or North Carolina, the Dominican Republic, the Philippines, or elsewhere, view themselves relative to the issues that have been identified here? How many of these other communities lack a building code that addresses wind and water impacts during hurricanes? How many are of the position that once code requirements are met there is nothing else to be done with respect to the design and construction of a new building? How many see the need to practice hurricane mitigation for the protection of life and property, and to reduce the potential for damage to the built environment?

I submit that all of the above "takeaway" points may be synthesized by considering all as an issue of risk. In this regard, we must then view risk as something we can identify, measure, assess, and also manage and mitigate through the practice of risk management.

Risk management involves, at a minimum, the following:

- Identification and assessment of risk
- Defining the level of acceptable risk
- Identification, assessment, and adoption of risk reduction measures
- Administration of available resources to control risk

It is not an objective here to offer an extended dissertation of risk management, but I am specifically interested in discussing what those who are already involved or merely interested in the development of projects in this paradise can do in order to design and construct hurricane-resistant buildings.

I recommend tackling this matter of hurricane-resistant buildings from two perspectives: (a) a systemic macro approach and (b) a project-specific approach.

MACRO APPROACH

First, it is always recommended to look at the big picture by using a macro approach to determine what needs to be done at a systemwide level. By system, I refer to the aggregation of regulatory agencies, laws, regulations, norms, and standards that would have the authority to oversee, govern, and regulate the practice of building design and construction in a given jurisdiction.

One of the most important actions to take at a macro level is for competent authorities at the state and municipal level to work together in the drafting and adoption of an *effective* building code and norms to regulate, with legal authority, all activities related to the design and construction of buildings and other structures be resistant to hurricanes. The Municipality of Benito Juarez took this initial systemwide step when it enacted its building code with wind provisions in April 2007. The state of Florida mandated counties and municipalities to adopt and enforce a building code (one of four recognized by the state) in the 1970s, and in 1998 enacted a law establishing the Florida Building Commission, which drafted a single statewide building code, the FBC, enacted into law in 2001. The FBC is currently in its fourth edition, that of 2010, which became effective as of July 1, 2012 and is based on the International Building Code and continues to incorporate the strongest antihurricane (wind) provisions in the country for what is known as the High Velocity Hurricane Zone (HVHZ) mandatory for Miami-Dade and Broward counties, but also used voluntarily by other jurisdictions or on a case-by-case basis elsewhere throughout the state.

Speaking of building codes, the word *effective* must be emphasized. Regardless of whether the specific building code in a jurisdiction is prescriptive or performance-based, it must be one central piece in a suite of components that will ensure the code is a live and effective instrument toward the objective of regulating building design and construction to address expected impacts of known hazards. In our specific case, we want a code that incorporates *antihurricane* criteria for building design and construction. Toward the effectiveness of the code, it is very important to consider having in place certified and approved infrastructure and protocols for testing materials and systems of construction to ensure and certify they meet minimum criteria of performance under expected combination of loads. Collaterally with such infrastructure, there is a need for a required official and certified system of product and approval to ensure that only those building products and systems meeting established minimum requirements may be used in actual construction. In addition to the above in pursuit of effectiveness, it is critically important to implement programs of applied research involving field studies to calibrate criteria and protocols used in testing laboratories. By verifying how a particular building material or system performs under known conditions in the field, which may be impossible to replicate exactly in a laboratory,

Hurricane-Resistant Buildings

testing protocols may be modified and calibrated to better reflect real expected conditions, allowing design professionals to adjust design criteria accordingly.

Effectiveness of the code will also be maintained by implementing an officially authorized and certified process and methodology for periodic updating and revision of the code, with the main objective of keeping it current with advances in the development of new materials, systems, and methods of construction; advances in design standards; and new scientific data and findings, to reflect progress and changes without losing sight of the need for balance between life safety and the protection of property, the needs of practice of involved professional sectors and of the construction industry in particular, with the need of keeping costs within acceptable levels in terms of expected benefits.

I recommend any hurricane-vulnerable jurisdiction that does not have a building code at all or, if it has one already, a code that incorporates wind design criteria, to give the highest priority to adopting and enforcing such a regulatory instrument. For those jurisdictions that have enacted a building code incorporating wind provisions, but do not yet have any of the other linked supporting components that I have identified above, I strongly recommend they make implementation of such essential infrastructure a high priority.

Communities such as Cancun (Municipality of Benito Juarez) that have already taken the first step by drafting and enacting into law a building code that includes hurricane winds provisions, or those just about to start the whole process from scratch, the good news is there are several rather good examples of these types of building codes and complementary infrastructure and procedures implemented by communities in other countries such as the United States (Florida), Australia, and Canada. I say good news because these existing examples allow Cancun and others embarking in this process to make good and quick progress by "copying the good" or adapting what has already been developed elsewhere. The idea is not to reinvent the wheel but rather to speed up the entire learning process by taking advantage of the efforts and years of experience already dedicated by others to the same issues.

Plenty has been said about stepping back and starting by taking a macro look, but before closing this section, I extend an invitation to my colleagues in the fields of building design and construction, vulnerability assessment, hazard mitigation and adaptation, resilience and sustainability, and emergency management to take into account that it takes a joint collaborative and multidisciplinary effort between the public and private sectors to create a hurricane-resistant, built environment and a resilient community. Toward that end, I urge those in the private sector to take a proactive role, in collaboration with state and local governments, to promote development and adoption of building code norms and prescriptive methods to address hurricane hazards, as well as the development and implementation of the building code support infrastructure that is so necessary.

PROJECT-SPECIFIC APPROACH

Against the above background of the "big picture," the complementary perspective focuses on specific design and construction criteria that are critical to the hurricane resistivity of individual buildings and structures to expected impacts that will often exceed minimum design criteria based on code requirements, and which every design professional and project director must carefully assess and incorporate in their practice above and beyond the minimum code requirements or even in the absence of an established building code.

I want to make this loud and clear: The knowledge required to design and build hurricane-resistant buildings already exists and is available to all; consequently, there is no need to wait for the adoption of a pertinent and relevant building code addressing hurricane hazards. Project directors and building design professionals practicing in hurricane-vulnerable communities can and must, as a matter of professional responsibility, incorporate criteria based on such available knowledge in every project they tackle from this point forward. By doing this, these professionals will make an important and much-needed contribution to mitigating the potential for damage to buildings and infrastructure from future hurricane impacts.

Even before discussing specific design criteria to produce hurricane-resistant buildings, I believe it is essential to carefully consider each of the following concepts:

- Beyond the aggregation of materials and components, a building must be considered as an interactive system of subsystems and components that behaves as a whole.
- Even more important than knowing how a structure of building remains standing is to know what factors may contribute to damaging it or to causing it to fail.
- The capacity of a building to resist external loads depends on the structural integrity of its materials and components, the connections between components, and anchoring methods.
- The foundation of a building must interact (work with) the ground and not just rest on it.
- Investing in the redundancy of systems and extra structural capacity when constructing a new building will return benefits that are several-fold the cost, in terms of damage avoided during future interactions with hurricanes.
- In addition to structural capacity, the shape and proportions, the form, of a building are important contributors to its hurricane resistivity.
- The shape, continuity, and the use of effective flow modifiers in the building envelope, as well as the materials, systems, and connections used in its construction, are critically important factors in the mitigation of potential damage from hurricane impacts.
- Building codes establish the minimum requirements to be met when designing and constructing a building. However, only the professional criteria of architects and engineers can define how resistant a building will be to the expected impact of hurricanes, by establishing criteria that will in most cases exceed said minimum requirements.
- Architectural and structural design criteria will define the capacity of a building to resist hurricanes, but it is the execution during the construction process that really ensures that such hurricane-resistant conditions will be achieved. In this regard, jobsite inspections to ensure strict adherence

Hurricane-Resistant Buildings 211

to plans and specifications as well as quality of construction are critically important and absolutely needed.

- Ideally, hurricane mitigation criteria must be incorporated during the design phase of a new building, as this is the most practical and cost-effective way to do so. But it is also feasible and recommended to incorporate hazard mitigation criteria for the benefit of existing buildings through a process of retrofitting or building rehabilitation. In this regard, the process of repair and reconstruction of buildings that have been damaged during a hurricane must be viewed as an ideal opportunity for the implementation of mitigation measures in a cost-effective manner.
- When incorporating hurricane-resistant measures during the design phase of a new projected building or during the rehabilitation, retrofitting, repair, or reconstruction of an already-existing building, there is a need to consider the matter of cost. Regarding this, it is critically important that all of those involved in the project, from design professionals to project managers and owners, consider costs in terms of the benefits to be derived from implementing such hurricane mitigation measures. To this end, the process of *benefit–cost analysis* must become an obligatory tool when considering these kinds of projects.
- Beyond protecting the building and reducing potential damages to it, other benefits to consider for purposes of benefit–cost analysis must also include protection of life, prevention of injury, protection of goods and property sheltered by the building, as well as continuity of function and the capacity for resuming operations as soon as possible after the hazard event.

Taking all of the above into account, as well as those aspects discussed in Chapter 5, let us now focus on those specific factors that will contribute toward hurricane-resistant buildings. In doing so, we must keep in mind that any one and all of the points put on the table for consideration are, in general, applicable to any hurricane-vulnerable building, but it is only through a building and site-specific study supplemented by wind tunnel studies, and research and testing when needed, that we can determine what and how the expected hurricane impacts will affect a building, and what design criteria and specific mitigation measures will be most effective in reducing the potential for damage.

SHAPE FACTOR

We have previously discussed how the shape of the building, its wind silhouette, and design of the envelope have a direct effect on the magnitude and characteristics of wind pressures acting on the building during a hurricane, as well as on the magnitude of resulting loads transferred to the main wind-force resisting system, the rest of the structure and foundations, and to components and cladding. Consequently, in terms of hurricane resistance, it is critical that design professionals and client owners, or project developers, consider the benefits of modifying the shape for optimum performance of the entire building under hurricane conditions. Research and testing, wind tunnel studies, and actual design and construction have shown how various

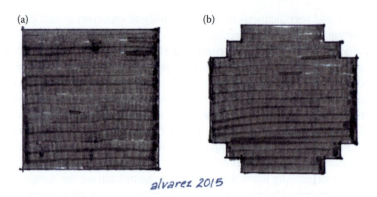

FIGURE 13.1 Schematic illustration of how the wind silhouette of a bluff body (a) can be softened by using stepped corners (b), which will promote a more streamlined flow of wind around the body. Both cross sections have the same area. This technique has been used effectively in buildings to reduce loading conditions on components and cladding and the structure during hurricanes.

shape strategies, such as softening of corners, using tapering, setbacks, varying cross sections, and twisting the building profile with height above ground and orientation, or the use of spoilers and porosity, have all proven effective in reducing excitation along surfaces, as well as extremes in pressures and loads and other effects such as overturning moments, torsion, and vortex shedding, which are root causes of potential damage to buildings during hurricanes (Figures 13.1 through 13.3).

Project owners and developers will do well to be informed and knowledgeable about the importance of shape relative to the performance of the building under hurricane conditions and the reduction of potential damages and to ask their design teams to give careful consideration to both shape and structure in the design of the building.

FOUNDATION

The foundation, the lowest load-bearing component of the structure of a building, fulfills two critically important functions:

1. The foundation *anchors* the building to the ground where it is built.
2. The foundation must resist the weight of the building and its contents plus other loads applied to it by its occupants and by external factors, to then transfer the same to the ground.

To function and perform effectively, the foundation must meet the following criteria: structural capacity and overcapacity to resist the maximum combination of dead, live, and environmental loads with a desired safety margin; redundancy to be able to continue performing safely in the event of failure of some individual component; and capability for interacting effectively with ground.

Hurricane-Resistant Buildings 213

FIGURE 13.2 A real-life example of the benefits of porosity in building construction. The house in the picture is located in Mahahual, in the state of Quintana Roo, Mexico, where it was impacted by Hurricane Dean (2007). The walls are reinforced masonry, and the openings were protected by solid wood doors and shutters. Despite being hit by a major hurricane, the house suffered little damage. The thatched roof, made of palm fronds, is rather porous and it allowed the wind to flow through, helping balance internal and external pressures and reducing the loads acting on the house. Some of the roof covering was lost, but other than that, the house suffered only cosmetic damage outside and no damage to the interior and contents.

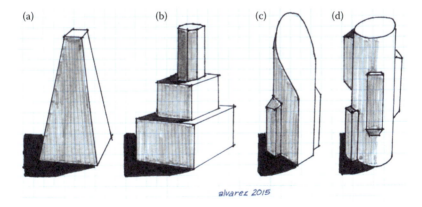

FIGURE 13.3 Figure illustrating different "shape factor" techniques used in tall buildings to manage wind flow, reduce loads, and improve performance while interacting with the wind. Tapering (a) has shown to be effective in reducing loads and turbulence of the flow; a combination of step-back and changes in cross section (b) with elevation offers a reduced profile and more streamlined shape to the wind; twisting of the building (c) to present different profiles with orientation and elevation has proven quite effective in improving wind flow around the building; and the use of building sections projecting beyond the surface (d) acting as "spoilers" also helps improve wind flow and reduce turbulence.

The only proven way to calculate the load-bearing capacity of the ground and determine how it will interact with the foundation to absorb loads transferred by this path is to conduct a site-specific soil study based on physical laboratory tests of actual samples. Pending the results of such studies and tests for a given specific building, and speaking in the most general of terms, we may assume that, except in rare cases of deep rocky soils, most coastal regions where sandy beaches prevail such as those discussed in this book in Cancun, in Florida, along the Gulf coast, and so many other hurricane-vulnerable regions, have sedimentary, sandy upper soil layers with minimal load-bearing capacity.

Also related to the load-bearing capacity of local soils, it is important to note that the water table, and in some cases, caverns and precursors to sink holes, such as are seen throughout the state of Quintana Roo and in Florida, are rather close to the surface, making the upper soil layers in some locations inadequate to resist the loads associated with most buildings.

In order to compensate for these weaknesses of local upper soils, and to ensure the foundation of a building will interact with layers possessing enough structural capacity to resist specific design–load combinations, it is necessary to use deep structural members, such as piles or deep footings reaching down to deep soil layers, as supports to anchor foundation members. This method of foundation construction is rather effective in resisting and transferring loads from building to ground while ensuring overall structural integrity, even in cases where soil erosion and undermining is caused by storm surge generated by a hurricane.

During field visits in Cancun and surrounding areas after Hurricane Gilbert (1988) and Hurricane Wilma (2005), I saw examples of buildings sustaining serious structural damage after their foundations had been undermined by storm surge and erosion. Without exception, foundations of these damaged buildings were rather shallow or consisted of floating concrete slabs basically at rest on superficial ground layers. Clearly, these foundations were totally inadequate to perform under forces generated by what should have been expected impacts. I do not know how prevalent the use of such shallow foundations was at the time or continues to be in that region, but in any case, such design and building practices are totally inadequate for hurricane-resistant construction in the coastal region.

Of critical importance is how the foundation is connected to the rest of the main structure of the building. It is such a connection that ensures an effective load path for the transfer of loads all the way from the highest points of the building to the ground that supports it. This specific main structure–foundation connection and all other structural connections in the building, including connection between components and cladding and the main wind-force resisting system, are of critical importance for hurricane-resistant construction, meriting the utmost careful attention during the design phase and the construction process.

Perhaps the most critical topic regarding the foundation of buildings located in the coastal region of hurricane-vulnerable areas is the corrosion of reinforcement in concrete that can lead to structural failure. This problem will become worse with time as sea level rise will continue to increase the exposure of reinforced concrete structures to salt water. Given this current and growing problem, if the objective is to achieve hurricane-resistant buildings, we must pay special attention to the hazards

Hurricane-Resistant Buildings

of storm surge, coastal inundation, salt water infiltration, and wave action, to how these can contribute to the problem of corrosion of reinforcement in concrete, and to what measures may be effective to mitigate the potential for damage caused by this problem.

Under normal conditions, reinforcement in concrete is protected from corrosion by the high alkalinity of the cementitious matrix of the concrete, which creates a protective oxide layer around the reinforcing steel. But on the other hand, concrete is porous and permeable to moisture, which means water can penetrate concrete. Moisture penetration increases when reinforced concrete is exposed to water, wave action, and flooding or storm surge. In a marine environment, such as we find in all the paradises in Florida, Cancun, and others we have alluded to in this book, moisture penetration carries the added factor of chlorides, in salt water getting into the concrete by a variety of mechanisms, such as permeation and capillary action. Reinforcing steel will start to corrode in contact with chloride, and, as we all know, the rust that is the by-product of corrosion occupies more space than the original material, causing the corroded reinforcement to generate an expansion force pushing on the concrete surrounding the rebars. Depending on a number of factors, principally how thick the concrete cover over the rebars is, cracks will develop in the concrete and eventually propagate and become visible first as small cracks on the surface of the concrete, and eventually as large cracks usually accompanied by heavy rust stain. Propagation of large cracks may eventually lead to spalling, a process where chunks of concrete are broken off the surface of the concrete member. While chloride-induced corrosion of the reinforcing steel is the worst example of this problem, it is also important to consider that corrosion can also be induced by contact of the concrete with the atmosphere, especially in locations where moisture penetration of the concrete is increased due to local environmental conditions, which can lead to carbonation-induced corrosion as CO_2 in the air penetrates the concrete and reacts with the reinforcing steel. Clearly, the possibility of carbonation-induced corrosion increases in a moist marine environment and will increase as the concentration of CO_2 also increases.

Here, we have a combination of problems for the reinforced concrete foundation of our buildings. The first problem is the possibility of corrosion of the reinforcing steel in the concrete, which is a really bad thing. Then we have the aggressiveness of the marine environment of the coastal region, where our hotels, other buildings, and important infrastructure are or will be located. A third problem is that climate change is now exacerbating and will continue to exacerbate the problem in two ways: by the increase in sea level generating salt water intrusion farther inland in contact with building foundations and by contributing to increased levels of storm surge and breaking waves during hurricanes that also increase the exposure of the buildings to the corrosive effects of chloride. Lastly, the concentration of carbon dioxide in the atmosphere, a driver of global warming, is continuing to increase, creating a more aggressive environment to contribute to carbonation-induced corrosion.

What a dilemma we have! As urban centers continue to grow along the coastlines of Florida, the Carolinas, the Gulf, Cancun, and in many other paradises around the world, there is a high probability that many existing buildings may already have foundations compromised by corrosion, affecting their life cycles. But these are the places where so many people want to be and so many tourists want to visit. These are the places where entrepreneurs and developers would like to build so many new buildings. Should we stop building in these locations? Should we stop visiting these wonderful places? Do we need to start retreating? What can we do with existing buildings?

Clearly, the threat is real and the problem complex. Mitigating potential damage to existing buildings will require a study that is beyond the scope of this book, but which must be included in any regional assessment of vulnerability in these locations. In the case of new buildings, there are several mitigation measures project owners, developers, and design professionals need to consider during the design process:

- Pay close attention to the type of cement used for the concrete mix, especially regarding the types of admixtures that are commonly used nowadays to increase the strength and workability of the concrete, as some of them (i.e., fly ash, ground granulated blast-furnace slag, or ggbs), which tend to have higher rates of carbonation, would contribute to corrosion.
- Tests and practice have shown that resistance to chloride increases with reduction of porosity in the concrete. Reduced porosity is a characteristic of high-strength concrete. The use of higher-strength concrete is recommended.
- Use surface protection in the form of impermeable or permeable coatings to prevent or reduce penetration of salt water. Consider using hydrophobic surface coating to repel salt water as another level of protection.
- Increase the concrete cover over the reinforcement, as this has proven effective in reducing cracking and propagation of cracks once they appear.
- Use glass-reinforced formwork, or other similarly impermeable formwork, to cast the concrete and leave in place permanently to provide a barrier to salt water and chloride penetration.
- Use corrosion-resistant reinforcement (CRR) rather than regular steel rebar (a.k.a. black rebar). There are numerous options available, ranging from epoxy-coated steel, hot-dip galvanized, double-coated thermally bonded steel, to new alloys and composite materials used in the manufacture of glass fiber and basal fiber-reinforced polymer rebars, and stainless-steel rebars. Caution in choosing the specific type of CRR is urged regarding this specific recommendation as the performance, handling and fabrication conditions, bonding to concrete characteristics, design life, life cycle cost, and other factors differ considerably among all the available options. What appears to be clear is that stainless steel, other alloys, especially using chromium and low carbon, and now composite materials, offer several advantages over coated materials. On this specific topic, it is highly recommended for design professionals to pay careful attention to standards for the use and performance of the various CRRs mainly established by the American Society for Testing Materials (ASTM) and the Concrete Reinforcing Steel Institute (CRSI), as these should prove quite helpful when comparing and selecting materials.

Hurricane-Resistant Buildings

STRUCTURE

The structure is to a building what the skeleton is to the human body. The main functions of the building structure are the following:

1. Resist, with an ample margin of safety, the combination of loads caused by the weight of the building, its contents, and occupants, plus external forces generated by environmental factors (wind, water, rain, flying or floating debris, seismic events, etc.) acting on the building.
2. Support and connect all building components (roof, exterior walls, components and cladding, interior partitions, electrical, plumbing and HVAC infrastructure, etc.) to the main load-bearing system and the overall assembly to the foundation.
3. Transfer all building load combinations to the foundation and then the ground.

The effective performance of the building structure must absolutely start with the use of realistic, factually based, design criteria regarding expected load combinations. For example, if we are designing a building in a coastal region with a historical record of hurricane 3-s wind gusts of 270 kph, it would make no sense using a basic wind speed of only 3-s 220 kph gusts as the design criterion.

Relative to the structure, it is important for project owners and directors to understand that the cost of the structure is really a fraction of the total cost of the building. Depending on several factors, it is not rare to have structures whose cost is less than 10% of the total cost of the building. With this in mind, it should come as no surprise that the cost–benefit ratio of our investment in structural enhancement is rather favorable.

On the topic of favorable cost–benefit for investing in structural enhancement to improve the hurricane resistivity of a building, the following is a real case of a project in which I participated as a hurricane mitigation consultant.

This was a nine-story new wing addition to a major hospital (850+ beds) in Florida, for which I provided vulnerability assessment and hurricane mitigation consulting services. Design criteria for the structure of this building was based on a basic wind speed of 3-s gusts of 192 kph for surface winds at 10 m above ground as required by the applicable building code. While the design criterion for wind loads complied with the building code, it was, in my opinion, inadequate for expected wind loads in the area even when taking into account the 15% safety factor required for hospitals.

I objected to the 192 kph criterion based on the following three factors:

- As recently as the 2004 hurricane season, three hurricanes had tracked over the area where this building was about to be built with at least one generating sustained winds of 215 kph and 3-s gusts of at least 250 kph, well in excess of the design criteria used for the building.
- This particular building would shelter a critical function as a new patient wing for a hospital facility.
- From a practical and realistic perspective, it is basically impossible to evacuate a large hospital ahead of an approaching hurricane. Except in the most

extreme instances, the preferred option should be to *shelter in place*, which requires the facility to be able to resist the impact of hurricane-generated loads while protecting the occupants, which in this case would include patients and health care staff.

The design phase for this particular building had just recently been completed and excavation and earth-moving work had commenced in preparation for foundation work, as the structural engineer on my team and I were reviewing the plans and design criteria. In view of the timeliness of this process, I suggested to the owner that we still had time to modify the structural design and change the plans to incorporate design criteria that more realistically reflected potential expected hurricane impacts and as a result have a truly hurricane-resistant critical facility.

I recommended using design criteria based on a basic surface wind speed of 3-s gusts of 224 kph, which would be equivalent to a minimum design wind-gust speed of 258 kph at the surface and proportionately and progressively stronger for higher floors and the roof of the building. Despite initial opposition by the engineer of record who claimed it would be too expensive to strengthen the structure on the basis of the new design criteria, the project owner agreed with my recommendation and authorized pertinent changes to the plans and specs. The net result of these actions was a stronger hurricane-resistant building at a total additional cost of just over $390,000, less than 1/2 of 1% of the total project cost of $86.0 million, and, what is even more important, the ability of the hospital to protect its patients and staff without exposing them to the traumatic and dangerous experience of an evacuation.

This anecdotal reference to a real case supports the recommendation that the structure of the building needs to be designed for expected impacts, which often means going beyond the minimum requirements of applicable building codes. It is further recommended to establish structural design criteria on the basis of expected impacts during the projected service life, the design life, of the building. This means the design team must take into account current expected impacts as well as changes in such projected impacts over time. With respect to buildings in the coastal region, this means much higher impacts from storm surge and breaking waves exacerbated by sea level rise, potentially stronger extreme rain events exacerbated by global warming. In summary, if the design life of a new building is 75 years, the structure should be designed for expected impacts taking place during that time span. This requires a forward-looking design paradigm rather than one based on historical data of past impacts.

Redundancy of the structure, meaning its capability to continue performing effectively even in cases where one or more components have been damaged or may have failed under the impact of a hurricane, must be considered a critically important contributor to a hurricane-resistant building. The same can be said about the connections between the various individual structural members.

BUILDING ENVELOPE

The building envelope, which covers all other building components, has two main functions:

Hurricane-Resistant Buildings

1. Protecting the building interior, its contents, and its occupants from the elements, mainly wind and water in the case of hurricanes
2. Sustaining external loads applied to the building by a hazard, such as a hurricane, transmitting them to the building structure

The building envelope consists of the exterior walls and the roof of a building. When it comes to hurricanes, the building envelope must be regarded as the *first line of defense* for the protection of the occupants, contents, and the interior of the building.

Based on many years of experience assessing building damages caused by hurricanes, when it comes to hurricane-resistant buildings, in my opinion, generally used building design methods, pertinent standards, and building codes, whether prescriptive or performance-based, are inadequate relative to expected impacts generated by major hurricanes; also, most design professionals, engineers, and architects focus mainly and almost exclusively on structural strength and only secondarily on the building envelope and architectural design aspects. Often, as a result of these practices, hurricane impacts have left buildings with standing-still functioning structures, but with severe and even catastrophic damage to the interior and contents.

In observing these kinds of hurricane damage, the only logical conclusion is that in each case, while the structure may have been strong enough to perform effectively and survive hurricane impact with little damage, the building envelope was no match for the loads generated by the hurricane.

To avoid these adverse results, it is essential that we consider the building envelope for what it really is, a critically important component of the building that must interact and work jointly with the structure in resisting and transferring loads during hurricanes.

On this topic, it is rather important that we recognize the tremendous effort of the building code process in Florida and elsewhere. Building codes were implemented and made a requirement in Florida in the mid-1970s, when jurisdictions were required to choose from one of four approved codes. The *South Florida Building Code* was the requited norm in Miami-Dade and Broward counties in 1992 when category 5 Hurricane Andrew devastated vast portions of southeast Florida. The disaster that followed triggered a major review of the South Florida Building Code, including new prescriptive methods and design criteria as well as innovative enhancements such as testing protocols to set a foundation for required product approval, the required use of impact-resistant materials to construct or protect all exterior openings, and other aspects, which became official in 1994. These code enhancements also motivated discussions about the need for a statewide building code in Florida, which led to the adoption of the FBC in 2001, incorporating the strong hurricane-related provisions of the South Florida Building Code into a section designated as the HVHZ, which is the strongest standard in the nation when it comes to hurricane-resistant design criteria and building construction. Currently, the FBC coordinates its contents and periodic changes with the *International Building Code Council* (IBCC).

In this regard, we must always remember that the building envelope is as strong as its weakest component.

Let us now discuss the function of each of the components of the building envelope and how each of these may contribute to hurricane-resistant buildings.

Exterior Walls

Together with the roof, exterior walls form the building envelope, that protective "box" around the interior of the building. Exterior walls may be structural, meaning load-bearing components capable of supporting a share of the combination of dead and live loads, or merely architectural or decorative features. Here, it is important to emphasize that all exterior walls, even those considered mainly as architectonic design, must by virtue of their function be load-bearing. So, in reality, all exterior walls must have structural capabilities.

Actual events have shown that the most effective exterior walls in terms of hurricane resistance are those built of solid substantial materials, capable of resisting the impact of flying and floating debris, as well as positive and negative loads exerted by wind pressure, with minimal deflection, or the impact of waves and exterior forces applied by hydrodynamic or hydrostatic pressures. Cast-in-place reinforced concrete walls, or walls made of precast reinforced concrete elements, or of reinforced masonry have in most cases proven rather effective in performing well under these impacts.

Curtain-wall exteriors consisting of large expanses of glass are spectacular, with great visibility filling building interiors with natural light, but are also much less resistant to the impacts of debris and suffer much larger deflection under external loads from wind-velocity pressure than those reinforced concrete and masonry walls described above. In my opinion, and as recent hurricane impacts have shown, glass curtain walls are not the most adequate for use in major hurricane regions such as Florida, the Gulf of Mexico, or Cancun and others in Mexico, even when we take into account advances in the development of impact and wind-pressure-resistant glazing materials that are now available.

Building design professionals should of course feel free to use glass curtain walls in their projects to incorporate the benefits of color, luminosity, and others into the architecture of the building, but in doing so, they must also take into account the limitations of the materials and the cost–benefit aspects of using them in hurricane-vulnerable locations. A rather critical aspect are the limitations of the product approval process, such as it exists in Miami-Dade County, Florida, that certifies the suitability of materials and components for use in such hurricane-vulnerable regions. Both the impact and wind-velocity pressure cycling testing protocols are based on criteria that replicate minimal conditions, which do not reflect much more adverse hazard conditions that can be generated during major hurricanes. While the product approval process ensures that the specified product meets certified minimum criteria of resistance to the impact of flying debris and the cyclic pressures, it is really up to the design professional of record to determine if expected impacts may generate external forces that surpass those used for product approval testing and, if so, take the appropriate course of action to protect the building. Along these lines also, it is important to learn how a product will perform under expected impacts. For example, impact-resistant glass is typically manufactured of two layers of glass with an impact-resistant layer of other material sandwiched in between. The testing protocol allows the exterior glass layer to break under impact, but requires the inner layer to remain intact or at worst develop a minimal number and size of minor breaches

Hurricane-Resistant Buildings

while keeping the inner layer intact. These results ensure that there will be no breach of the envelope of a building, and the interior and contents will remain protected under certain categories of hurricane impacts. What the design professional of record and the project owner must consider is that under real hurricane conditions, such approved glass products will be damaged and will have to be replaced, which introduces an important element of cost to be included in an analysis of cost–benefit.

The strength and effectiveness of connections between exterior walls and the main structure of the building are critically important in determining how well the entire building will perform during hurricanes. It is essential then for architects and engineers to pay careful attention to the design criteria used in all connections.

In the context of all of the above, the main recommendation is for the design team and project owners to make sure the materials and methods used to construct exterior walls, including components and cladding, reflect the realities of expected hazard impacts specific to the site where the building is located for its projected service life (design life), with the clear objective of reducing the potential for damage from recurring impacts.

Roofs

The roof, another component of the building envelope, also protects the interior of the building from the elements, including rain and other forms of precipitation, while also resisting positive and negative pressures applied by the wind, transferring resulting loads to the main structure.

Connections between the roof and its supporting structure are the critical elements that ensure an effective interaction between these two components of a building.

In general, most high-rise hotels and other commercial buildings have flat roofs, which makes them susceptible to the highest negative loads (suction) exerted by wind pressure during hurricanes. This becomes an important aspect to consider when defining design criteria for hurricane-resistant buildings.

When addressing the matter of hurricane-resistant buildings from the perspective of the roof, as a component of the building envelope, the following are several other factors that must be considered:

Roof Covering

Regardless of shape, it is customary to cover roofs with a wide range of roof-covering materials for utilitarian and/or decorative purposes. Some of these roof-covering materials act as insulation against exterior temperature, as waterproofing to keep water out from precipitation, or, as already mentioned, as an architectonic decorative element.

A variety of coverings are generally used for sloped roofs, including clay or ceramic tile, aluminum, galvanized steel, copper, shingles, and other similar materials, which are installed over a waterproofing membrane and a substrate that is attached to a supporting structure. The configuration of the finished roof will vary depending on the type of covering and substrates used. In Cancun and surrounding areas, most of the sloped roofs used clay tile for the covering as well as aluminum sheets, but to a lesser degree.

During the post-Wilma assessment of damage in Cancun, Cozumel, Playa del Carmen, and neighboring resort areas, I recorded a high incidence of damage and failure in sloped roofs with clay tile covering. Building practices in this area used three basic methods to install clay tile coverings on sloped roof. The most prevalent method, which I will characterize as *chemical*, used a full mortar bed to set the tile on a waterproofed reinforced concrete substrate. The second method, used in just a few cases, combined *chemical* and *mechanical* means to install tile. In addition to using mortar, each tile was either nailed to, or tied by, galvanized steel wire to a wooden batten attached to the waterproofed concrete substrate. The third method relied only on mechanical means, either a nail or a tie wire, to attach each tile to a simple wood structure. This last method was generally used for decorative roofs over balconies or terraces. While failure and damage was widespread in clay tile roofs, regardless of the method of installation used, by far the highest extent of damage occurred with roofs using only the mechanical method of attachment.

With the objective of increasing the hurricane resistance of tile roofs, I recommend using a combined chemical–mechanical method of attachment, where in addition to each tile being nailed or tied in place by galvanized wire ties, it is also set in place by using adhesive foam instead of the customary cement mortar bed. Also, the combination of chemical and mechanical means of anchoring for each tile adds redundancy to the complete installation, which enhances performance under hurricane conditions. I would recommend preferably using adhesive foam for tile installation, which proved during the passage of Hurricane Wilma through South Florida in October 2005 to be far superior to cement mortar in terms of adhesive strength and in providing full embedment for each tile. Regarding methods of installation, I submit that more applied research and testing is needed to enhance the performance of ridges and hips in tile roofs. I base this recommendation on the damage to these specific tile roof components that I observed in the aftermath of several hurricanes in Florida, the Gulf of Mexico, and Quintana Roo, Mexico from 1988 through 2005, which showed these to be most susceptible to damage under hurricane conditions. In my opinion, it is clear that improved methods for constructing tile roof ridges and hips must be developed in order to enhance performance under hurricane impacts.

Most hotels, timeshares, condominiums, and other commercial buildings in Cancun and other resorts in the area, as well as in Florida and most other international tourism destinations, have flat roofs. In the specific case of Cancun and other resorts in the region, save for a couple of exceptions, most of the flat roofs consist of a reinforced concrete slab supported by reinforced concrete structures covered by a variety of waterproofing materials, from elastomeric membranes to specialty coatings (paints). In a few cases, where the roof of a portion of the building also serves as an exterior space, a terrace, for adjacent rooms or public areas, covering materials include ceramic floor tile or pavers installed on the waterproofed reinforced concrete substrate.

In most cases, these flat roofs and coverings performed effectively under the impact of Hurricane Wilma in 2005. Damage to the roof covering could be attributed to a few root causes, such as use of single covering membrane that could not sustain the negative pressures (uplift) generated by hurricane winds; too small of an overlap

Hurricane-Resistant Buildings

between adjacent strips of membrane, resulting in tears along the seams and water penetration; or physical damage caused by dislodged roof-mounted equipment or by windborne debris causing tears on the covering membrane, which lead to further damage.

During our field inspections, it became clear that the damage to the covering and the flat roof itself was much more severe in cases of roofs supported by metal structures than for coverings installed on a substrate consisting of a reinforced concrete slab.

Based on the observed failure of roof covering, the mode of damage to flat roofs in the Cancun area when compared to flat roof construction practices commonly used in South Florida, I recommend changes be made in the method of construction and materials used in Cancun and other resorts in Quintana Roo, to enhance the performance of flat-roof covering and of the flat roof themselves under hurricane impacts. Recommended changes include the following: using multilayer membrane roof covering, including two separate waterproofing membranes (moisture barriers), installed transversally with respect to each other, to provide redundancy; increasing the overlap between adjacent strips of membranes; conducting field uplift tests on newly installed roofs, after a prudent period to allow for proper curing, to verify the adhesive strength to hold the assembly in place under expected negative pressures; providing redundancy and a safety margin in drainage capacity through a combination of in-the-field roof drains and perimeter scuppers or rain spouts; providing structural points of attachment to anchor all roof-mounted equipment to prevent it from being dislodged; and causing damage to the roof under hurricane forces.

In summary, when it comes to roof coverings, whether for sloped or flat roofs, and at a risk of sounding repetitive, everything hinges on the strength of anchors and connections and on built-in redundancy, to ensure effective performance and a reduction of potential damage when the building interacts with a hurricane.

Parapets

Many flat roofs are built with parapets around their perimeter. These parapets fulfill two basic functions: to serve as an architectonic device to hide roof-installed equipment and to provide a controlled method for evacuating rain falling on the roof.

Parapets may also fulfill a third function: providing protection from wind loads to roof-mounted equipment, noting that such protective capability would depend on the type and size of the parapet.

For example, a low parapet 50 cm or less in height would offer very little protection from wind loads to roof-mounted equipment. But a high parapet, say 2–3 m in height, would offer significantly more protection for equipment and infrastructure on the roof, but creates potential structural problems under wind pressures that will need to be addressed to ensure effective performance under the impact of the hazard. To illustrate, consider a 2-m-high reinforced masonry parapet supported by reinforced concrete structural members that would shield roof-mounted equipment and infrastructure from wind and the impact of windborne debris. Structurally, this parapet cantilevers above the building, where wind pressures are the strongest, acting as a sail catching a lot of wind because of its large surface area. It is easy to visualize the tremendous total external loads this parapet would sustain during a hurricane. If this parapet lacks buttresses or other structural bracing, there is a high probability that it may suffer damage under the effects of wind pressures on its surfaces. In fact, I have documented several cases of parapet failure in South Florida due to the coincidence of conditions just described above.

To benefit from the protection that can be provided by a high parapet while also reducing the potential for structural damage, I recommend using an approach that has proven effective in Florida: build a semiopen rather than a solid high parapet braced by structural members for additional support against lateral loads. A semiopen parapet takes advantage of the concept of porosity to present less surface area to the wind and reduce loads transferred to the main structure, dampening the force of the wind flowing through it and resulting in much smaller wind loads on the roof-mounted equipment and infrastructure. The net result of this method of parapet construction is a reduction in the potential for damage to the parapet itself, and to the equipment and infrastructure behind it on the roof top, in other words: mitigation!

Roof-Mounted Equipment

It is common for buildings in tropical tourism resorts to depend on air conditioning and ventilation equipment to regulate the interior climate for the comfort of their guests and occupants. It is a common practice, in Florida, Cancun, and almost everywhere else, to use the roof to install a wide range of equipment for these purposes. In addition, in Cancun and other destinations, it is also common for solar heaters, photovoltaic cells, and water storage tanks to be installed on roofs.

In this respect, it is important to be reminded that wind speed increases with elevation above the ground, and that wind pressure increases in direct proportion to the square of the wind velocity. What this means is that wind forces will be strongest at the highest point of a building. Consequently, roof-mounted equipment and infrastructure will be impacted by some of the most damaging wind effects sustained by a building during a hurricane (Figure 13.4).

In view of this, the apparent lack of attention paid to the installation of roof-mounted equipment is always puzzling. In case after case, in the aftermath of hurricanes in Florida, Mississippi, Alabama, Quintana Roo, and in other places, I have documented countless examples of roof-mounted equipment lacking adequate anchoring or tie-downs. The results, as have been documented in this book, are damaged and dislodged equipment, damaged roofs, water penetration, a breach of the envelope, and even structural roof damage, all caused mainly by the lack of attention to the installation and anchoring of roof-mounted equipment.

Toward the objective of reducing potential damage to roof-mounted equipment, here are some recommendations:

- Anchor support frames and bases for roof-mounted equipment directly to the structure of the building, not the roof covering or substrate.
- Design anchoring devices and connections between pieces of equipment and their supports on the basis of expected wind pressures plus a healthy

Hurricane-Resistant Buildings

FIGURE 13.4 Example of poorly anchored roof-mounted equipment atop a multistory building in the coastal region, which in addition shows evidence of corrosion. The potential for damage under hurricane conditions is high in this case.

safety margin, keeping in mind the exposure of the building and the height of the installation area above ground.
- Reinforce and supplement the attachment of pieces of equipment to their supporting frames or bases by using additional means of tie-down, such as galvanized or stainless-steel cables, galvanized sheet steel straps, or industrial-strength fabric straps equipped with tensing mechanisms, placed over a piece of equipment and connected to anchoring devices attached to the building structure. The performance effectiveness of this tie-down system has been amply demonstrated during hurricanes in Florida. The tensile strength of the restraining devices is critical as is the angle at which they go from their anchoring points over the piece of equipment, which should be between 30° and 45°. A structural engineer must design and specify these tie-downs based on-site-specific parameters.
- Shield the area where roof-mounted equipment is installed, or the entire roof with a porous wall or parapet supported and braced by structural elements designed for the expected wind pressures at the specific elevation above ground, to protect the equipment from potential impacts of wind-borne debris (Figure 13.5).

Roof Drainage

The roof is the main barrier keeping rain out of the building. The roof fulfills this function by incorporating waterproofing and moisture barriers in its construction,

FIGURE 13.5 Illustration of a good example of the use of a porous and braced high parapet to protect roof-mounted equipment.

a gravity drainage system that may include several components, and by using sloping fields to move water toward points of water evacuation via the drainage system.

The effectiveness of the drainage system is a critical factor in the case of flat roofs, especially those surrounded by a parapet. In this regard, consider that during extreme rain events when the rainfall may reach or surpass 100–120 mm/h, it is entirely possible for the rate of precipitation to exceed the total drainage capacity of the entire roof, allowing water to pond and build up, generating a substantial live load, which may in some cases exceed the design capacity for the roof and its supporting structure.

To illustrate, take a flat roof with a total area of 1000 square meters surrounded by a parapet. It is entirely possible for a torrential rain event such as described above to overwhelm the installed drainage capacity causing water to rapidly accumulate to a depth of 30–50 mm or more. A simple calculation shows that for every 10 mm of water depth, an additional live load of 10 metric tons would be generated, which means we could have anywhere from 10 to 50 kg per square meter of additional load over the entire roof, which will be transferred by the roof to the building structure and all the way down to the foundations and the ground. Picture this occurring during a hurricane simultaneously and in combination with loads generated by wind pressures. Will the existing structure, as designed, be capable of sustaining these additional loads generated by accumulated rain water without failure?

To address events and overloads such as I have just described, and toward the objective of hurricane-resistant buildings, I recommend the following:

- Building design professionals as well as project owners and developers must pay the same level of careful and dedicated attention to the issue of roof drainage that is given to other critical design aspects of the project.

Hurricane-Resistant Buildings 227

- Design the total drainage capacity of a roof-drainage system to include the additional loads that may be generated by expected extreme rain events that may occur during the projected service life of the building.
- Consider that global warming is increasing the capacity of the atmosphere for retaining moisture, which in turn leads to more frequent extreme rain events in some regions that will gradually grow worse in the future. Because of this, design criteria for roof drainage must take into account not only historical local rain data but also that which could be expected in the future during the projected service life of the building.
- Incorporate additional loads generated by the accumulation of water on a flat roof during extreme rain events, into the combination of loads used to establish design criteria for the structure of the building.

Exterior Openings

All building envelopes require openings for means of access and egress, to allow daylight in, as means of natural ventilation, to evacuate smoke, and others reasons.

In hotels and other buildings in tourist resorts, large windows and expanses of glass are basically a requirement for guests and visitors to enjoy the spectacular views of the sand, the ocean, and the sun.

The benefits of having such glazed openings are not incompatible with the design of hurricane-resistant buildings, as long as design professionals, project owners, and developers implement all necessary measures to preserve the integrity of the building envelope during interaction with hurricanes. All exterior openings must be designed to perform without failing under the cyclic loading of wind pressures, and to resist the impact of windborne debris, preventing breaching of the envelope. Regarding this, it is encouraging to see how much progress industry continues to make by way of research and development in the production of new and stronger materials and systems, including impact-resistant glass, used for hurricane-resistant openings.

Doors

Doors are indispensable components in every building, as means of ingress/egress, to control access, for safety and security, and for privacy. It is important to carefully consider the various kinds of doors that may be installed in a building. In the case of hotels, such as have occupied much of the narrative in this book, we will commonly find double or large single exterior glass doors with a wide range of supporting and operating hardware, including aluminum, stainless steel, nickel, and others, in most public and common areas at ground level and elsewhere. There will be wooden, metal, or fiberglass doors for guest rooms. In guest rooms, we may also find other exterior doors leading from the room to a balcony or terrace. In support areas of the hotel, there will be a need for very large doors, such as roll-down metal doors or grilles, metal doors with ventilation louvers for certain spaces, and doors to provide access to roof areas.

In compliance with life-safety norms, there is also a need for emergency doors to be installed at each level of a multistory hotel to provide access to the exterior of the building at ground level or to fire escape stairs leading to the exterior. Emergency doors cannot be locked by key, but may have a locking mechanism that can be opened by way of panic hardware from the interior of the building. The purpose of these kinds of doors is life safety and evacuation of a building in case of fire or other emergencies. When considering the special functions and requirements associated with emergency doors, or other specialty exterior doors, we must not lose sight of the need for hurricane-resistant construction for the protection of life and property.

My recommendation, when dealing with exterior doors, is that all exterior doors must meet the following criteria:

- All exterior doors must be constructed of impact-resistant materials or be protected by impact-resistant devices, such as hurricane shutters, in order to prevent breaching of the building envelope. Use only doors and devices that have been certified to be impact resistant by an officially designated agency, or which have been tested by a certified testing laboratory under accepted protocols. On this specific point, it must be made clear that under the FBC (Florida Statutes S. 553.73), there is a required product approval process for building product to be used for building construction in the state. Miami-Dade County had a product approval process since 1994 that predates the adoption of the FBC. Products that have been approved under this process receive a "Notice of Approval" or NOA with a unique identifying code.
- All exterior doors must be certified, by an officially recognized agency, to be capable of sustaining expected loads generated by the combination of wind pressure and internal building pressure, and the impact of windborne debris. It takes both the design and materials used in manufacturing the doors and the method of installation, and the use of an external impact-resistant shutter, to ensure effective performance under such loads. In this regard, it is critically important, for project owners and developers, to know that hurricane shutters and other such type of protective devices are designed to protect against the impact of flying debris, but they *do not* protect against wind pressure, so it is possible for an exterior door to be damaged by wind pressure even when protected against impacts by a hurricane shutter.
- At the ground level, or lower levels of a building vulnerable to the impact of storm surge and waves during hurricanes, it is critically important to install exterior doors capable of sustaining the hydrodynamic pressure of the rushing water and the impact of breaking waves or of floating debris, as well as hydrostatic pressure from flooding. When it might not be cost effective to meet such criteria for all exterior doors at specific building levels, a recommended alternative is to install such type of doors only on those spaces, sheltering equipment, and/or functions that are critical for the operation of the facility, such as generator vaults, communication equipment rooms, electrical control and switch gear rooms, mechanical equipment rooms, and others. This ensures the continuity of function of a facility. A word of caution in this regard: when pursuing the recommended alternative, it is essential that where surge-resistant flood doors are installed, the spaces themselves must be protected on all sides and made floodproof. This includes interior walls and doors.

Hurricane-Resistant Buildings

Windows

Windows let natural light into a building, allowing occupants to look outside and enjoy the view while being sheltered from the elements. When windows are operable, they contribute to natural ventilation and may provide means of evacuation in case of fire or other emergency.

Windows are important components of the building envelope. It is recommended that all exterior windows meet the following criteria in order to contribute to hurricane-resistant buildings:

- All exterior windows must be manufactured with impact-resistant materials (both glass and frame) and be installed in a manner that makes the entire assembly resistant to the impact of flying debris, or be protected by impact-resistant protective devices such as hurricane shutters. Both the window assemblies and external protective devices must be certified and have an NOA issued by the pertinent agency in Florida or elsewhere.
- Impact-resistant windows could themselves also be protected by impact-resistant devices, such as hurricane shutters, to provide redundancy and to avoid the need for replacing costly windows when the exterior glass may have been shattered by flying debris during a hurricane event.
- Design criteria for the full window assembly, both glass and frame, must make it strong enough to resist cyclic (positive and negative) loading from wind pressure.
- The method of anchoring and installation of the window assembly must makes it capable of resisting loads generated by wind pressure, ensuring that such loads do not exceed the carrying capacity of any single individual anchoring device.
- Locking mechanism and other security hardware in operable windows must be capable of maintaining the window shut while resisting loads generated by wind pressure.
- For sliding glass (horizontally or vertically), the track must have enough depth and wall thickness (gauge) to prevent the movable portion of the window from being dislodged by wind pressure during hurricanes.
- All exterior windows, whether fixed or operable, must have substantial weather stripping to prevent moisture or water penetration, into the building interior, under the extreme conditions encountered when a building interacts with a hurricane.

Skylights

All skylights, regardless of shape or size, must be treated as windows on the roof and, as such, be evaluated under the same criteria discussed in the previous section.

There is no doubt that skylights are spectacular architectural elements that create impressive effects in bathing interior spaces with natural light. Skylights make it possible to design and build hotels with interior balconies and gardens facing into a central sky-lit space.

In the context of aiming for hurricane-resistant buildings while considering the use of skylights, the following recommendations are appropriate:

- All materials used in the manufacture or construction of a skylight must be certified impact-resistant or protected by certified impact-resistant devices. I do not know of any ready-made, impact-resistant barrier manufactured specifically to protect individual skylights, but there are several certified products in Florida that can be customized as impact-resistant barriers for this purpose. There are several examples of hurricane mitigation projects in Florida, in which I have participated, where skylights of various shapes and sizes were not only protected in this fashion but also performed quite effectively during the passage of Hurricane Wilma through the area in 2005.
- The full skylight assembly, including any supporting structure or anchoring system, must be attached to the structure of the building, not just the roof covering or substrate.
- The full skylight assembly and its method of installation must be designed and constructed to withstand expected forces generated by positive or negative wind pressures during a hurricane event. Since most skylights are ready-made or custom-made devices manufactured by others, it is critically important for the project engineer of record to specify the design criteria to be met or to certify that the assembly as "built-by-others" meets design criteria established for the project. Equally critical for the project engineer-of-record is to either design and specify the method of installation for the skylight assembly, including type of fasteners and fastening schedule, or certify that an installation system specified by others meets the required design criteria for the project.
- In the case of large skylights crowning large interior spaces, which are typically fabricated *in situ* using components manufactured and supplied by others, the safety factor for loading should be increased by the structural engineer, to account for the possibility that a breach of the building envelope at some lower level may allow hurricane winds inside the building, generating a well-distributed positive pressure pushing up on the underside of the skylight combining with possibly negative pressure from above, which will result in a total load exceeding the design criteria for the system leading to damage, and possibly structural failure (Figure 13.6).
- With regard to individual skylights, we must acknowledge the efforts of the industry to meet product approval requirements under the FBC, including the more stringent ones for the HVHZ, which has resulted in the wide range of wind- and impact-resistant skylights that are now available.

Ventilation Components

The tropical and subtropical climates that prevail in South Florida, Quintana Roo, the Caribbean, and many other resort destinations worldwide make air conditioning of hotels and other buildings obligatory for the comfort of guests and occupants.

Hurricane-Resistant Buildings 231

FIGURE 13.6 Example of a large skylight that has been protected by a custom-designed wind and impact-resistant barrier that also allows light to pass through. All materials used in fabricating the barriers have been certified and approved by Miami-Dade County, Florida.

The basic operation of most air conditioning and ventilation systems requires outside air to be inserted into the building for the system to cool it and remove some of its moisture content to then distribute it throughout the building, and at certain prescribed intervals, exchange already "used" conditioned air by exhausting to the exterior for "new" fresh exterior air to be brought in through ad hoc air intakes. The intaking and exhausting requires openings of various kinds and sizes on the roof and through exterior walls requiring duct work through the building envelope. The system often includes exhaust fans to mechanically remove large volumes of air, especially from spaces such as kitchens, cafeterias, bathrooms, laundry rooms, or mechanical and electrical rooms, where installed equipment generates excessive heat.

The ductwork requires a range of covers, from metal grating or louvers for air intake, to ventilation hoods, cowlings for various devices, operable louvers or flaps, and other coverings. We have all seen these devices protruding through or surface mounted on exterior walls and roofs. Some may have also seen, as have I, the extensive damage sustained by such devices under the impact of hurricane winds and flying debris, which has often led to water penetration from rain (Figure 13.7).

Because of the need for these various components and the degree of damage they can sustain under hurricane conditions, it is worrisome that these continue to be manufactured of light-gauge sheet metal held together by a few metal screws or other fasteners that are no match for winds of a tropical cyclone or the impact of flying debris. It is also worrisome to see that in most places, with the possible exception of Southeast Florida, there is little to no effort made to strengthen the methods of installation and anchoring for these devices. This perpetuates the inadequacy of these

FIGURE 13.7 An example of a typical ventilation hood covering ductwork through the wall of a building. This type of device has an elevated propensity to being damaged under hurricane conditions.

pieces of equipment for supporting hurricane wind loads and the potential for failure and damage, including possible breaching of the building envelope (Figure 13.8).

Much remains to be done by way of enhancing and strengthening these components. Toward that end, the following recommendations are offered:

- Project owners and developers need to be aware of the inherent weaknesses of many of these components of an air conditioning and ventilation system and address effective protective measures with building design professionals involved in the project.
- Manufacturers of these products should focus their research and development efforts toward the production of stronger, improved products with enhanced capabilities for sustaining loads and impacts under hurricane conditions.
- Architects and engineers responsible for the design of a building should pay special attention to these building components and design anchoring and tie-down systems as well as barriers to protect against debris impacts, with the goal of improving performance and reducing the potential for damage during hurricane event.

Hurricane-Resistant Buildings

FIGURE 13.8 Another example of the vulnerable ventilation devices already mentioned; these are installed on the roof of the building.

Other Building Envelope Components

Because of their specific use or function in certain buildings, some spaces must be designed and built as semiopen to meet natural ventilation requirements. These include electrical vaults where transformers, switchgear, and electrical panels generate excessive heat, and also elevator machinery rooms, communication equipment rooms, emergency power generator rooms, and other spaces requiring natural ventilation.

The generally accepted practice is to provide these spaces with a specified area of opening to satisfy the required volume of natural ventilation into the room and to outfit these openings with specially designed fixed or operable louvers that allow for the required ventilation into the room (Figure 13.9).

One problem with this practice is that hurricane winds will penetrate these semiopen spaces and affect equipment installed there. Are these pieces of equipment capable of resisting such strong winds without sustaining damage? A second problem has to do with penetration of wind-driven rain into the space and the potential for damage to the equipment inside. This problem can be solved by installing especially designed louvers incorporating slats of a particular cross section and other devices to keep rain out and guide any water collecting in the unit toward the exterior, but such specialty louvers are not widely used. A third problem is the impact of windborne debris on these devices, which are not really designed or tested for such occurrences.

In summary, these semiopen spaces present an important challenge for design professionals, but one that must be addressed head-on even if in a case-by-case basis in order to reduce the potential for the damage described above.

FIGURE 13.9 Photo illustrating typical ventilation louvers installed in a mechanical room atop a multistory building, which unless designed for wind pressure and to keep rain out, and protected against impact, may be damaged and allow wind and rain inside the building.

My main recommendations regarding how to protect such spaces are as follows:

- Install impact-resistant operable louvers that can be shut down during periods of peak wind intensity as part of an emergency plan.
- When specifying fixed ventilation louvers, use the kind that have specially shaped slats designed to keep wind-driven rain out of the interior space, and consider bracing such louvers to increase their resistance to wind forces and the impact of flying debris.
- Provide interior barriers and protective devices inside the space, available space permitting, to protect installed equipment from rain and wind that penetrate the interior.
- Consider designing and installing ad hoc impact-resistant barriers outside louvered openings, making sure the required amount of opening to allow proper ventilation is maintained. This will require calculations by a mechanical engineer.

BUILDING SHAPE AND PROPORTIONS

We have discussed previously (Chapter 5 and earlier in this chapter) how the shape of the building, its wind silhouette if you will, can be used as a tool to mitigate hurricane impacts of a building. The shape of a building both in plan and elevation define in great measure how it will interact with and perform during a hurricane. The project design team, especially the architect of record, together with the building owner, will define the shape and proportions of the final building. It is important then for the project architect and engineer to jointly evaluate all design decisions to ensure

Hurricane-Resistant Buildings 235

these will not lead to characteristics that may contribute to increasing the potential for damage during interaction with a hurricane.

Architects, engineers, and others responsible for the many hotels and other buildings to be built in our paradise of interest, be it Miami, Cancun, or another place, will need to pay special and careful attention to the hurricane vulnerability of the region and the project site, and to what the damage a tropical cyclone may cause when attacking the coastal regions that hold such attraction for all of us. We all need to visualize how the shape and proportions of the planned building you design will affect how it performs while interacting with the wind and the water during a hurricane.

Given the critical importance of learning about the linkage between the shape and proportions of a projected building and its performance under hurricane conditions, a prevalent practice is to conduct wind tunnel studies using scaled models of the proposed building and its vicinity that replicate surface roughness and local topography to obtain data on expected wind pressures and behavior, identify possible problems, and to help establish realistic design criteria for a hurricane-resistant building. Wind tunnel studies are mainly used to assist in the design of tall or special-shape building. In addition, project owners and developers and their design teams would do well by engaging experts in vulnerability assessment and hurricane hazard mitigation into their teams to identify potential weaknesses in a proposed design and recommend hurricane mitigation criteria to be incorporated during the design process.

Regarding the building shape and proportions, the following aspects should be considered during the design phase of a new building.

Slenderness

The ratio between the height of a building and its horizontal cross section determines its *slenderness*. This slenderness may contribute to accentuating the effects of drift, positive and negative forces generated by wind-velocity pressure, and the overturning moment under the force of the wind, which will be reflected mainly in oscillations of and possibly torsional effects on the building under the impact of a hurricane.

Such swaying motion and the accentuation of drift will increase the potential for damage to the building. Given such potentially adverse consequences, it may be best to avoid, to the extent possible, designing tall and narrow (slender) buildings in regions that are vulnerable to major hurricanes.

Continuity of the Building Envelope

We have already discussed how structural continuity is essential to ensuring an orderly transfer of building load combinations from top to bottom to the foundations and the ground. This same principle makes continuity of the building envelope a highly desirable characteristic to ensure an orderly flow of wind around and over the building when it interacts with hurricane winds.

A continuous building envelope is one that covers the entire edifice without major interruptions, or drastic and frequent changes in direction.

A continuous building envelope precludes neither architectural elements or relief changes on the building facades nor the use of stepped corners, porosity, variations in cross section with height, twisting of surfaces with orientation, or using spoilers to modify wind behavior, and mitigate wind effects.

On this topic of continuity of the building envelope, we will do well to remember how topography and related factors, such as surface roughness, exert considerable influence on the wind as it flows over the terrain, increasing turbulence.

This brings to mind my history of an architecture professor in college, who in rather clear terms conveyed to us how the visual appearance of a building, its architectural character, reflects the characteristics of the place, its vulnerability to specific hazards, and its use or function. My professor illustrated these lectures with a vast collection of slides showing, for example, buildings with rather high sloping roofs located in regions of high precipitation; buildings elevated above adjacent terrain or built on stilts and pilings located in flood zones; buildings constructed of solid materials, thick high walls without openings in their lower levels, indicating a purpose of defense against possible attackers; buildings with rather thick walls painted white, with small windows covered by louvers, with living quarters around a central courtyard with a pond or a water fountain, all as protection from a local climate of extreme sun and heat. In summary, the clear message was: *The architecture of a building is a reflection of the environment and vulnerability of its location.* Conversely, *the architecture of buildings located in hurricane-vulnerable regions must clearly reflect such vulnerability, in terms of their shape, proportions, and the character of their envelopes.*

Sails and Wind-Catchers

Earlier (Chapter 5), we addressed the topic of sails and wind-catchers. At this time, I only want to add a couple of comments under the concept of hurricane-resistant buildings.

It is practically impossible to avoid sails in a building. Any exterior wall will catch the wind and the larger its surface area, the larger the wind load will be. By calculating the total wind loads, such sails will sustain and transfer to the main structure of the building, the engineer of record can establish design criteria and the necessary safety margins. From this, we may conclude that sails should not be a problem as long as the building design team recognizes their potential effects under hurricane conditions, and addresses the same by implementing appropriate and effective structural design criteria (Figure 13.10).

There could be problems however, in the case of *unrecognized sails*, or those lacking adequate structural anchoring or connections, or when the sail is a cantilevered wall such as a parapet, or when it comes in the form of something added to an already-existing building. Large advertising signs, tall parapets, or certain kind of tall infrastructure installed or built on the roof of an existing building could easily become an unrecognized sail and a potential contributor to damage under hurricane conditions.

Just as it is impossible not to have sails, wind-catchers should be totally avoidable by paying attention during the design phase of a building. If the shape and building envelope characteristics include wind-catchers, it is because the responsible design professionals included these in their design. They are responsible for such features being there (Figure 13.11).

Design teams as well as project owners and developers would do well to not include wind-catchers while designing buildings in hurricane-vulnerable regions.

Hurricane-Resistant Buildings

FIGURE 13.10 An example of an "unintended sail." The objects shown are metal cabinets housing cellular telephony gear for a communication company renting space atop this roof. These cabinets are attached to a supporting bracket by just two bolts through steel angles welded to their backs. These pieces of equipment are at 40+ m above the ground on a building near the open waters of Tampa Bay, Florida. Because of their exposure, inadequate anchoring, and the fact that they cantilever above the roof acting as "sails," the potential for damage is high.

And, in those cases when due to the function of the building or the absolute necessity for making a dramatic architectonic statement it becomes totally necessary to include a wind-catcher, to thoroughly assess the consequences this may have in the building performance under hurricane conditions, and then address them through sound and effective structural design criteria.

Wind Tunnels

There are two types of wind tunnels (see Chapter 5) in buildings: those that are deliberately included as part of the design of the building by the responsible design team, making them totally avoidable, and those that result from proximity with nearby buildings, which may be avoidable or not, but should in all cases be recognized and addressed in structural terms by those responsible for the building (Figure 13.12).

238 Hurricane Mitigation for the Built Environment

FIGURE 13.11 An example of "wind-catchers." These large parabolic antennas (satellite dishes), which are attached to the roof of this building will "catch" plenty of wind during hurricanes, transferring these loads to the building structure.

FIGURE 13.12 An example of a "wind tunnel" created by design. This building sustained the impact of Hurricane Wilma (2005) in Cancun. Damage to the structure inside the "tunnel" is clear.

Hurricane-Resistant Buildings

The recommendation is to avoid designing wind tunnels in a building to be built in a hurricane-vulnerable region. If possible, avoid creating wind tunnels when a new building is to be constructed near already-existing buildings, as may happen when you add a new wing to an existing building or when you site a new building on a campus where several other buildings already exist. If it proves totally impossible not to create a wind tunnel by proximity between buildings, the design team should recognize the situation and address it by incorporating effective mitigation measures to reduce the potential for damage to both the new and the already-existing buildings, which may result from hurricane winds flowing through such wind tunnel, by taking advantage of wind tunnel studies to model the effects of such wind flow.

INTERNAL INFRASTRUCTURE

The capacity of a building to resist the impact of a hurricane is measured not only in terms of its structure and building envelope, resisting such impact without sustaining major damage, but also in terms of the capacity of the building's internal infrastructure to continue functioning during or in the immediate aftermath of a hurricane event, including one where a breach of the building envelope may have occurred, allowing wind and water inside the building.

The professional team responsible for the design of a new building and the director of plant operations of an existing building must take effective and necessary measures to protect the internal infrastructure of a building and mitigate the potential for damage in case of a breach of the building envelope during a hurricane, making sure the building or facility will maintain an ample degree of functionality during and in the aftermath of a hurricane impact.

Not surprisingly, the same as with other components of a building, effective anchoring, connections, and redundancy are all important factors to consider with respect to the functionality and resiliency of internal infrastructure.

While all internal infrastructure components must be assessed for vulnerability in terms of potential damage from a hurricane impact, I would like to briefly discuss key components of the internal infrastructure in most buildings.

Electrical

No hotel or building can function without electrical energy. For this reason, protecting the entire electrical system of a building, from the point of initial intake and metering, to transforming, switching, and distributing, becomes a high priority both during the design phase and under the drafting of an emergency plan for the facility. Relative to protecting the electrical system, I make the following recommendations:

- To protect against potential damage from storm surge, wave impact, and flooding, all critically essential components of the electrical system, including the main intake point from the utility, transformers, main breakers, and switch gear, must be elevated above the expected worst-case water level. In most cases for buildings located in the coastal region, this will mean installation on a second floor or higher. If we are talking about an existing building, then relocating these critical components to higher levels or retrofitting

existing spaces to make them water tight and resistant to the hydrodynamic pressure generated by storm surge and impact loads from breaking waves, would be alternatives to consider (Figure 13.13).
- In addition, all critical components of the electrical system must be located in spaces protected against the impacts of wind, water, and flying debris during a hurricane.
- The project owner or developer, and the design team when speaking of a new building, or the director of plant operations for an existing building, will need to consider the probability that even if the electrical system of the building is fully protected and capable of maintaining functionality during and in the aftermath of a hurricane, it could very well be that it is the electrical utility that suffers major damage to its transmission and/or distribution systems resulting in the interruption of the public power supply. It is recommended to anticipate such an eventuality by installing emergency power-generating equipment, preferably capable of dual-fuel operation (i.e., natural gas–diesel), with plenty of generating capacity and fuel reserves to

FIGURE 13.13 An example of a second line of mitigation measures. In this particular case, electrical equipment has been elevated about 0.5 m above ground inside an electrical room in a building that has installed surge/flood protective devices.

run all critical services in the building for a minimum of 2 weeks or until the utility service is restored. In support of this preparedness and recovery plan, it is also recommended that the design team and operators of a building protect the fuel supply, and the facility for fuel resupply, against the hazards already mentioned by using the same approach of elevating above a certain levels and protecting against specific expected impacts. Fuel tanks for emergency power generators must be double-hauled and firmly anchored to the ground by way of deep footings and strong points of attachment to prevent damage from floating debris impact, and also to prevent the tank itself from being uplifted from the ground by extreme buoyancy forces generated by fully saturated soil. Additionally, ventilation pipes for these fuel tanks must be high enough to ensure their openings are elevated above expected high water and wave levels. All manifolds and valves used to fill the fuel tanks, and access to these, must also be so elevated and protected against impacts.

- In the case of alternate fuel, such as natural gas or propane gas, for emergency power generators or for other uses in the building, I have two recommendations depending on whether the fuel is stored on-site in tanks that are refilled by tanker trucks, or if it is piped to the site from the gas company. In the case of on-site storage tanks, almost everything that has been recommended for the diesel tanks in terms of the design, strength, method of anchoring to the ground, height of ventilation pipes, etc. also applies here. But, if the gas is piped to the site by the gas company through a distribution system, then the recommendation is to have an alternate source of supply on-site in case the gas company needs to interrupt the supply due to hurricane damage. A recommended alternative, successfully implemented in several hurricane mitigation projects I have been involved in, is to have special fuel-supply staging areas at key location throughout the building outfitted with manifolds and valves that are part of the building's internal gas lines, where a supply of bottled gas would be stored, ready to be used in case of interruption of supply from the utility.
- A final recommendation for enhancing the hurricane-resistant characteristic of the electrical infrastructure is to make sure all electrical outlets and switches on the ground floor are waterproof and elevated much higher than what the normal practice is. All circuits for outlets and switches on the ground floor should be separate and totally independent from those supplying other levels of the building, clearly identified, and disconnected from the power supply at a set time under an activated emergency plan when water impact from an approaching hurricane is expected.

Mechanical

To operate a major hotel or a large multistory commercial building requires a full array of systems and equipment, supporting infrastructure, and continued preventive maintenance. Mechanical systems include boilers, chillers, air handlers, furnaces, air conditioners, condensers, evaporators, cooling towers, refrigeration equipment,

242 Hurricane Mitigation for the Built Environment

water heaters, incinerators, various kinds of pumps, fire-extinguishing systems, conveyors, elevators and lifts, etc.

Typically, much of this mechanical equipment is installed in large mechanical rooms inside the building, while other pieces of equipment are mounted on the roof of the building, and others such as cooling towers for air conditioning, incinerators, or other rather large pieces are installed outside on the grounds around the building.

Toward the objective of a hurricane-resistant building, one that is based on current terminology, we would refer to a *resilient building*, the main purpose relative to all mechanical equipment being to protect it from damage in such a way that it will continue to function during and in the aftermath of a hurricane impact.

To achieve this, the following is recommended:

- Mechanical equipment installed inside the building will be protected to the degree that the building itself has been made hurricane-resistant. However, in view of the possibility of a breach in the building envelope, which would allow wind and/or water inside the mechanical room, a second line of mitigation measures within the space itself is highly recommended. Mounting equipment above the floor level by using elevated mounting frames or concrete pads and elevating all power connections and controls would reduce potential damage from flooding in case of water penetration. These measures could be complemented by the installation of sump pumps and float switches to evacuate water from the room and stop sensitive equipment should water reach a critical level.
- Make sure the air intake for indoor equipment that requires natural ventilation is designed to resist the impact of debris without failing and will also keep wind-driven rain out of the room. If storm surge and waves are a concern, then appropriate external measures, such as dedicated flood walls to protect the air intake, need to be considered.
- For equipment installed outdoors on the grounds of the facility, the approach needs to be the same: elevate above a critical level to avoid water damage from surge, waves, and flooding; elevate fuel and power supplies and controls; and protect against wind and flying debris by installing appropriate impact-resistant barriers around key pieces of equipment. In addition, make sure all infrastructure related to these pieces of equipment, such as pipes, manifolds, valves, fuel supply lines, electrical controls, etc. are equally protected against the impacts of wind, water, and debris.
- These recommendations also apply to mechanical equipment mounted on the roof. At this point, I refer to the discussion of roof-mounted equipment on page 224 of this chapter.
- Beyond the specifics discussed above, one recommendation for the protection of this equipment and the objective of a hurricane-resistant building, especially in regard to continuity of function in the event of a hurricane, is for the director of plant operations to adopt and enforce a strict program of preventive maintenance with emphasis on outdoor equipment installed outdoor in the coastal region where sea water and ocean spray are highly corrosive (Figure 13.14).

FIGURE 13.14 One example of what corrosion can do in a marine environment near the water. In this case, the supports and anchoring devices of a large structure are seriously compromised by erosion and most probably by lack of preventive maintenance. There is a high probability that this structure could suffer serious damage if impacted by wind and surge during a hurricane.

- Corrosion weakens anchors and pieces of equipment themselves, which in turn increases the potential for damage under the impact of a hurricane. A second general recommendation is that all pieces of equipment that are essential for the operability and continuity of function of the facility must be connected to the emergency power supply.

Plumbing

Building owners and developers, and the design team in case of a new building, need to consider the plumbing system as a critical component of infrastructure and take all possible and effective measures to protect it against impacts and external forces during hurricanes. The plumbing system ensures the supply of water for human consumption, sanitation, fire-fighting, and for other purposes, and waste evacuation.

Project owners, developers, and designers will need to accept as a given the possibility that public water and wastewater services may fail and be interrupted, perhaps for extended periods of time, as a consequence of hurricane impact. The high possibility of such interruption of essential services requires the implementation of mitigation measures to ensure the continuity of water supply and the discharge of wastewater, for however long it should take for these public services to be restored.

244 Hurricane Mitigation for the Built Environment

Potable Water

To ensure continuity of supply of potable water for human consumption, food preparation, and hygiene and sanitation, in the event of interruption of the public supply caused by a hurricane, the following is recommended:

- Design, install, and maintain an alternate emergency source of potable water on-site. This could be done by building/installing elevated water storage tanks that could operate by gravity or be assisted by pumps if needed. An alternate method is to have a cistern, usually installed underground or at ground level, to collect rain water. This system will need to be complemented with pumping equipment and filtration devices to ensure the potability of the water and the means for distributing it throughout the building. A cistern is only viable in locations where the amount of annual rainfall is adequate for this purpose.
- Explore the feasibility of drilling a well on-site as a source of fresh water. The well could be outfitted with a pump to facilitate storing the water in an elevated tank or in a cistern. In considering this alternative, it is critical to test the well water for potability and mineral content, and to ensure the underground reservoir from which the well will draw is not contaminated by salt water, as it is often the case along the coastal region. If analyses confirm that the well water is potable and fit for human consumption, it is important to install filtration equipment somewhere along the distribution line. Should this well water turn out to be unsuitable for human consumption, it could still be used for other purposes such as waste evacuation or irrigation of landscaping.
- Regardless of which of the above alternatives is adopted, a distribution infrastructure is an essential component of the potable water system. A mixed gravity–pump-assisted system is quite practical and one in wide use in many locations. What is important in this case is to connect all pumps to the emergency electrical power system.
- To provide some level of redundancy to an on-site emergency potable water supply, I would recommend adding other sources by selecting from several alternatives, ranging from portable bottled water fountains that could be distributed throughout the hotel or building, to having staging areas throughout the facility to store adequate emergency supplies of individual-dosage bottled water to be distributed to hotel guests or building occupants as needed. Another alternative is the use of special equipment that manufactures water from moisture in the atmosphere through processes associated with emergency power generation or air conditioning. There are several manufacturers offering these types of systems.

Wastewater

With respect to wastewater and the objective of maintaining the functionality of the facility during a hurricane or the interruption of public wastewater/sewage services in its aftermath, there are various alternatives to consider for ensuring continuity in

Hurricane-Resistant Buildings 245

the discharge of sanitary fixtures and evacuation of wastewater for treatment. In this regard, I would recommend the following:

- Build an on-site septic tank, or tanks, and filtration fields capable of processing all wastewater for the facility for a minimum fixed period of time, say, for example, 15–30 days. Such a system should also include pumping equipment and a conduit to pump accumulated waste from the septic tank to the public system once service is restored.
- A variation of the above would be to install several of these combinations of septic tank and filtration fields throughout the grounds of the facility in order to increase capacity and operate independently of the public wastewater system for a longer period of time.
- A third alternative that warrants consideration is to build a fully functional wastewater treatment plant on-site to make the facility totally self-sufficient in this regard. When building such a system, the public wastewater utility could be considered as a back-up emergency system. This alternative requires a careful analysis of cost and benefits before deciding as the initial investment could be significant.
- To complement any of the above alternatives that are ultimately selected and to provide a specified level of redundancy, the facility owner, or management team, or the design team in case of a planned new building, could purchase or have a rental agreement for a number of chemically operated portable toilet systems to be deployed throughout the building during the activation of a hurricane emergency plan.

Communication Systems

To ensure hurricane resistance on a hotel or commercial building in terms of communication systems, a first step is to address the protection of critical components, such as antennas, towers, transmitters, switchboards, and batteries, essential for the operability of the entire system. In this regard and considering that some of these components must be installed outdoors, often atop a building, the following recommendations are offered:

- The building itself will provide hurricane protection to indoor communication equipment. However, it is important to use the same approach recommended before in terms of providing a secondary line of protection against wind and water for these pieces of equipment, in case a breach of the building envelope allows these hazards inside. It is equally important to consider implementing measures to ensure natural ventilation and protection for specific pieces of equipment.
- To protect those components of the communication system installed outdoors, especially towers, antennas, and cables, the emphasis must be on the means of anchoring and attachment, as well as on the design of specific components. For example, communication towers installed outdoor or atop the building will perform more effectively under hurricane conditions if

manufactured with tubular rather than angular components and if designed as a unit attached to a structure or foundation rather than one that is supported by guy wires.

- As important as the design aspects and strength of anchoring and connections to ensure a desired level of hurricane resistance, including effective performance during a hurricane and continuity of function in its aftermath, is consideration that a building's communication system will depend on public or private external infrastructure operated and maintained by others, making it virtually impossible to ensure continuity of service because even when the owned system is protected and capable of surviving hurricane impact without major damage, it is probable that some of the components of the external infrastructure, such as towers or antennas, or cables will suffer damage leading to interruption of services.
- A tested and effective approach toward ensuring continuity of functionality of the communication system is to create various levels of redundancy. For example, starting from a wired telephone system, a back-up system could be a wireless Wi-Fi VoIP telephone system. A second level of redundancy could be the cellular telephone system, to which we could add satellite telephones. Additional levels of redundancy to maintain communications services for the building and its occupants could be by way of one of more radio-communication systems, including the quite reliable and trusted workhorse used worldwide: ham radio! In summary, the approach is to provide the highest level of physical protection to the components of the communication system to reduce the potential for damage from hurricane impacts, while collaterally creating several levels of redundancy as described above to ensure continuity of service while the external public or private infrastructure may be out of commission because of hurricane damage.
- A similar approach needs to be used relative to other elements of a communication system, such as cable television and Internet service. The backup for both these services could be secured by installing satellite antennas to pull down signals from communication and broadcast satellites. In this regard, it is important to note that the technology associated with these services is a rapidly advancing field, where new systems and equipment are constantly coming on line, enhancing the quality and reliability of these services. So, it is important to keep track of where the state of the practice is at any given time and to take advantage of new and more effective products and services toward ensuring hurricane-resistant systems and buildings.

I would like to add that communication systems are critical and essential components of local, state, and federal emergency and response plans, which give priority to the restoration of communication services of all kinds in the aftermath of a hurricane impact. This may mean that interruption of public communication services may in most cases be of relatively short duration, except for catastrophic hazard events, which is a positive thing but only to the extent that our own system shall have been

Hurricane-Resistant Buildings

made capable of maintaining functionality after a hurricane impact by implementing some of the recommendations made here.

Waste Management

Let us say that as owners, developers, or designers of a new project, we have designed and built a hurricane-resistant building, or that we have achieved an enhanced level of protection by retrofitting an existing building. Let us also say that our hotel or other building has already survived a hurricane impact with some damage but is fully capable of continuing to operate as soon as pertinent authorities allow it.

Reactivating operations is a critically important goal for a hotel, or a commercial building, especially in financial and marketing terms. Regarding this, it is essential for the hotel or company management to have a business continuity plan ready to be implemented as soon as possible after a hurricane impact.

Of the many concerns to be addressed in such continuity plan, waste management is one of the most challenging, especially when taking into account the interruption of public services such as waste pick-up, that may last from several days to weeks or even longer. What alternatives are there for resolving such a problem?

- One recommendation is for the hotel to invest in the installation of non-perishable waste-compacting equipment as well as incineration equipment. This allows for managing the disposal of nonperishable waste on-site until public services are restored.
- A second, complementary, alternative is to hire transportation services to take bundled compacted nonperishable waste to a public dump site or recycling center.
- Managing the disposal of perishable waste is a totally different story because of health and hygiene issues associated with this, so the first recommendation is to be familiar with all public health and waste management requirements applicable to the collection and disposal of this type of waste in your specific jurisdiction. Beyond this, other options include incineration on-site, collection, and disposal via private transportation service, chemical treatment, and various alternatives for safe packaging, which may allow for temporary storage on-site for eventual disposal via private transportation service to a proper authorized public waste treatment facility or transfer station.

BUILDING INTERIOR AND DÉCOR

If we were to implement many or most of the concepts and recommendations discussed so far in this book, we would go a long way toward achieving a hurricane-resistant building, which in turn reduces the potential for damage to the building itself, its interior and contents and, above all, to its occupants.

In spite of this, it is recommended to always plan for a worst-case scenario, such as when nature once again surprises us with the intensity of its attacks, or when the confluence of coincidences is such that the result is a breach of the building envelope, allowing wind and water and other forces of nature into our hotel (Figures 13.15 and 13.16).

FIGURE 13.15 Example of damage to external infrastructure and the building envelope caused by storm surge, breaking waves, and wind. This is the kind of occurrence that will bring the hazards to the interior of a building, causing extensive damage to contents and décor.

Regardless of how low the probability of such an eventuality may be, a building owner or manager needs to invest in mitigation measures to reduce adverse consequences from such impacts. Toward that objective, I recommend considering the following with regard to interior walls and partitions:

- Consider it a given that nonstructural interior walls and partitions, regardless of what a low probability such an occurrence would be, may at some

FIGURE 13.16 Example of damage to the interior of the building once storm surge, waves, and wind have penetrated inside after a breach in the envelope.

Hurricane-Resistant Buildings 249

point during their projected service life sustain loads generated by wind pressure because of a breach of the building envelope during a hurricane, as well as possible impacts from flying debris.

- When dealing with interior walls made of drywall or similar types of non-structural panels, the metal-stud structure should be strengthened by using at a minimum gauge 16 (1.61 mm) galvanized steel "C-shaped" studs for vertical members, attached to top and bottom channels firmly anchored to the floor and ceiling slabs, and cross-braced by horizontal members of the same gauge.

Finishes, Decorative Elements, and Built-In Furniture

These same criteria are also applicable to interior finishes, décor, built-in pieces, and also to regular furniture and decorative objects regularly found inside buildings. From a practical perspective, it is important to make the assumption that at some point, the interior of the buildings, and all of its components and contents, may be subjected to external loads generated by wind pressure, the impact of flying debris, wind-driven rain, and all of the effects of wind and water as damaging components of a hurricane.

In considering such eventuality and visualizing the outcome, one important question to ask is, which or how many of these artifacts, pieces of furniture, and other components of the building interior have been designed and built to withstand these kinds of impacts? None of course.

Based on previous discussion, we know damage to these kinds of objects and pieces will be directly related to the quality and strength of materials used, the methods and devices used for anchoring, and the strength and effectiveness of connections used in installing them.

It is also important to recognize that materials and methods used in some of these installations, or when it comes to free-standing furniture and various decorative objects and artifacts, may be fragile and quite susceptible to damage. Consequently, it is critical for emergency plans to include appropriate and effective measures to protect them in case of a hurricane. A practical example of how to do this was already discussed (Chapter 11) and it comes from the emergency plan implemented during Hurricane Wilma by one of the hotels visited in Cancun. The message is clear, design criteria and construction methods contribute to hurricane resistance of a building on a permanent basis, while preparedness actions taken while executing an emergency plan can be equally effective in reducing potential damage during a hurricane.

EXTERNAL INFRASTRUCTURE

Having addressed all of the components of a building, from foundation and structure, to roof and building envelope, and all interior components, we may conclude that our job in terms of ensuring a hurricane-resistant building has been accomplished. But this would be erroneous as we still need to evaluate the external infrastructure, which includes swimming pools, outdoor terraces, gardens and landscaping, and

250 Hurricane Mitigation for the Built Environment

leisure and recreational areas, that contributes so much to the enjoyment of hotel guests. A wide range of equipment and outdoor installations that support the plant operation and services for guests and occupants are all part of the external infrastructure that must be protected against the impacts of hurricanes.

Toward the objectives of achieving a hurricane-resistant facility and damage avoidance, the following is recommended:

- Store all free-standing pieces of furniture and objects such as outdoor chairs, tables, umbrellas, and similar items inside protected covered spaces behind locked doors.
- Secure larger, heavier, difficult-to-move pieces of furniture by using temporary methods to tie them in place by using straps, netting, or cables anchored to preinstalled structural points, to prevent them from being blown about or pushed by surge as well as to protect them from the impact of debris.
- Moved potted plants, especially those in hanging pots, to protected indoor spaces.
- Brace and secure trees, especially younger, not-yet fully established ones, by attaching cables or straps anchored to the ground that will provide additional support counteracting overturning forces from hurricane winds.
- Practice the preventive antihurricane pruning (see Chapter 11) originally developed in South Florida, which has proven quite effective over the years in reducing hurricane damage to trees. The objective of antihurricane pruning is to improve the performance of the tree by reducing canopy volume to enhance the flow of wind through it by presenting less resistance, and reduce the generation of flying debris. This technique has been so successful that the local Agricultural Extension Service in Miami-Dade County offers classes on how to practice antihurricane preventive tree pruning several times a year for professional landscapers as well as homeowners.
- Use plants native to the hurricane-vulnerable area as much as possible when creating new landscaping and gardens and to gradually replace existing landscaping.
- It is recommended that building owners and property managers conduct a comprehensive assessment of vulnerability of their facilities under the direction of qualified professionals in this field. The main objectives of this assessment are to characterize expected site-specific impacts from future hurricanes, identify weaknesses in buildings and infrastructure, and identify and recommend effective hurricane mitigation measures to achieve a hurricane-resistant facility.

VICINITY

Beyond an emphasis on achieving a hurricane-resistant facility through the implementation of hurricane mitigation measures, building owners and management must not lose sight of the fact that its vulnerability and desirable hurricane-resistant character will be directly affected by the character of the vicinity and environment around it.

Hurricane-Resistant Buildings

In view of this, owners, developers, managers, and design professionals need to define the character of the vicinity around the site by researching and asking questions that should include the following:

- What are the characteristics of area around the site, beyond its topography, and proximity to the beach and water?
- Is the vicinity a fully developed urban area where hotels and multistory residential and commercial buildings are the norm?
- Is the vicinity mainly a residential area of detached single-family one- or two-story houses or perhaps low-rise multifamily buildings and tree-lined streets?
- Is the vicinity a semirural area where open spaces, isolated buildings, and vegetation prevail?
- Is the vicinity mainly a natural area with plenty of trees and other vegetation, a river, or other body of water, where a facility will become a first step toward urbanization and commercial development?

There are three specific objectives in defining the character of the vicinity, as follows:

- In terms of site-specific vulnerability, it is critical to identify local factors that may act as impact modifiers affecting how a building will interact with and perform during a hurricane. Identifying and assessing such potential impact modifiers will provide relevant and important knowledge to owners, managers, and design professionals.
- Help identify and assess possible sources of flying or floating debris that may pose a threat to a facility.
- Determine the type and characteristics of public infrastructure that exists in the area.

If you have ever seen movies or video of flying debris during a hurricane, I am sure you will agree that I cannot overemphasize the need to identify and assess potential sources of flying debris present in the vicinity of a planned or existing building, so that appropriate mitigation measures may be implemented. I recommend looking for the following as potential sources of flying debris, both in the vicinity or in the grounds of your site:

- Buildings and houses with tile roofs
- Roof-mounted equipment on buildings
- Buildings with sheet-metal roofs
- Buildings that may still have gravel-ballast roofs
- High-rise buildings with metal coping on parapets
- Commercial buildings with signs mounted on their roofs or attached to exterior walls
- Communication towers with various kinds of antennas and equipment attached to them

252 Hurricane Mitigation for the Built Environment

- Commercial establishments where unsecured objects, materials of various types and sizes, and dumpsters containing various kinds of waste are normally stored outdoors
- Commercial and/or recreational establishments where outdoor furniture and other objects are normally present
- Trees that are young and not yet established, especially nonnative species, in landscaped areas or along streets

Identifying such potential sources of flying debris within a prudent radius of a site allows us to assess the threat each one poses by gathering relevant information such as the following:

- Elevation above ground and distance from a target site for each identified potential source
- Type, materials, and average size of missiles that would be generated by each identified source
- General conditions, in terms of physico-structural quality, maintenance, and age of each building or facility identified as a potential source
- In the case of trees, species, height, canopy characteristics, and condition (Is it a healthy, well-maintained specimen or quite the contrary?)

This information is useful in calculating the potential energy of impact, possible trajectory, and elevation of possible impact by type of debris and potential source, as well as in mapping out and characterizing expected impacts by building sector. In turn, this contributes to the identification, design, and deployment of effective mitigation measures to be incorporated into the design of a new building or the retrofitting of an existing one.

Possible mitigation measures must include the possibility of eliminating or controlling the generation of flying debris at the source itself. These measures must also include what can be done by paying special attention to potential sources within your own site, which may be expected to exist in the case of large grounds or a campus where more than one building and other structures and appurtenances are built, such as happens with hotels, hospitals, office or industrial parks, government installations, and housing complexes.

Any assessment of the vicinity must include the site for your own project whether already built or still in its design phase. Keep in mind, flying debris originating from your own site will come from sources that are much closer to your building, but which are also under your control.

The same approach described above should be used to identify and assess potential sources of floating debris that may threaten our site.

Assessing the character of the vicinity will reveal the kind of public infrastructure servicing the area and provide valuable information to respond to the following:

- How vulnerable are its various components to the impact of wind and water during hurricanes?
- More importantly, what is the probability that services such as electric power, public lighting, potable water, storm water, sewage and wastewater

Hurricane-Resistant Buildings

treatment, telephone, cable television, traffic signals, the Internet, and other services may be interrupted, and for how long, as a consequence of a hurricane?

- What local factors exist that may place components of public infrastructure at higher risk of damage or extended failure? For example, nonnative trees, not-yet-established young trees, and poorly maintained trees may all contribute to downed power and communication lines by way of broken limbs, or broken water or sewer lines when trees overturn under wind forces.

In our quest for hurricane-resistant buildings, I recommend our mind-set must be one of controlling all that is within our power and capability to do using effective design criteria and construction materials and methodology, both in cases of new buildings and the retrofit of existing facilities. This must be complemented by the careful identification and assessment of external factors beyond our control, in order to design and implement effective mitigation measures to protect against them.

14 Climate Change
An Exacerbating Factor

Global climate change, global warming in particular, as I have already referred to in this book (see Chapter 12), is now and will continue to be a contributing factor to hurricanes.

I want to take some time to share various issues and concerns that I have regarding the role of climate change as an exacerbating factor in future hurricane impacts on the coastal regions of Southeast Florida, Cancun, and many other such vulnerable places around the country and the world.

While the opinion and comments I will express are based mainly on my observations, research, and experience with hurricane mitigation projects in Florida, mainly in Miami-Dade County, these are certainly and totally applicable to hurricane-vulnerable coastal regions everywhere, including Cancun, Playa del Carmen, the Maya Riviera, and other areas of Quintana Roo, where I have conducted most of the field work and observations that constitute the core foundation of this book.

To put these comments in context, let me recount that I began looking into the issue of sea level rise in 1994/1995 in the context of floodplain management related to coastal flooding, storm surge, and hurricane mitigation for buildings and infrastructure in various regions in Florida in the aftermath of Hurricane Andrew (1992), but I only became "officially engaged" in the larger topic of global climate change in 1998 through my participation in the first National Assessment of Global Climate Change Consequences in the United States (NA), when I acted as managing director for the *Climate Change and Extreme Events Workshop* (July 21–23, 1998 in North Miami, Florida) for the region comprising the U.S. South Atlantic coastal areas of Florida, Georgia, North Carolina, South Carolina, Puerto Rico, and the U.S. Virgin Islands, which was sponsored by the NOAA Office of Global Programs (OGP), the U.S. Global Change Research Program (USGCRP), and the White House Office of Science and Technology Policy (OSTP) as one of several regional workshops conducted during 1997–1999 in support of the National Assessment and its associated report required to be submitted to the President and the Congress of the United States by January 1, 2000.

To set a foundation for meaningful and challenging discussion of relevant issues during the workshop, I wrote a paper, *The Need for Action to Confront Potential Consequences of Global Climate Change on a Regional Basis*, in which I summarized our state of knowledge with respect to global climate change and regional consequences, and posed a wide range of relevant questions, including some about the link between climate change and hurricanes and the special vulnerability of the coastal region.

That was about 17 years before the writing of this book, a time when we knew much less than we do now about drivers and consequences of global climate change.

255

That was a time when existing climate models were so coarse in resolution that hurricanes and certain regions were not even discernible. It was a time when the Intergovernmental Panel on Climate Change (IPCC) offered the following timid finding: "… evidence suggests that there is a discernible human influence on global climate," while also offering that "the amount of that influence is unknown due to uncertainties in key factors."

Those were days when a high degree of uncertainty prevailed relative to drivers of global climate change and their potential effects on cyclogenesis and hurricane intensity. Those were days when the main focus was on the greenhouse effect and GHG emissions.

Those were also days when the worst kind of politically motivated opposition to climate science amounted to a Republican calling the USGCRP as *Al Gore's*, meaning a Democrat, *thing*. That was before the onslaught of ideological propaganda against climate science and scientists working to improve our understanding of climate.

By contrast, those were also the days, and this may be surprising to some, when both the United Nations Framework Convention on Climate Change (UNCCC) and the United States through its USGCRP had taken a proactive approach based on what in international law is known as the *precautionary principle*. Under such precautionary principle, the United States had taken a pragmatic approach to tackling the potential national consequences of climate change and variability. The first part of the approach was recognizing that there was an existing, evolving, and long-term problem. The second part of the approach was recognizing the need for setting objectives and for taking action sooner rather than later, even though actual effects from climate change may not be fully recognizable for some time. Under such precautionary principle, the UNCCC proposed there are activities that have the potential for adverse or irreversible damage, such as those that may contribute to climate change, which can be restricted or prohibited *before* there is absolute scientific certainty about their effects. It also proposed that this precautionary principle is founded on the understanding that the ability of humankind to combat the adverse effects of certain environmental problems may be seriously compromised, or be taken away altogether, if final scientific proof of cause and effect is required before actions can be taken. In other words, to wait for such final proof would be *too late*.

Those were the days when the first National Assessment of Climate Change Consequences in the United States was completed and delivered to the President and the Congress in the year 2000.

Fast forward to 2014 and what do we find?

- We find there was a huge gap of more than 8 years, between 2000 and 2009, when no new NA reports (now known as National Climate Assessments or NCA) were produced, a clear violation of the Global Change Research Act (GCRA, the Law) requirement to deliver a report every 4 years. Sadly, this wasted opportunity to inform was driven by ideology and nothing else.
- We find new NCAs were completed and delivered in 2009 and 2013.
- We find the latest NCA, completed in 2013, includes innovations that go beyond the basic requirements of the GCRA, making for a richer, more complete and usable document. These innovations include the following:

Climate Change

    a. It identifies research needs and knowledge gaps.
    b. It provides a vision for an ongoing assessment process.
    c. It examines mitigation and adaptation responses.

- We find the IPCC completed its 5th Assessment Report (ARS), which includes explicit, frank, strong, and needed statements on important topics, including the following:

    a. "We are headed for pervasive and irreversible impacts."
    b. "Statistically speaking there is at least 95% confidence that more than half of this warning (over the past 50 years) is due to human activities."
    c. "Continued emission of greenhouse gases will cause further warming and long-lasting changes in all components of the climate system."
    d. "Adaptation will be necessary to weather a changing climate regardless, but that job becomes much easier if we minimize that climate change."
    e. "Everything we know tells us that immediate action is warranted both ecologically and economically."

- We find that in 2012, the IPCC published a special report linking extreme events and climate change with an emphasis on adaptation: *Managing the Risks of Extreme Events and Disasters to Advance Climate Change Adaptation*, a special report of the Intergovernmental Panel on Climate Change. Finally, after we here in South Florida back in 1998 proposed the linkage between climate change and extreme events, there is now official word directly from the highest organization in the world addressing climate change that confirms such connection.

- We find climate models that have seen tremendous improvement in resolution, both statistically and dynamically, making them capable of projecting events and consequences of climate processes at the regional level.

- We find a total of 14 states that as of November 2014 have formally adopted *Climate Change Action Plans* while nine others are in the process of drafting or reviewing proposed climate change action plans. Not surprisingly, 13 of the 14 states that have already adopted climate change plans are coastal states. A common theme often heard during the process that led to adoption of these state plans pointed toward the lack of action at the federal level, and the reality of the threat as drivers for their own initiatives. These states just got tired of waiting for an ideologically polarized and ineffective Congress to act and used the already-mentioned precautionary principle to act now, before it is too late.

- Encouraging as the examples of these states that have already taken action are, we also find cases that make you cringe in disbelief at the level of ideological idiocy that drives partisan legislative decisions regarding climate change in some states. One particular example is North Carolina where a partisan state legislature voted to ignore scientifically based sea level rise projections from a panel of experts, forbidding state agencies to consider projections beyond a 30-year horizon for planning purposes. There are also reports from several states, including Florida, that state authorities are discouraging and even preventing staff from using the term climate change in verbal or written communications pertaining to state business, which is rather sad and disappointing indeed.

- We find that numerous counties and municipalities across the country are following the example of some states, deciding to enact their own climate change initiatives to drive action at the local level now rather than waiting for policy to come from the state or national governments. Worthy of notice because of its unique and groundbreaking approach is the *Southeast Florida Regional Climate Change Compact,* also known as the *4 County Climate Change Compact* (4 County CCC), adopted in 2010 by the Boards of County Commissioners of Broward, Miami-Dade, Monroe, and Palm Beach counties. These four counties, recognizing that expected impacts of sea level rise and hurricanes do not stop at the county line, cut across political boundaries, and real cultural, economic, and partisan differences as well as legitimate competitive rivalries, and decided that the only approach that makes sense is to confront expected climate threats as a region. The 4 County CCC drafted the *Southeast Florida Regional Climate Action Plan* (2012), which has been adopted by each of the four participating counties. Remarkable initiative indeed.
- On the political front in the United States, we find that matters have deteriorated significantly. We now find a nasty, misguided, misleading, and pervasive ideological propaganda effort funded by special interests to confuse the general public about what is happening with the climate, the role of science and scientists, and the need for action to confront expected consequences. We find cases of legislators engaging in witch hunts, in clear abuses of authority and power, against scientists who have contributed to the effort of understanding climate change and its consequences for various sectors in the United States. We find a willingness by some legislators to court favor with the same special-interest sources of funding in exchange for continuing the business-as-usual approach and undercutting critically important scientific enterprise, without stopping to consider that this undermines the long-held leadership of the United States in many fields, counteracts development and job creation, and places growing numbers of people and infrastructure at risk from future expected impacts of sea level rise, storm surge, and hurricanes, among other natural hazards. A clear example of this is the recent charade in the U.S. House of Representatives where after lengthy debate and self-serving pompousness, climate change deniers approved a motion declaring that climate change is real, but it is not caused by humans. What purpose did such action serve? What benefit did this clear dereliction of duty bring to the people these legislators are paid to serve? Why not invest equally precious time debating what measures we need to take as a country to mitigate the adverse consequences of climate change?

In summary, after some 20 years of engagement in the climate change arena, I see a mixed bag of good and bad news, of progress on some fronts and regression in others. Even in places where climate action plans have been adopted and there are initiatives underway based on the same, I see the need to move from the rhetorical,

Climate Change

the regulatory, and theoretical toward implementation and the application of pragmatic and effective solutions. This is particularly true with respect to coastal urban regions vulnerable to hurricane impact and the exacerbating factor of climate change.

In looking back at the time I started on this path and reading the new NCA and IPCC 5th ARS, I believe both these reports provide valuable updates to the available knowledge relative to our changing climate and its expected consequences, and they do so with much more detail, clarity, emphasis, as well as with a sense of urgency, but the more I think about these reports, the more I realize what they tell us about the core issues could very well have been written 20 years ago.

In my opinion, what is most concerning about all this is that despite all the new and improved knowledge and excellent information in these periodic reports, the response from most sectors and nations across the face of Earth has been quite dismal, particularly when it comes to adaptation.

Against this background, I want to focus my closing comments in this chapter on what is happening closer to home, or in any of the coastal regions addressed in this book, relative to hurricanes and what I view as the exacerbating factor of climate change.

First, I want to highlight the difference between approaches that are prevalent in Quintana Roo, Mexico and in Florida, the two regions on which this book is based.

In Cancun and in the whole state of Quintana Roo in Mexico, the civil protection (emergency management) sector has always considered the hazards generated by climate change, such as global warming, sea level rise, and other extreme weather events, as their purview as they do with hurricanes.

In Florida specifically and in the United States in general, the emergency management sector, while always directly involved with hurricanes, has for the most part stayed away from climate change issues until very recently when it began to look at sea level rise as a hazard and contributor to coastal inundation and storm surge.

This divide between sectors in the United States, climate change versus emergency management, has been there for the longest time, so much so that even the terms used by one or the other sector have contributed to confusion. For example, the term *mitigation* has been used by the U.S. emergency management sector for 30 years or so to describe actions to reduce the potential for damage to human activity from hazards. In contrast, the climate change sector started using the term *mitigation* only in the mid-2000s to describe what humans can do to minimize our impact on climate and the term *adaptation* to describe exactly what emergency managements consider mitigation. How much more confusing can this be?

There is one more example of this divide that I want to share. Back around 2001/2002, I was invited to serve as a member of the State (of Florida) Hazard Mitigation Plan Advisory Team (SHMPAT) charged with drafting the first state hazard mitigation plan to comply with the newly enacted Hazard Mitigation Act of 2000, which for the first time required states to adopt a statewide hazard mitigation plan in order to qualify for hazard mitigation funding in the event of a major disaster declaration. Our charge as a team was to follow the process and meet the requirements established in 44 CFR 201—mitigation planning to draft the state plan, which would then be submitted to FEMA for review and approval so that the state could then officially adopt it as the state plan. One of the required components of the plan is a "State Risk Assessment" identifying the vulnerability of each county to specific hazards, the magnitude of potential damage, and annual probability per occurrence.

As a member of the advisory team, I recommended including *sea level rise* as one of the specific hazards to be evaluated in the risk assessment. Despite my best and most eloquent arguments, my proposal was voted down by the group, because most team members felt emergency management and hazard mitigation had nothing to do with climate change. Fast forward to 2012 when Florida once again has convened its SHMPAT to review and update its mitigation plan, in compliance with the law, so that it can be submitted to FEMA for review and approval. Guess what! 10 years later, this latest plan (*Florida Enhanced Hazard Mitigation Plan: Section 3—State Risk Assessment*) approved in 2013 includes *sea level rise* not as a separate natural hazard but as a contributor and exacerbating factor of coastal flooding, storm surge, and salt-water intrusion contaminating fresh water aquifers in the coastal regions. As a result of this, we now see more emergency managers getting involved in climate change issues, particularly sea level rise, so the divide is being bridged, but there is a long way to go before we can have the unified approach that they have in Cancun and Quintana Roo in Mexico.

On the other side of the divide, those involved in the climate sector have slowly recognized the critical need to dedicate an equal or greater effort to *adaptation* that they have dedicated to *mitigation*. In doing this, climate managers have begun to grapple with identifying and implementing actual adaptation solutions, and in the process are encountering the same problem emergency managers here in Florida had, some 20 years ago, in trying to convert regulatory hazard mitigation language to actual solutions in the field. Climate managers are now confronting the challenge of converting their theories and rhetoric about adaptation into actual effective real measures in the field. It is clear that both sectors would benefit greatly by closer and more frequent interaction at this stage; emergency managers would learn more about climate issues and climate managers would also acquire much needed knowledge about adaptation (hazard mitigation).

There are encouraging signs that many of the players involved on both sides are in fact aware of the need for close collaboration between sectors and have taken actions toward that end. An excellent example of this is found in the recent report "Recommendations to the President" presented to the President in November 2014 by the State, Local, and Tribal Leaders Task Force on Climate Preparedness and Resilience (www.whitehouse. gov/administration/eop/ceq/initiatives/resilience/taskforce), established by Executive Order 13653 "Preparing the United States for the Impacts of Climate Change" of November 1, 2013 (http://www.whitehouse.gov/the-press-office/2013/11/01/executive-order-preparing-united-states-impacts-climate-change). Among the several report themes that were subjects of discussion and recommendations by the task force, there is one on "Supporting Climate-Smart Hazard Mitigation, Disaster Preparedness and Recovery." In my opinion, the "climate-smart" qualifier for what have been core emergency management activities not only says it all, but it is also a powerful statement coming as it does from a task force of 26 governors, mayors, county officials, and tribal leaders from across the United States.

Climate Change

Toward such recommended climate-smart hazard mitigation, I submit the undeniable link between climate change and hurricanes via sea level rise (Alvarez, *Natural Hazards Observer*, May 2009) provides ideal common ground for both these sectors, emergency management and climate management, to collaborate and develop a common approach based on shared knowledge and expertise.

On the need for such collaboration relative to links between climate change and hurricanes, I submit this need not stop with the field of tropical cyclones and the climate research community, but must in fact engage several other sectors beyond the two already identified such as building design and construction, higher education together with professional licensing.

I further submit that this process must aim beyond the obvious goals of informing and the exchanging of knowledge across fields and disciplines. It must aggressively pursue objectives that will foster contributing, participating, collaborating, and the taking of action by practitioners in fields that up to now may have barely acknowledged each other, like ships passing in the night.

In this regard, I will argue that it is not enough to want to and agree to collaborate. Also, it is not enough to incorporate the other sectors I have mentioned and agree that the ultimate objective will be the taking of actions for the benefit of vulnerable coastal communities everywhere. I will argue that to avoid engaging in yet another rhetorical, theoretical, or utopian intellectual exercise, and in order to have truly productive and effective collaboration focusing on the topic of mitigating adverse consequences from the exacerbation of hurricanes by climate change, there must also be agreement on the following:

- Specific problems to solve
- Specific links between climate change and hurricanes and resulting hazard impacts
- Expected consequences from continuing with a "business-as-usual" approach
- The need for a paradigm shift and on what elements it should be based
- A deliverable action plan consisting of a set of recommendations and timelines for execution

Toward these expected points of agreement for our proposed collaboration enterprise, I will contribute the following.

SPECIFIC PROBLEMS

Currently, to build in a hurricane-vulnerable coastal location, the design team uses accepted standards (American Society of Civil Engineers standards ASCE-7 and ASCE-24) to establish minimum design loads for buildings and other structures, including those exerted by wind, flood, storm surge, and wave impact. In the case of storm surge impacts, applicable parameters for calculating such minimum design loads on a site-specific basis come from a range of sources that are largely based on historical events, do not include wave action, and usually ignore the effect of continuous sea level rise requiring corrections to establish accurate parameters for

262 Hurricane Mitigation for the Built Environment

storm surge depth and wave height at the specific project location, which is seldom if ever done.

Another problem is that the building design professions, the architectural and engineering sectors in particular, have been largely absent from the climate change arena, especially with regard to the need for adapting the built environment to potential impacts from climate change. A commonly held view among architects and engineers in this regard is that all you are required to do is meet the pertinent building code. Unfortunately, even the strongest building codes only establish minimum design requirements and no criteria for expected natural hazard impacts that will exceed such minimum requirements.

LINKS BETWEEN HURRICANES AND CLIMATE CHANGE

All hazards incorporate damaging components capable of causing direct damage to the built environment and human activity. Wind pressure, hydrodynamic pressure, and impact loads applied to buildings and infrastructure by storm surge and breaking waves during hurricanes are all examples of damaging components.

Damaging components of climate change include global warming and sea level rise.

Sea level rise is already exacerbating storm surge during hurricanes and will continue to do so into the foreseeable future. Sea level rise results in deeper coastal waters, leading to higher faster-flowing storm surge and higher waves. The net results are much stronger hydrodynamic pressure and impact loads acting on buildings affected by storm surge and waves during hurricanes.

Global warming has increased the capability of the atmosphere for holding moisture and may be elevating the threshold for precipitation to occur. As a result, empirical data shows an increase in the incidence of extreme rain events in certain locations. These conditions will exacerbate the potential for damage during "wet" hurricanes.

The connection between sea level rise and the exacerbation of storm surge, and between global warming and extreme precipitation events, is clear. Based on this, the link between climate change and hurricanes is undeniable.

EXPECTED CONSEQUENCES OF BUSINESS-AS-USUAL APPROACH

New buildings are being built today using minimum design criteria based on historical data and outdated points of reference that, in the specific case of storm surge, do not include the current and future effects of sea level rise.

Because of this, new buildings in coastal locations may suffer external loads from storm surge and wave impact during the course of their projected service life, which may exceed their original design criteria by factors of 150%–200%, creating the potential for catastrophic damage.

New and existing buildings on sites currently outside the influence of storm surge impact or subject to minimal levels of storm surge and waves may find themselves in more hazardous storm surge zones in the future as a result of sea level rise and potentially subject to loads from hydrodynamic pressure and from wave impact that will exceed the minimum design loads used to build them. Sea level rise will also drive

Climate Change

salt water intrusion landward from current locations, which will expose increasingly larger numbers of reinforced concrete buildings to the dangers of chloride-induced corrosion of reinforcing steel in their foundations and structures, a danger that may remain largely hidden for long periods, but which increases the risk of damage and failure from hurricane impacts these buildings face.

A large portion of the existing stock of buildings and structures in the coastal region of Florida, Quintana Roo, and other hurricane-vulnerable states and countries is at risk of catastrophic damage from storm surge and wave impact. This is a problem of gargantuan proportions not only in terms of the value-at-risk represented by the replacement cost of the built environment, but also mainly because of the value of human life and the full range of human activity sheltered by all those buildings, including governance, health care, education, commerce, manufacturing, research, and a wide range of critically needed services.

A PARADIGM SHIFT IS NEEDED

Continuing with the business-as-usual approach when it comes to buildings in the coastal locations of Florida, Quintana Roo, or so many other hurricane-vulnerable regions will not cut it. I would argue significant and immediate change needs to take place across many sectors.

The scientific community needs to acknowledge the influence of climate change in the exacerbation of specific damaging components of hurricanes.

The emergency management community must consider specific components of climate change as hazards, hence as sources of potential damage to the built environment, human activity, and the natural environment.

The scientific community in collaboration with the engineering sector and the emergency management community needs to pursue research with the objective of enhancing capabilities for establishing realistic parameters for future storm surge elevation, velocity of flow, and wave heights under the continuous influence of sea level rise, which can be used in defining design criteria for building construction.

Building design professionals, architects, and engineers must radically change the current approach to building design and embrace a method that is based on future potential loads, especially in the case of storm surge and wave impact exacerbated by sea level rise, that may occur during the expected service life of a new building needs to replace the existing approach. Nothing but a paradigm shift in design methodology will suffice.

Higher education communities need to upgrade their curricula to reflect these critically needed changes and equip future building design professionals, emergency managers, and scientists with practical tools to reduce the potential for damage from the impacts of hurricanes and extreme events affected by climate change through the adaptation of buildings, structures, and infrastructure using forward-looking design and hazard mitigation criteria.

The regulatory community will need to incorporate pertinent requirements in the professional licensing process to ensure that professionals in many fields are equipped with the knowledge to confront current and future impacts of climate change on the built environment and human activity.

RECOMMENDATIONS AND TIMELINES

All recommendations for hazard mitigation and adaptation solutions must directly address local conditions. Consequently, I will not dwell on this topic other than to say that my previous comments here may be useful as guidelines for those who will act at the local level. When it comes to hazard mitigation and adaptation of the built environment to the expected local impacts of climate change-exacerbated hurricanes, there is no one-size-fits-all solution. It has been stated, quite correctly, that all mitigation is local. I submit that this book, with the many actual examples and shared empirical knowledge and recommendations for mitigation, makes a practical and comprehensive blueprint for those who will be tasked to lead and manage similar efforts in their own communities.

In closing and always on the topic climate change as an exacerbating contributor to hurricanes, I would like to leave you with two thoughts:

1. Know your hazards

   If you are a design professional, or a planner, or a policymaker, or just someone thinking about what to do to protect your property from expected combined impacts of future hurricanes and climate change, it is imperative that you know your hazards. By this I mean knowing and understanding the causes of direct damage generated by the hazard.

   In the case of hurricanes exacerbated by climate change, it is critically important to understand how sea level rise will contribute to those causes of damage.

   I believe the following points will contribute to such understanding:
   a. It is all about the depth of water.
   b. Water, in the form of storm surge and waves, is the most damaging component of a hurricane.
   c. The capacity of water for causing damage derives from its characteristics as a dense, incompressible, and isotropic fluid.
   d. Hydrodynamic pressure, the force generated by the rushing waters of storm surge against buildings and objects in its path, grows in direct proportion to the square of the velocity of flow.
   e. The velocity of flow of storm surge is water-depth dependent. The deeper the water, the faster it flows and the higher the hydrodynamic pressure becomes.
   f. The damaging impact force of waves breaking against a building is directly proportional to wave height.
   g. Wave height is also water-depth dependent. The deeper the water, the higher the wave and the stronger its energy of impact becomes.
   h. Since sea level rise contributes to water depth, it is also a contributing exacerbating factor to the energy of impact of storm surge and breaking waves and, consequently, their capacity for causing direct damage.
   i. Salt water intrusion is also directly related to water depth. Consequently, sea level rise is a direct contributing exacerbating factor in salt water intrusion.
2. Think of regional protection

Climate Change

If I have learned one important thing over the many years I have been involved in the field of hazard mitigation, it is that you must put your preconceptions aside and consider all possible solutions before you can assess effectiveness, compare alternatives, and recommend a preferred measure.

What I have seen over the years in actual practice is that some possible hazard mitigation alternatives are discarded without any kind of analysis because of perceived "high cost"; this without even bothering to complete a cost–benefit analysis. Others are ignored or discarded because "you will never get this approved" or "where will the funding for this come from?" And still other potentially effective and cost-beneficial mitigation alternatives are dismissed on the basis of real or perceived problems, but without bothering to research for possible solutions that may make it possible to implement such measures.

Such is the case of regional "Dutch-style" protective works for, say, southeast Florida that are dismissed or attacked by some with the argument that the limestone substrate of the region makes it impossible to build such types of structures because water will seep through anyway under such structures. However, to my knowledge, no comprehensive dedicated research effort has been undertaken to determine if the porosity of limestone problem can be solved at the scale needed for regional protective works. On the other hand, there are plenty of engineering projects in the region where the exact same problem has been successfully solved albeit at much smaller and limited scales. But solved anyway, so why can we not invest in research to determine if we can extrapolate what we have learned to find a solution that will work at the regional level?

I do not know if it is possible or not to build a major protective barrier that will keep the sea, storm surge, and major wave impact away, preserving our way of life and the developed urban communities as we know them, preserving our beaches, ensuring the continuity of the longshore sand supply, preserving existing ecosystems and benthic communities, while also allowing for commercial and recreational navigation and preservation of annual migrations of protected sea turtles. It sounds like an awfully tall order, but we will never know whether it is feasible unless we put it on the list with every other hazard mitigation measure we can think of that addresses the same hazards.

By using a building-by-building approach, or a community-by-community approach, we are attempting very limited solutions that still leave our projects highly vulnerable and may in fact create unintended consequences, increased vulnerability, and risk for others around them.

Take for example the case of beach erosion, due to sea level rise, surge, and other hazards, and the many, constant, and costly beach nourishment projects taking place in Florida. This approach ignores the fact that human intervention has disrupted the continuity of coastal regions and sandy beaches by cutting inlets to allow for navigation from the intracoastal waterways to the open ocean. So what is happening is that projects and measures are permitted and implemented on a community basis even when the specific area shares a beach with other neighboring communities. For example, one community at the north end of a shared sandy beach is granted permission by pertinent authorities and allowed to build groins or otherwise armor their portion of the beach with serious adverse consequences for the community at the southern end of the same beach. Or when a community on the north side of an inlet uses sand to counteract erosion of its beach and does not allow enough sand to bypass and continue to supply the beach on the southern side of the jetty, which then aggravates erosion problems on that side. Many of these problems would be solved if a regional approach would be taken requiring all affected communities to collaborate in the search for more effective and permanent solutions.

The same kind of adverse outcomes result when a building-by-building approach is used to apply hazard mitigation measures. Say, for example, one project owner decides to elevate his building to mitigate against potential damage from storm surge and waves and in the process increases the potential for damage to other properties in the area by changing the flow and volume of rain runoff or flood waters. Or, for example, take a community where all property owners agree to, and implement, hazard mitigation measures to protect against sea level rise and hurricanes, but public roadways and other infrastructure remain unprotected, which will make all of those "protected buildings" vulnerable to interruptions of public services. Also, an individual building approach, even when many building owners join in the effort, will always be a piecemeal time-consuming approach that would still leave the community or the entire region vulnerable to expected impacts of, say, sea level rise-exacerbated storm surge and waves. A consequence of this is that in case of a future hurricane impact, there may be numerous buildings sustaining moderate to minor damage because of the installed protective measures, but most of the buildings around them are severely damaged and rendered nonfunctional, turning such "protected buildings" into unsustainable "island buildings" that would have to be evacuated.

It is clear that a building-by-building approach has serious drawbacks that will need to be seriously considered in any mitigation and cost-effectiveness assessment, and comparison with other identified alternatives.

In my opinion, a regional approach to hazard mitigation in the case of the storm surge-waves-sea-level-rise hazard has several advantages over the piecemeal building-by-building approach, not the least of which is that it preserves the character and way of life of every community, and that it avoids the major disruptions associated with such an approach even if it could be successfully implemented in a cost-effective manner.

For all of the stated reasons, a regional approach to hazard mitigation of the built environment in coastal regions affected by the impacts of hurricanes, exacerbated by climate change, must be included in any list of identified alternatives and given the same attention and analysis so that it can be compared with all other such alternatives.

This is the challenge in front of us. To confront it, some will need to stop hiding behind stereotypes, such as the limestone porosity, and start proving whether it is solvable or not. Some will need to stop issuing doomsday predictions without offering solutions to the problem. Some will need to step out of their comfort zone, whether this is in the halls of academia, or the business sector, or in the chambers of legislative policy making. This is the time to show what we are made out of, the time to let our actions define who we are and what we intend to do to make our region a

Climate Change 267

resilient and sustainable community for the current and future generations of South Floridians.

Theories and utopian ideas will not do because we do not have the luxury of a clean slate. The region is fully built-up and dedicated to a wide range of human activities. What we need is to stay the course and follow a methodological and concerted approach to consider, assess, dissect, test for effectiveness, and compare all possible alternatives to reduce the potential for damage to our region from the combined impacts of storm surge and sea level rise. Only by proceeding in this fashion will we be able to identify, categorize, and rank the individual alternatives or combinations of alternatives that will be effective in mitigating expected impacts.

Only by proceeding in this manner will we learn which may be most effective: to implement one type of solution to be followed by another as the effectiveness of the first diminishes, or to implement a range of solutions, some collaterally and some in sequence. Only in this way will we be able to decide that we may need all three classes of hazard mitigation measures as opposed to just a preferred one. Whatever the ultimate outcome of this analysis may be, let us exhaust our efforts to test whether regional protection may be an effective and feasible option for South Florida.

As I said earlier in this book, leave all preconceptions behind and use your imagination, put all of the options on the table, concentrate on the big picture and on effectiveness first, and then proceed to the matter of design and construction details and cost estimates. Let the method work. I am neither advocating for a regional approach nor against a building-by-building approach. It may very well be that we will need both approaches collaterally or in tandem so that our vulnerable coastal communities can remain viable for a long time, but we will not be able to decide one way or the other until we put both alternatives through the same analytical and comparative process that has been described here.

Let us go forward and mitigate those future hurricanes to protect our built environment, wherever that may be, and the precious life, property, and vibrant array of human activities taking place in these buildings and homes!

Index

A

Absolute vulnerability, 30
ACV, *see* Air conditioning and ventilation (ACV)
Aerodynamic drag, 48
Aerodynamic force, 48
Aerodynamics, 86, 95–96
Air, 37
    atmosphere, 37, 38
    stratopause, 39
    transparent layers of Earth's atmosphere, 38
    troposphere, 37
Air conditioning and ventilation (ACV), 191
American Society for Testing Materials (ASTM), 216
American Society of Civil Engineers (ASCE), 43
Ammonia (NH_3), 37
Angle of attack, 48
Anthropogenic factors, 202
    factors, 203
    future hurricane impacts, 203–204
Argon (Ar), 37
ASCE, *see* American Society of Civil Engineers (ASCE)
ASTM, *see* American Society for Testing Materials (ASTM)
Atlantic hurricane season (1880), 108
Atlantic hurricane season (1979), 102–103
Atlantic hurricane season (1988), 103
Atlantic hurricane season (2005), 103–104
Atmosphere, 37
    boundary layer, 42
    pressure, 39

B

Balconies, 174, 184
Beach damage, 149, 150; *see also* Building damage; Damages
    damage to sandy beach, 151
    from hurricane, 150
    mitigation, 151–152
    natural beach reconstruction, 149–150
Benefit–cost analysis, 211, 265
Bernoulli's equation for incompressible flow, 41
Black rebar, *see* Regular steel rebar
Bluff bodies, 45
Boundary layer, 45
Building-by-building approach, 265, 266
Building axes, 48
Building damage, 152; *see also* Beach damage

balconies, 174
building interior, 188–192
contents, 192–194
decorative artisan roofs, 164–165
exterior-mounted equipment, 177
exterior ceilings, 174–175
exterior lighting, masts, and traffic lights, 178–179
exterior walls, 170–172
external infrastructure, 172–173
foundations, 152–154
landscaping and gardens, 181
metal roofs, 163–164
mitigation, 182–188, 193–196
parking lots, 177
piers, 180–181
railings, 174
reinforced concrete, 166–170
retaining walls, 173
roof-mounted equipment, 175–176
roofs, 155–161
signs and billboards, 181
skylights, 161–163
structure, 154–155
swimming pools, 174
terraces, 174
tiki huts, 180–181
Building envelope, 78, 165–166, 188–189, 218; *see also* Project-specific approach
    building codes, 219
    catastrophic occurrence, 80
    criteria, 79
    damage to, 120–122
    doors, 227–228
    exterior openings, 227
    exterior walls, 220–221
    functions, 78
    hurricane winds, 233
    IBCC, 219
    perimeter, 80–81
    roof, 221–227
    skylights, 229–230
    ventilation components, 230–233
    ventilation louvers, 234
    windows, 228–229
Building interior, 188
    ceilings, 189–190
    electromechanical equipment, infrastructure, 191
    interior walls, 188–189
    salt water flooding, 192

269

270 Index

Built environment, 75
    aerodynamics, 86, 95–96
    building envelope, 78–81
    centricity, 86, 91–93
    components, 75
    continuity, 86, 93–95
    exterior infrastructure, 82–83
    foundation, 76–77
    hurricane, 98–99
    hydrodynamics, 86, 96
    sails, 84–86
    structural integrity, 97–98
    structure, 77–78
    symmetry, 86, 90–91
    wind-catchers, 84–86
    wind tunnels, 84–86
Buoyancy, 61
Business-as-usual approach, 126, 203
    consequences, 262–263

C

Cancun, 101
    Atlantic hurricane season (1979), 102–103
    Atlantic hurricane season (1988), 103
    Atlantic hurricane season (2005), 103–104
    City of Cancun proper, 101
    Papantla Flyers, 102
    paradise, 104–105
    southern beach in, 126
Carbon dioxide (CO_2), 37
Carbon monoxide (CO), 37
Ceilings, 189–190
Center of gravity, *see* Centroid
Center of mass, *see* Centroid
Centricity, 86, 91
    floor plans of buildings, 92
    structural centricity, 92
    torsion and overturning combination, 93
Centroid, 90
Climate change, 198, 255–256
    climate-smart hazard mitigation, 261
    consequences of business-as-usual approach, 262–263
    encouraging signs, 260
    findings, 256–255
    global warming, 198–200
    links with hurricanes, 262
    NCA and IPCC, 256, 259
    paradigm shift, 263
    recommendations and timelines, 264–267
    sea level rising, 200–201
    SHMPAT (State [of Florida] Hazard Mitigation Plan Advisory Team), 259
    specific problems, 261–262
    State Risk Assessment, 259–260
Common salt, 58

Communication systems, 245–247
Community-by-community approach, 265
Concrete Reinforcing Steel Institute (CRSI), 216
Continuity, 86, 93
    building envelopes, 95, 235–236
    critical factor, 94
Coriolis force, 42
Corrosion-resistant reinforcement (CRR), 216
Coupled ocean–atmosphere system, 40
Critical factor, 94
CRR, *see* Corrosion-resistant reinforcement (CRR)
CRSI, *see* Concrete Reinforcing Steel Institute (CRSI)
Cyclogenesis, 201
Cyclone, 27

D

Damages, 31; *see also* Beach damage; Building damage
    components, 31
    floating debris, 35
    flooding, 33
    hydrodynamic pressure, 33–34
    torrential rain, 32–33
    wave impact, 34
    windborne debris, 32
    wind pressure, 32
DCA, *see* Department of Community Affairs (DCA)
Debris, 70
    floating debris, 70–71
    flying, 70
    storm surge from Hurricane Gilbert, 72
Decorative artisan roofs, 164–165
Department of Community Affairs (DCA), 137
Detailed method, 63
Disaster Mitigation Act of 2000 (DMA 2000), 29
Domino effect, 157
Doors, 227–228
Drag, 48–49
Drift, 52
Dvorak method, 17
Dynamic pressure, 41

E

Eddies, 54
Education, 28–30
EIFS, *see* Exterior insulation finishing system (EIFS)
Einstein equation, 32
Electrical system, 239–241
EM, *see* Emergency management (EM)
Emergency management (EM), 4
Energy of impact, 32
Erosion, 68

Index

Exosphere, 39
Exterior-mounted equipment, 177
Exterior ceilings, 174–175, 184
Exterior infrastructure, 82–83; *see also* Internal
    infrastructure
Exterior insulation finishing system (EIFS), 171
Exterior lighting, 178–179
Exterior openings, 227
Exterior walls, 170
    components, 170–171
    EIFS, 171
    mitigation, 172
External infrastructure, 172–173, 249–250

F

FBC, *see* Florida Building Code (FBC)
Federal Alliance for Safe Housing (FLASH), 9
Federal Emergency Management Agency
    (FEMA), 2
FIU, *see* Florida International University (FIU)
FLASH, *see* Federal Alliance for Safe Housing
    (FLASH)
Flat roofs, 159
    damage under uplift forces, 160
    flat-roof damage assessment, 159
    mitigation, 160–161
Floating debris, 35
Floating missiles, 35
Flooding, 66
    causes of damage, 68
    tropical cyclone, 67–68
Floors, 190–191
Florida Building Code (FBC), 206
Florida International University (FIU), 137
Flying debris, 70
4 County Climate Change Compact (4 County
    CCC), 258
Frontal impact load, 62

G

GCRA, *see* Global Change Research Act (GCRA)
ggbs, *see* Ground granulated blast-furnace slag
    (ggbs)
Glass and architectural metals, 167
    causes of damage, 167–168
    mitigation, 168–170
Glazing systems, 167–168
Global Change Research Act (GCRA), 256
Global warming, 198, 255, 262
    damaging wet hurricanes, 200
    extreme hurricane-generated rain, 199
    hurricanes, 198
Greenhouse gases, 37
Ground granulated blast-furnace slag (ggbs), 216
Ground zero, 117

H

Hazard, 2
Hazard mitigation, 1, 2; *see also* Global
    warming; *see also* Mitigation
    benefit, 9
    in 44 CFR, 2–3
    hazard impacts, 7
    methodology, 5
    phases of EM, 4, 6
    sustainable development, 8
    theory of mitigation, 5
Heat-strengthened glass curtain wall, 167
Heating, ventilation and air conditioning
    (HVAC), 177
Helium (He), 37
High tides, 58
High velocity, 34
High Velocity Hurricane Zone (HVHZ),
    206, 208
Hurricane-resistant buildings, 205; *see also*
    Project-specific approach
    Hurricane Gilbert, 206
    macro approach, 208–209
    risk management, 207–208
    theories and methodology, 205
Hurricane-vulnerable coastal regions, 96
Hurricane(s), 11, 31, 98–99; *see also* Hurricane
    Gilbert (1988); Hurricane Wilma
    (2005)
    amnesia, 24
    damages, 31–35
    Dvorak method, 17
    education, 28–30
    40-passenger twin engine jet-prop, 21
    human side of hurricane impacts, 22
    hurricane amnesia, 24
    Hurricane Andrew, 20, 21
    Hurricane David, 13, 15, 16
    links with climate change, 262
    natural hazard, 27–28
    protagonists, 25
    tropical cyclones, 11, 18, 27
    tropical wave, 12
    vulnerability, 30–31
Hurricane Gilbert (1988), 113
    atmospheric environment, 113–114
    balance, 115–116
    beach, damage to, 118
    building envelope, damage to, 120–122
    building interior, damage to, 122
    damage causing by, 117
    foundations, damage to, 120
    from lesson book, 116–117
    outdoor infrastructure, damage to, 118–119
    satellite view, 115
    track, 114

272   Index

Hurricane Wilma (2005), 129
  balancing, 132
  beach destruction, 138–139
  building interior, damage to, 145–147
  damages causing by, 137
  damages, 131
  envelope, damage to building, 142–144
  external infrastructure, damage to, 140
  foundations, damage to building, 140–142
  Hurricane Gilbert vs., 133–134
  industrial-type building, 143
  lesson book, 134–137
  satellite observations, 130
  water-vapor satellite, 131
HVAC, *see* Heating, ventilation and air
      conditioning (HVAC)
HVHZ, *see* High Velocity Hurricane Zone
      (HVHZ)
Hydrodynamic pressure, 62–63
  due to flooding, 34
  from storm surge, 33–34
Hydrodynamics, 86, 96
Hydrogen (H_2), 37
Hydrologic cycle, 57
Hydrostatic pressure, 60
  load patterns, 60–61
  saturated soil, 61
  on walls of building, 62

I

IBCC, *see* International Building Code Council
      (IBCC)
IBHS, *see* Institute for Business & Home Safety
      (IBHS)
IBHS FORTIFIED Program, 9
IHRC, *see* International Hurricane Research
      Center (IHRC)
Impact momentum, 32
Inches of mercury (in Hg), 39
Institute for Business & Home Safety (IBHS),
      137, 196
Institute for Public Opinion Research
      (IPOR), 137
Intergovernmental Panel on Climate Change
      (IPCC), 256, 257, 259
Interior walls, 188–189
Internal infrastructure, 239; *see also* External
      infrastructure
  electrical system, 239–241
  mechanical system, 241–243
  plumbing system, 243
International Building Code Council
      (IBCC), 219
International Hurricane Research Center
      (IHRC), 137
International System of Units (SI), 32

Interplanetary space, 39
IPCC, *see* Intergovernmental Panel on Climate
      Change (IPCC)
IPOR, *see* Institute for Public Opinion Research
      (IPOR)
Isotropy, 39

K

kN/m^2, *see* Newtons per square meter (N/m^2)
Krypton (Kr), 37

L

Landscaping and gardens, 181
Leveling-off, 68–70
Local Mitigation Strategy (LMS), 29
log-law, *see* Logarithmic law (log-law)
Logarithmic law (log-law), 42–43
Low tides, 58

M

Macro approach, 208–209
Main tile roofs, 156–157
Main wind-force resisting system
      (MWFRS), 91
Mechanical system, 241–243
Mesopause, 39
Mesosphere, 39
Metal roofs, 163–164
Methane (CH_4), 37
Missiles, 54–56
Mitigation, 1, 2, 182; *see also* Hazard mitigation
  beach damage, 151–152
  corrosion-resistant materials, 188
  damage to external infrastructure, 182
  decorative artisan roofs, 164–165
  flat roofs, 160–161
  measures, 135
  metal roofs, 163–164
  outdoor infrastructure, 183–187
  skylights, 162–163
  tile roofs, 158–159
Moon, 38
Multidecadal cycles of tropical cyclone activity,
      201–202
Multivitamin broth, 37
MWFRS, *see* Main wind-force resisting system
      (MWFRS)

N

National Climate Assessments (NCA), 256–257,
      259
National Geodetic Vertical Datum (NGVD), 200
National Hurricane Center (NHC), 12

Index

273

National Institute of Building Sciences (NIBS), 9
National Oceanographic and Atmospheric
    Administration (NOAA), 107
Natural factors, 197
    climate change, 198–201
    multidecadal cycles of tropical cyclone
        activity, 201–202
Natural hazard, 27–28
NCA, *see* National Climate Assessments (NCA)
Negative pressure, *see* Suction
Neon (Ne), 37
Newtons per square meter (N/m^2), 34, 60, 62
NGVD, *see* National Geodetic Vertical Datum
    (NGVD)
NHC, *see* National Hurricane Center (NHC)
NIBS, *see* National Institute of Building Sciences
    (NIBS)
Nitrogen (N$_2$), 37
Nitrogen oxides (NO$_x$), 37
Nitrous oxide (N$_2$O), 37
NOA, *see* Notice of Approval (NOA)
NOAA, *see* National Oceanographic and
    Atmospheric Administration (NOAA)
Notice of Approval (NOA), 228

O

Office of Global Programs (OGP), 255
OGP, *see* Office of Global Programs (OGP)
OSTP, *see* White House Office of Science and
    Technology Policy (OSTP)
Overcapacity, 78
Overturning, 52–53
Oxygen (O$_2$), 37
Ozone (O$_3$), 37

P

P-Delta effect, 53
Palapa, *see* Tiki huts
Papantla Flyers, 102
Paradigm shift, 263
Parapets, 223–224
Pascals, 60, 62
Perimeter, 80–81
Piers, 180–181, 186
Plumbing system, 243
Positive force, 62
Positive pressure, 46–47
Potable water, 244
Power law, 42–43
Precautionary principle, 256
Predisaster Mitigation, 29
Pressure gradient force, 42
Project-specific approach, 209; *see also* Building
    envelope; Hurricane-resistant
    buildings

building interior and décor, 247–249
building shape and proportions, 234–239
external infrastructure, 249–250
foundation, 212–216
hurricane-resistant buildings, 210
internal infrastructure, 239–243
potable water, 244
shape factor, 211–212
structure, 217–218
vicinity, 250–253
wastewater, 244–247

Q

Quintana Roo cyclones, 107
    Atlantic hurricane season (1880), 108
    annual probability of tropical cyclone impact,
        110
    Re-Analysis Project, 107
    tropical cyclone impacts, 109–111

R

Railings, 174, 184
Re-Analysis Project, 107
Redundancy, 77–78
Regular steel rebar, 216
Reinforced concrete, 166
    glass and architectural metals, 167–170
    mitigation, 166
Relative vulnerability, 30
Resilient building, 242
Retaining walls, 173, 183
Roof-mounted equipment, 175–176, 184, 224–225
Roof(s), 155, 221
    covering, 221–223
    drainage, 225–227
    flat roofs, 159–161
    main tile, 156–157
    mitigation, 158–159
    parapets, 223–224
    roof-mounted equipment, 224–225
    secondary tile, 157

S

Sails, 84, 236–237
    billboards, 84
    solar water heaters, 85
Saturated soil, 61
Sea
    level rising, 200–201, 262
    surface water temperature, 59
    water, 58
Secondary tile roofs, 157
Semidiurnal tides, 58
Shaking, 49

Index

"Shape factor" techniques, 211–212, 213
SHMPAT, *see* State (of Florida) Hazard
Mitigation Plan Advisory Team
(SHMPAT)
SI, *see* International System of Units (SI)
Signs and billboards, 181, 187
Simplified method, 63
Skylights, 161, 229–230
as architectural elements, 162
mitigation, 162–163
Slenderness, 235
Slow velocity, 34
Sodium chloride (NaCl), 58
Specific vulnerability, *see* Relative vulnerability
Specific weight of water, 57
Stagnation, 51–52
State (of Florida) Hazard Mitigation Plan
Advisory Team (SHMPAT), 259
Static pressure, 41
Storm surge, 65–66, 135–136
from Hurricane Gilbert, 72
hydrodynamic pressure from, 33–34
Storm tide, 63
Stratopause, 39
Stratosphere, 37, 39
Streamlined bodies, 45, 46
Structural centricity, 92
Structural integrity, 97–98
Structural redundancy, 78
Suction, 47–48
Sulfur oxides (SO_x), 37
Swimming pools, 174, 183–184
Symmetry, 86, 90–91

T

Tempered-glass curtain wall, 167
Terraces, 174, 183–184
Thermosphere, 39
Tides, 63
Tiki huts, 180–181, 186
Total pressure, 41
Traffic lights, 178–179
Tropical cyclones, 11, 13, 18, 27, 33, 98–99, 103,
107, 110, 201
Tropical depression, 17
Tropical wave, 12
Tropopause, 37
Troposphere, 37
Tropospheric ozone (O_3), 37
Turbulent flow, 43–44, 45
Typhoon, 27

U

United Nations Framework Convention on
Climate Change (UNCCC), 256

Unrecognized sails, 236
Uplift, 53–54, 77
U.S. Global Change Research Program
(USGCRP), 255, 256

V

Ventilation components, 230
air conditioning 231
ventilation hood covering ductwork, 232
ventilation systems, 231
vulnerable ventilation devices, 233
Vibration, 49–50
Vicinity, 250
hurricane-resistant buildings, 253
mitigation measures, 252
objectives in, 251
Vorticity, 50–51
Vulnerability, 30–31, 123
Hurricane Gilbert impact, 123
potential for damage, 125–127
preliminary assessment, 124–125

W

Waste management, 247
Wastewater, 244
communication systems, 245–247
waste management, 247
Water, 37, 56
characteristics of water flow, 57–58
debris, 70–72
effects, 60
erosion, 68
flooding, 66–68
heavy and incompressible fluid, 57
hydrodynamic pressure, 62–63
hydrologic cycle, 57
hydrostatic pressure, 60–62
leveling-off, 68–70
in oceans, 58–59
pressure, 57
sea surface water temperature, 59
sea water, 58
storm surge, 65–66
tides, 63
waves, 63–65
whirlpool, 72–73
Waves, 63
for causing damage, 64
magnitude of wave-induced loads, 65
rule of thumb, 64
Weather, 37
Whirlpool, 72–73
White House Office of Science and Technology
Policy (OSTP), 255
Wind-catchers, 84, 236–237

Index

architectural design, 87
billboards, 84
examples, 86
solar water heaters, 85
Wind, 40
axes, 48
characteristics of wind flow, 42–43
drag, 48–49
drift, 52
eddies, 54
effects, 44
guy-wire communication tower damaged by,
177
missiles, 54–56
movement of air, 40
overturning, 52–53
positive pressure, 46–47
shaking, 49
silhouette, 91
stagnation, 51–52
static wind pressure, 41–42
streamlined bodies, 45, 46
suction, 47–48
tunnels, 86, 88, 237–239
turbulent flow, 43–44, 45
uplift, 53–54
vibration, 49–50
vorticity, 50–51
wind speed, 40–41
Windows, 228–229

X

Xenon (Xe), 37